HEALERS, INVENTORS & ENTREPRENEURS

Dartmouth's Pioneering Graduate Schools

By Jeffrey Good

Geisel School
of Medicine

Thayer School
of Engineering

Tuck School
of Business

Guarini School
of Graduate and
Advanced Studies

SHIRES✺PRESS

4869 Main Street
P.O. Box 2200
Manchester Center, VT 05255
www.northshire.com

Healers, Inventors & Entrepreneurs:
Dartmouth's Pioneering Graduate Schools
Copyright © 2021 by Jeffrey Good
All rights reserved

ISBN Number: 978-160571-529-2

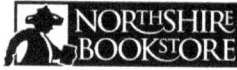

NORTHSHIRE
BOOKSTORE

Building Community, One Book at a Time
A family-owned, independent bookstore in
Manchester Ctr., VT, since 1976 and Saratoga Springs, NY since 2013.
We are committed to excellence in bookselling.
The Northshire Bookstore's mission is to serve as a resource for
information, ideas, and entertainment while honoring the needs of
customers, staff, and community.

Printed in the United States of America

For my parents, Arnold and Marcia Good
Where my history began

Book One

A painting of the Dartmouth College campus, circa 1803, by George Ticknor. *Image courtesy of Dartmouth College Archives.*

Eleazar Wheelock. *Image courtesy of Dartmouth College Photographic Files.*

"THIS, SIR, IS MY CASE! IT IS THE CASE NOT MERE-
LY OF THAT HUMBLE INSTITUTION, IT IS THE CASE
OF EVERY COLLEGE IN OUR LAND!... IT IS, SIR, AS
I HAVE SAID A SMALL COLLEGE, AND YET ..."

Daniel Webster at the argument of the Dartmouth College case.
*Image courtesy of Hood Museum of Art, Dartmouth College:
Gift of the Estate of Henry N. Teague, Class of 1900.*

Chapter 1
A Voice in the Wilderness

Before there was a Geisel School of Medicine, a Thayer School of Engineering, a Tuck School of Business, a Guarini School of Graduate and Advanced Studies; before Daniel Webster made his fiery case before the U.S. Supreme Court that his alma mater was a "small college — and yet there are those who love it;" before the nation won its independence from Great Britain and grew into a superpower hungry for young men and women equipped to lead it into the 21st century — before all of these things, there was a preacher who heard a voice crying in the wilderness.

Eleazar Wheelock, who founded Dartmouth College in 1769, grew up on a Connecticut farm. He was the grandson of Capt. Eleazar Wheelock, "a commander of a corps of cavalry in the Indian wars, but in times of peace a recognized friend of the savages," Leon B. Richardson wrote in his masterful two-volume *History of Dartmouth College* published in 1932. [1]

At age 16, young Eleazar decided on a life in the ministry. Aided by his grandfather's bequest, he attended Yale and got his license to preach. He was good at it. Connecticut historian Benjamin Trumbull observed: "Wheelock was a gentleman of a comely figure, of a mild and winning aspect, his voice smooth and harmonious ... His preaching and addresses were close and pungent and yet winning beyond almost all comparison, so that his audience would be melted even into tears before they were aware of it," according to Richardson.

In his parish in Lebanon, Conn., Wheelock got swept up in the Great Awakening led by hellfire evangelist Jonathan Edwards. As many as 25,000 or 30,000 people were converted by the Great Awakening and, of these, some credit Wheelock "with a goodly share."

But Wheelock was not satisfied with saving only fellow white settlers. He set his sights on preaching to Indigenous people, "the Indians." Encouraged by the success he had in tutoring Samson Occom, a young member of the Mohegan tribe whom he invited to study at the college preparatory school he was running in Connecticut, Wheelock expanded his efforts. By the end of 1760, he had eight Indigenous youths under his tutelage.

One observer said that while some teachers might appear "as scrupulous legislators or stern judges, he was always the gentle and affectionate father of his tawny family," Richardson wrote. By 1765, Wheelock had added eight English boys and was looking for a way to financially support the enterprise. "He was a most skilled beggar, plausible, persistent tactful and, through it all, possessed of a keen sense of dignity and self-respect," wrote Richardson.

For financial support, Wheelock looked back to England and to his early pupil, Occom, who was now 42. To potential benefactors in the old country, Occom proved irresistible. "The advent of a native Indian with the garb, mannerisms, language and habits" of a Puritan minister opened the purses. Among the benefactors was William Legge, second Earl of Dartmouth, who was "a torchbearer for the Great Awakening in England"[2]; John Wentworth, the newly appointed governor of the British Colony of New Hampshire; and even King George III, who chipped in 200 pounds at Lord Dartmouth's suggestion.

Wheelock wasn't satisfied with running a prep school; he wanted to start a college, which in pre-Revolutionary times required a charter from the Crown. Sensing, correctly, that Yale would oppose his efforts to secure one in Connecticut, he looked to New Hampshire, where Gov. Wentworth offered a charter and a grant of land to boot. Wheelock and his benefactors settled on a location with few English settlers but much promise — Hanover.

The beauty of the place was undeniable. "To the east were rugged, densely wooded hills, presently to rise into bare and towering mountains. On the level plateau selected as the location for the college, giant pines nearing three hundred feet in height shut out the very sun, save at noon, and calmed the fiercest blasts of upper air into a cathedral quietitude," Wilder Quint wrote in a passage quoted in the 1999 anthology *Miraculously Builded in Our Hearts: A Dartmouth Reader.* [3]

" 'Tis most central on the river — and most convenient for transportation up and down the river — as near as any to the Indians," Wheelock himself wrote, in a passage from an earlier anthology, Francis Brown's 1969 *Dartmouth Reader*. His college would rise up "on a beautiful plain, the soil fertile and easy of cultivation." [4]

Wheelock offered to name the new school after Gov. Wentworth, but the dashing young Brit demurred, supporting instead the idea of naming it after Lord Dartmouth. The royal charter was granted on Dec. 13, 1769. The Rev. Wheelock was now the president of Dartmouth College.

Wheelock brought 30 students to Hanover, only three of them Indigenous. Most were English charity students. "Although a suitable number of Indians would continue to be admitted, the main reliance in the future must be on white boys, trained to serve as missionaries" bringing the gospel to Indigenous populations, wrote Richardson.

The first commencement was held Aug. 28, 1771. Four students, including Wheelock's son, John, graduated, although their diplomas went temporarily unsigned because a quorum of trustees was unable to make the trek.

Dartmouth was the ninth of America's colonial colleges, the last to receive a royal charter.

While Wheelock is often portrayed in historic images as a "merry squire," he was more complex — patient and amiable at times, but also "fretful, dictatorial and peevish," Ralph Nading Hill wrote in *The College on the Hill: A Dartmouth Chronicle*, a collection of historical essays published in 1964. [5]

And what of Wheelock's educational philosophy? His primary goal was Christianizing Indigenous youths and while he wrote of "liberal education" in his letters, "there is no evidence that he devoted any serious thought to educational problems as such," wrote Richardson. He did, however, come up with an inscription for the college seal: *Vox clamantis in deserto*.

While the wilderness had its charms, it also held its challenges. If Wheelock had known that his little college would nearly a century later establish a graduate school to train some of America's top engineers, he might have wanted to send for one. After finishing construction of a house for him and his family, he wrote that they dug two wells but found "no prospect of water." After digging a half-dozen wells, his crew finally found water, relocated the residence and welcomed Wheelock's family and "near thirty students." [6]

Enrollment at Dartmouth grew at a steady clip. During the last decade of the 18th century, its 362 graduates were second only to Harvard's 394. Yale (295) and Princeton (240) lagged behind. While his college would thrive, Wheelock did not live to see much of that life; he died on April 24, 1779 at age 69.

Among his last wishes were that his son, John,

succeed him as president. The younger Wheelock would lead the college through its next three and a half decades — a time in which Dartmouth's very existence would face a severe test even as it took its first step toward educating not just undergraduates, but also students wanting to use graduate school as a stepping stone to careers in the professions.

The "Johnny Appleseed of Medicine" begins a school

While Dartmouth has prided itself from the beginning on providing undergraduates with a solid foundation in the liberal arts, its graduates from the beginning have sought the training needed for professional lives. Of the 1,177 young men who graduated during the years when the college was led by Eleazar Wheelock and his son John in the late 18th and early 19th centuries, nine in ten became doctors, lawyers, preachers or teachers. [7]

The future physicians didn't have to go far. Despite its rural location, Dartmouth in 1797 founded the nation's fourth medical school. And as had been the case with the college itself, it began with the audacious vision of a single man, Nathan Smith.

At time of founding, "the nation itself was still young and raw," Constance E. Putnam wrote in her 2004 history of the medical school's first two centuries, *The Science We Have Loved and Taught.* Only three other medical schools had been founded, all of them in urban settings: Philadelphia, New York and Boston. Hanover was hardly a metropolis: the population had just climbed past 1,000, including students at the college. [8]

Smith came of age in the small village of Chester, Vermont. There, at age 22, he found his calling one day when an itinerant surgeon, Josiah Goodhue, came to town to perform an amputation and called for a volunteer to assist him. While many would shrink from such an assignment, Smith embraced it – and asked the doctor on the spot if he could become his apprentice.

As they roamed the backroads together, the future Dr. Smith impressed Dr. Goodhue with his pluck. "Neither the darkness of the night, the mud to his horse's knees, or the violence of the storm were any impediments to him," Goodhue would later write. "If it should be asked what laid the foundation of Doctor Smith's eminence, the answer is industry. If it should be asked what brought him to the pinnacle of the profession, the answer is the most unremitting industry."

After his three-year apprenticeship with Goodhue, Smith moved in 1787 to the village of Cornish, N.H., to establish his own practice. Eager for more formal training, he enrolled in Harvard Medical School and became, in 1790, that school's fifth graduate.

Smith returned to Cornish, built his practice and hatched a broader ambition. In 1796, he sent a letter to President John Wheelock and the Dartmouth Board of Trustees proposing that they allow him to establish a medical school at the college. In addition to broadening the college's educational offerings, he said, it would help to supply well-trained physicians to a rural New England badly in need of their services. Smith wanted to travel to Scotland for further education to prepare him for the role, but offered to cover that expense himself. (The loan would take him 20 years to repay, perhaps evidence that his medical acumen exceeded his financial smarts.)

While Dartmouth trustees did not provide any cash to support Smith's study abroad, they did not discourage him. "Although still struggling to establish the College at the time, the Trustees accepted the offer," James Wright, a historian and Dartmouth's president from 1998-2009, wrote in his introduction to Putnam's book. "They knew a good thing when they saw it."

On Nov. 22, 1797, Smith gave the first of his lectures at Dartmouth. He did so without any formal blessing from college trustees. "Thus did Dartmouth Medical School come into being — quite unobtrusively, with no fanfare and no formal declaration of its existence," Putnam wrote. It wasn't until the next year, in August 1798, that trustees took a formal step toward "a medical establishment at this University."

Students who had already earned a bachelor's degree in another subject could earn their Bachelor of Medicine by following two 10-week courses of lectures — in the areas of anatomy, surgery, chemistry, materia medica (pharmaceutical remedies) and the theory and practice of medical healing — all capped by a two-year apprenticeship with a practicing physician. Those who lacked a bachelor's in another subject had to spend an extra year in apprenticeship and pass exams demonstrating their mastery of not only medical subjects but also Latin, math, geography and philosophy. [9]

As was standard at the time, medical students paid their tuition not to the institution, but directly to the faculty. With the exception of short stints by lecturers in chemistry and anatomy, that faculty from 1797-1810 consisted largely of Smith, Richardson noted. In 1805, Smith was making $200 a year from his work at Dartmouth. [10]

The lectures given by Smith and others didn't serve just to supplement textbooks; they *were* the textbooks. Professors spoke slowly to allow students to write down the important information. Student notebooks from the time show a range of care, from slap-dash notes to ones that are "very complete, neat, and expensively bound in leather."

In the beginning, the school made its home in the north end of Dartmouth Hall. And while Smith got little financial support directly from the college, he proved an effective lobbyist for state help, securing from New Hampshire nearly $4,700 to build the medical school building on land he agreed to donate, Richardson wrote. The structure was built in 1811.

The school was a success from the start. By 1806, there were 45 medical students and nearly as many undergraduates taking courses there. While debates would rage in the decades and centuries that followed about whether graduate study and research detracts from the quality of undergraduate education at Dartmouth, undergrads from the beginning took advantage of the medical school's offerings, flocking to lectures by Smith, said by some to be "the best teacher in Hanover." (Smith was not quite as charitable in his assessment of his colleagues on the liberal arts faculty, whom he dismissed as "a pack of literary drones.") [11]

Students weren't the only ones attending Smith's lectures. College President John Wheelock sat in on one and was so taken with what he heard that he regaled students in a chapel service with an especially scientific prayer. "Oh, Lord, we thank Thee for oxygen gas, for the hydrogen gas, for the mephitic gas," he professed. "We thank thee for all the gases."

Then, as now, students found ways to blow off steam, including alcohol in portions that sometimes kept them from exhibiting deference toward authority figures. At one point, Smith and Wheelock came across young revelers who failed to show the proper respect. Smith admonished the student, "Silence, young man, don't you see this is President Wheelock?" The student replied, "Ah! President Wheelock. I am happy to meet so distinguished a character, as I am no less distinguished."

In addition to the lessons they got in the classroom, students also had the opportunity to learn by accompanying the still-active physician on his rounds through the rural region. Smith was known as a doctor who applied common sense to the treatment of diseases and, as a surgeon, as a "bold and daring operator." He also had a sense of humor, joking with students that if someone in his family got sick, he didn't completely trust his skills but instead "sent for old Mrs. Dewey."

In 1813, a typhoid epidemic left one local boy with a serious leg infection. While amputation was the standard cure, Smith saved the leg by removing the damaged parts of the bone. The patient, Joseph

Smith (who was no relation to his doctor), grew up to become the prophet of the Mormon faith.

That same year, Smith departed Dartmouth, going on to play a role in founding medical schools at Yale, Bowdoin and the University of Vermont. In this way, President Wright observed, he came to be known as "the Johnny Appleseed of American medicine." [12]

At Dartmouth, he left as a physical legacy the "New Medical House," the first structure built in the United States to serve purely as a medical school, Putnam wrote. The building remained the centerpiece of Dartmouth Medical School until 1963, when it was razed — and, among many who wanted it to endure even longer, mourned.

"There are those who love it"

In 1818, one of Dartmouth's favorite sons, Daniel Webster, appeared before the U.S. Supreme Court to defend a "small college" that for a time was at risk of becoming a state university. The court's ruling would not only secure the independence of Dartmouth but also establish a bulwark that for centuries to follow would keep government from reaching too deeply into the affairs of private entities.

The "Dartmouth Case" began with a theological fistfight and growing conflict between then-President John Wheelock and the college's Board of Trustees, Richardson wrote.

In the beginning, the board's membership ran heavily to supporters of the strong-willed president. But sympathies shifted after Wheelock tried to impose his choice for a pastor at the College Church. Rather than continuing to endure a preacher known for his "monumental dullness," a group of congregants went into open revolt. Before long, "the controversy was changed from a quarrel between warring factions in the church to one between Wheelock and the board," Richardson wrote. [13]

Wheelock's intransigence on the church issue fed a growing sense among trustees that it was time for him to take his leave from governance not only of the church but also of the college. A series of clashes ensued — including the trustees' effort to weaken the position of Wheelock's chief faculty ally, medical school professor Dr. Cyrus Perkins. Wheelock, frustrated by his inability to navigate Dartmouth's internal shoals, took his case to the public in a collection of not-so-anonymous pamphlets that gave the reader an "impression of trustee arrogance, bigotry and incompetence."

The embattled president's next stop was the New Hampshire Statehouse, where in 1815 he asked lawmakers to "investigate definite perversions in college management." The trustees responded by firing Wheelock, and a private college's feud became a very public matter. It seemed Wheelock might prevail, as "a majority of the people of New Hampshire were convinced that a liberal and forward-looking college executive was being driven from office by the bigotry of a reactionary cabal."

The state elections of 1816 had at their heart the college dispute, Richardson wrote, as candidates lined up on either side of the question. The pro-Wheelock Democrats prevailed, sweeping

Federalists from power and rewarding Wheelock by changing the name of the institution from Dartmouth College to Dartmouth University, packing the board with Wheelock supporters and effectively placing the school under state control.

The trustees fought back, asserting that the state takeover violated the terms of Dartmouth's royal charter, which they asserted was a private contract immune to government meddling. By 1817, Hanover played host to two competing institutions: the trustee-controlled Dartmouth College, which enrolled most of the students but had lost custody of most of the buildings, and the Wheelock-led Dartmouth University, which controlled the structures but had precious few students to instruct.

For the most part, relations between students of each were friendly, even as the conflict between their elders simmered. There were, however, a few notable dustups.

The first came in 1817 when the commencement exercises for both institutions were scheduled at the same time in College Church. The College students took over the church the day before, arming themselves with stones, canes and clubs. The University students remained at a safe remove.

Later that year, a dispute over who controlled the books used by students of both institutions led to a clash of partisans with "upraised axes." Happily, "the melee terminated without a blow being struck on either side."

Shortly before these clashes, on April 4, 1817, John Wheelock died of dropsy and his son-in-law, Francis Brown, took over as president. The next spring, on March 10, 1818, the dispute ended up at the U.S. Supreme Court. There, Webster, class of 1801, delivered his now-famous argument against the state takeover of his alma mater.

Webster and his fellow lawyers argued that the state had overstepped its authority by interfering with a private contract between the king and the college's trustees. If allowed to proceed, the argument went, private entities of all sorts — colleges, corporations, charities — would be subject to heedless state interference and control.

"Shall our state legislature be allowed to take that which is not their own, to turn it from its original use, and apply it to such ends or purposes as they, in their discretion, shall see fit?" Webster asked Chief Justice John Marshall and his fellow jurists. "Sir, you may destroy this little institution; it is weak, it is in your hands. I know it is one of the lesser lights in the literary horizon of our country."

"You may put it out, but if you do you must carry through your work!" he continued. "You must extinguish, one after another, all those great lights of science which, for more than a century, have thrown their radiance over the land!"

And then thundered the line for which Webster has been forever known: "It is sir, as I have said, a small college — and yet there are those who love it."

Webster was then 36, having served two terms representing New Hampshire in the U.S. House of Representatives, but hardly the national figure he would become. According to an account of Professor Chauncey A. Goodrich of Yale, later woven into

Rufus Choate's eulogy of Webster, the young orator's speech had a profound effect on the nation's highest court — an effect produced by both the power of the legal argument and the passion with which it was delivered.

"The court-room during these two or three minutes presented an extraordinary spectacle," Goodrich wrote, in a passage quoted by Richardson. "Chief Justice Marshall, with his tall, gaunt figure bent over as if to catch the slightest whisper, the deep furrows of his cheek expanded with emotion, and eyes suffused with tears; Mr. Justice Washington at his side with his small emaciated frame, and countenance more like marble than I ever saw on any other human being, leaning forward with an eager troubled look, and the remainder of the court at the two extremities, pressing, as it were, toward a single point, while the audience below were wrapping themselves round in closer folds beneath the bench to catch each look and every movement of the speaker's face."

Nearly a year later, on Feb. 2, 1819, the court ruled in the college's favor, finding Dartmouth's royal charter had the power of any other private contract and could therefore not be subsumed by the state. Dartmouth University was no more, and the "small college" of Dartmouth could continue in most any way it chose. The court's decision would become one of its most historically significant in court history, serving as a "bulwark of private property" and its right to exist free of government control.

In Hanover, the ruling had a power that extends

to this day. Rather than setting down the path to become a state university, with an ever-broadening collection of graduate programs as well as under-graduate ones, Dartmouth would remain — in fact and, more significantly, in the collective imagina-tion — a "small college."

Upon hearing of the court ruling, Congressman Joseph Hopkinson wrote to then-Dartmouth Presi-dent Brown to congratulate him on the victory over "legislative despotism," according to *A College on the Hill*. "I would have an inscription over the door of your building, 'Founded by Eleazar Wheelock, Refounded by Daniel Webster.' " [14]

The protracted battle had left Dartmouth spir-itually exhausted and financially depleted, and it would require a long climb back to vigor. But the court ruling also ensured that the college — and others like it — could raise money without fear that the government would tell them how to spend it.

In a 1945 memoir, sociology professor John Moffatt Mecklin wrote that the judgment "assured the college corporate security and independence and made possible the accumulation of millions of endowment." Without that, he said, "the freedom of the great Eastern colleges was hardly possible." [15]

Chapter Two
The Medical School Thrives

The long siege had left the college independent, but financially depleted. As the overall institution struggled to shore up its budget, though, Nathan Smith's medical school throve. Even a "small college," it seemed, had room for a growing professional school.

With Smith gone to Yale, two other professors, Drs. Reuben D. Mussey and Cyrus Perkins, worked to fill the void. Mussey was known as an accomplished physician, popular teacher and well-respected member of the community "despite certain outstanding peculiarities, such as an extreme devotion to the cause of vegetarianism," Richardson noted.[16] Dr. Perkins was the one member of the medical faculty who aligned himself with the Wheelock/University contingent; he resigned to private practice once that cause was lost.

A new professor, Dr. James Freeman Dana, was a Harvard graduate and a professor who loved research at least as much as teaching. He published papers on subjects including the new science of electromagnetism but "did not find the atmosphere of the college favorable to investigation" and in 1826 departed for the College of Physicians and Surgeons in New York. There, the attendees at his popular lectures included Samuel F. B. Morse, a portrait artist who was so inspired by Dana that he went on to help invent the telegraph.

The departure of Dana, and his research, was an early sign of the tension that would continue to simmer in the decades that followed. Could a "small college" be home to both cutting-edge research and inspiring instruction?

At the medical school, Dr. Mussey kept busy not only training future doctors but also leading a "vigorous temperance agitation, which, "to judge from faculty records … was probably much needed," Richardson wrote.[17] Mussey was also a researcher who wasn't afraid to immerse himself in his experiments. To prove that human skin was absorbent, for instance, he soaked himself in tubs of water full of chemicals while making careful notes on the results, Putnam wrote. He brought fame to the school and himself with his successful ligation of a carotid artery, a feat the school used to advertise itself. [18]

Two decades after an ecclesiastical wrestling match set in motion the conflict over Dartmouth's future that had to be resolved by the nation's highest court, a smaller but no less lively contretemps sent waves through the medical school, Richardson wrote in his history of the college.

Benjamin Hale, a chemistry professor who had joined the faculty in 1827, was a devout Episcopalian who began holding small services attended by one of his colleagues, Professor Daniel Oliver, and a handful of students. For a time, he held the services in the medical building, but that drew a protest from some faculty members who objected to using the college building. Hale agreed to move the services to his home.

He didn't stop there, however, going on to organize a small worship group in Norwich, the small town just across the Connecticut River from Hanover. A few members of that town's Congregational assembly joined him, to the vocal displeasure of their former pastor. Did Hale keep quiet and allow the controversy to blow over? Hardly.

"He showed his satisfaction over the Norwich converts rather too publicly and set forth, moreover, high pretensions to superiority over the evangelical ministers of the vicinity," Richardson wrote.[19]

Well. Some of those ministers took their displeasure to Dartmouth trustees, who — having already had an earful about Hale's medical school services — decided in 1835 to show him the door. They didn't fire him directly, but instead hired another professor of chemistry, thus rendering Hale's services largely unnecessary. Showing their appreciation for irony, though, they still asked "Hale, now without title or rank, to help them out for the time being by giving the lectures in chemistry" for the remainder of the term.

Hale, no shrinking violet, fired back. After wrapping up the term, he distributed a pamphlet entitled "Valedictory Letter to the Trustees of Dartmouth College," in which he catalogued not only the injustices done to him personally but also their lack of support for scientific studies generally, as well as their disrespect for the nonsectarian character established by the college charter of 1769. Shortly after that, a competing pamphlet appeared to accuse Hale of being the one to diminish the quality of scientific instruction. Further, the pamphlet asserted, "a better teacher could be secured at a cheaper rate."

When it came to the college's support for serious scientific scholarship in this era, that truth seemed to be on the side of Hale. It appeared that not much had changed since when Hale's predecessor, Dr. Dana, said physical science at Dartmouth "was like a log anchored in the stream which only served to slow its velocity." The brouhaha didn't slow Hale's velocity; he went on to become the well-regarded president of Hobart College.

In 1839, Samuel McGill became the first Black student to earn a Dartmouth medical degree. He had left the United States as a child and spent the rest of his youth in Liberia, but then returned to study medicine at Washington College in Maryland. After students there protested his presence, Dartmouth opened the door.[20]

Some of the school's alumni rose to positions of prominence. One, Charles Knowlton, graduated in 1824 and eight years later published a small book, *The Fruits of Philosophy.* Its title notwithstanding, the book was not a philosophical tract but instead a highly practical guide to birth control for couples who wanted to carefully plan their families, Putnam wrote.

The book proved a best seller not only in the United States but also in the United Kingdom. It also caused an uproar, "particularly among a certain class of pious, self-appointed protectors of public morals." Knowlton underwent three trials, one of which resulted in a three-month jail sentence. And his British publishers also faced criminal prosecution for publishing an "indecent, lewd, filthy, bawdy, and obscene book."[21]

Nearly a century later, in 1934, writer Lewis Mumford would publish an article about Dartmouth in *The New Republic* in which he not only waxed poetic about the college and the Baker Library frescoes of Jose Clemente Orozco but also, briefly, about Knowlton's humble beginnings as a medical student.

"Six miles up the Connecticut Valley from White River Junction lies Hanover," Mumford wrote. "Here, Eleazar Wheelock, dreaming to turn the Indians into rational citizens of Heaven, planted something the New England farmer once valued almost as much as piety and thrift and hard labor: a college."

Just as the undergraduate college attracted students of Webster's caliber, Mumford wrote, so did its graduate program. "(T)o the Dartmouth Medical School, the first of its kind in America, came as a young man the foremost American advocate of birth control, bearing an overripe corpse in his wagon to defray the costs of tuition."[22]

From the school's beginnings, faculty members and students struggled to come up with a steady supply of corpses to dissect during anatomy classes. Regular midnight incursions of local cemeteries stirred ill will among local residents, though, sometimes leading to a call at the medical school from the local constable. In 1809, medical school student E.D. Cushing was indicted by a grand jury for "raising the dead."

The body snatching also led to some creative pranks by medical students, who brought their finds to the chapel where undergraduates and medical students alike gathered each day. "More than once, a corpse from the medical school was ghoulishly propped up in the freshman section to shock those fresh from guileless homes."[23]

Nathan Lord and the university question

In 1828, the trustees named one of their own to assume the presidency. The Rev. Nathan Lord (like all but the junior Wheelock, a man of the cloth) left behind the ministry to try his hand at administration. He became the first of the college's presidents to prepare a formal inaugural address, during which he turned — as so many had and would — to the question of whether Dartmouth should continue to be first and foremost a college devoted to educating undergraduates in the liberal arts.[24]

Lord's answer, according to Richardson, was an emphatic yes. He mentioned "the possibility of eventually enlarging the institution to the status of a university," but just as quickly rejected it in the near term because 'the attempt to magnify the college'" while it was still a fledgling institution risked diluting its purpose.

While the college's curriculum was "introductory to professional study," it was not "designed for individuals who were to engage in mercantile, mechanical or agricultural operations," he declared. It should emphasize first a mastery of the classics. "It is not probable that the name of scholar will ever be awarded to one who has not loved to spend his days and nights upon the pages of antiquity nor drunk deep from those original sources of taste and genius and philosophy," he continued.

By 1841 — 13 years into what would be a 35-year tenure — Lord's thinking on the university question shifted after he had confronted the fragile state of the college bank account. Mindful of the Dartmouth Case and determined not to turn to lawmakers for financial support, he turned instead to winning over New England ministers in hopes they would help open channels of private donation. Why not, he mused, add to the medical school professional schools in divinity and law?

"Another step will then place the College in the position of a University, to which the Div. Providence has been so evidently leading it and for which the public opinion is, in a great degree, prepared," Lord wrote. "There will hardly be a doubt to those who look carefully into this subject that professional students, as well in law, as in Medicine and Divinity, may be drawn to the Institution in sufficient numbers to meet the wants of this portion of the country and to sustain such Departments even upon slender endowment."

Opportunities found and lost at the medical school
While the law and divinity schools did not materialize during the administration of Lord or any of his successors, the medical school continued to operate — if not to grow dramatically. Attendance consistently stood at about 100 in the early years, and the practice of students paying their tuition directly to the professors meant that the three faculty members each earned a better wage than did their colleagues teaching undergraduates at Dartmouth College.

"The receipts, divided among them, gave to each an income (for 14 weeks of active teaching) considerably in excess of that which the academic professors received for the work of the entire year," wrote Richardson. The professors didn't just teach; aided by their students, they also treated ailing residents, establishing Hanover as the medical hub of a region far removed from the hospitals of Boston and other cities.[25]

The school had its turmoil. In the middle of the 1830s, all three faculty members left in rapid succession. The first, Hale, was "summarily ejected from his office" by trustees; the second, Oliver, quit in protest; the third, the beloved Dr. Mussey, resigned to take a job at the Cincinnati Medical School. By 1847, competition from other schools had cut the student body in half.

A succession of other professors followed the original three, including some who would go on to become Dartmouth legends. Some of those legends only stayed a short while, including Dr. Oliver Wendell Holmes, who taught anatomy and physiology at Dartmouth in the late 1830s before going on to a long and distinguished life as a professor at Harvard, a Boston author and father of Supreme Court Justice Oliver Wendell Holmes, Jr.

Holmes had decidedly mixed feelings about the school's rural location, writing on one occasion to fellow professor Dixi Crosby that "contrary to my expectations, I arrived in Boston in one whole piece. I thought I should have been a living museum of comminuted fractures before I had ploughed through twenty miles of what you call *The Road* by a singular misnomer, in New Hampshire," Putnam wrote.[26]

Crosby stayed in Hanover much longer, serving as professor of surgery from 1838 to 1869. He taught from a background of "skill and daring" at the operating table, Richardson wrote. While apprenticing with his surgeon father, Crosby had performed a successful amputation on a man whom his father had given up as a lost cause. Another time, he and his father found themselves at a distant emergency without their instruments.

"Whereupon the young Dixi secured the family carving knife, sharpened it upon a grindstone, whetted it on a razor hone, and with this and a hand saw the pair proceeded to the task." The patient survived.

Crosby enjoyed a storied career at Dartmouth and in New Hampshire's medical community. "Dr. Dixi's Hospital" on North College Street was the first in town. In 1846, Crosby observed the new ether dome in operation at Massachusetts General

Hospital and introduced anesthesia at his hospital on North College Street in Hanover.

He became a beloved figure in Hanover and its rural environs: "a robust, imposing man with a large nose and full beard, exuding cheerfulness and confidence, as he lectured to his students, as he traveled the countryside in sulky and sleigh."

Crosby had an inventive and entrepreneurial spirit. Also in 1846, he teamed up with Valentine Mott and members of the nearby Shakers religious sect to develop Syrup of Sasparilla, which became a popular remedy. In 1853 he played a key role in America's budding oil industry. Intrigued by Kier's Rock Oil, a petroleum being marketed as a health balm, Crosby and chemistry professor Oliver Payson Hubbard examined it and found it to contain more than medicinal benefits. It wasn't long before the Pennsylvania crude was being proclaimed "an illuminating material superior to anything in use."[27]

As was the case with the college, the medical school student body was all-male. In addition to giving lectures open only to the official medical students who came bearing admission tickets, members of the faculty also gave public lectures that were well-attended by a full range of townspeople — including females.

Their presence did not go unremarked. According to Putnam, one student, Parsons Whidden, in 1828 wrote a note suggesting that he regretted that "the Girls don't attend the Chimical Lectures as they have heretofore." Another man fretted that women attending one lecture might, when presented with the material, "tumble to pieces."

In 1852, Dartmouth missed a "dramatic opportunity to set a historical precedent" when it briefly considered, but then rejected, a request from Emily Blackwell of Cincinnati to attend lectures as a full-fledged student. The three professors agreed that "in the opinion of this Faculty we should not be justified by the medical profession of New England in complying with her request." Undeterred, Blackwell successfully applied to Western Reserve Medical College in her home state of Ohio, from which she earned a degree in 1854. Putnam concluded, "Women applicants just were not taken very seriously at Dartmouth."[28]

And what of the students — all men — who were admitted? Most students during the 19th century underwent oral exams from their professors, who left a paper trail not of As and Bs but of adjectives ranging from "poor" to "excellent," with the occasional "tolerably" tossed in, Putnam wrote. In 1882, Professor Lyman B. How would be less vague in his assessment of the 18 students who had failed his anatomy and physiology examination. The list of names bore his header: "Strangulati pro bono publico." Happily for their future patients, 23 other would-be physicians had passed the exam.

Moral character carried as much weight as academic performance, it appears. According to the Statutes of the Medical Institution of Dartmouth College published in 1842, "satisfactory evidence" of "good moral character" was required for graduation. That didn't mean, of course, a complete lack of youthful energy along the way. Professor Edwin Bartlett provided a glimpse:

The order of a medical school was self-regulated and peculiar. The jovial medic, cramped and constrained during a long morning spent on the hard seats of the amphitheater, had a way of easing joints and nerves before and after lectures by singing, stamping and the most boisterous horse-play, sometimes passing a man up from the lowest tier of seats to the top with shrieks and howls of artless glee; but the minute the lecturer entered the room all noise stopped as though the sportive crew had been changed to stone.[29]

Old Medical school buildings: Vail and Remsen. *Image courtesy of Geisel School of Medicine.*

Chapter Three
The Move Toward Becoming a University

President Lord's openness to new, university-like avenues of study was tested by a fat bequest with troublesome strings attached. In 1851, a Harvard graduate and successful businessman, Abiel Chandler, left Dartmouth $50,000 to establish a school to provide instruction "in the practical or useful arts of life composed chiefly in the branches of mechanics and civil engineering, the invention and manufacture of machinery" and so forth, delivered with a foundation of modern languages, literature, bookkeeping and "the careful inculcation of the principles of pure morality, piety and religion."[30]

While vesting Dartmouth faculty and trustees with the power to oversee the new school, Chandler's will required that a board of visitors be established to oversee — and exercise veto power over

31

— that decision making. Neither Lord nor trustees were pleased with those conditions nor sanguine about the prospects of success, but they found it impossible to turn down such a big gift. The Chandler School of Science and the Arts was born.

While its mission presaged in some ways the offerings of the Thayer School of Civil Engineering that would come a decade and a half later, the Chandler School did not integrate its students or learning with that of the central college. It did, however, stir considerable ill will there.

Because Chandler's bequest specified that students be accepted only after establishing that they had studied "subjects taught in the common schools of New England," Chandler undergraduates tended to arrive in Hanover less prepared than their Dartmouth College brethren. While some members of Dartmouth faculty taught Chandler students, others fretted that the lower admission standards would debase the currency of a Dartmouth degree.

While Dartmouth science professors made extra money teaching Chandler students, their colleagues in classics, language and literature had no such opportunities — and came to resent the resulting income gap. While the passage of time eased tensions somewhat, "the salary scale was, nevertheless, a point of friction as long as the Chandler School endured."

By the time the 20th century arrived, international financier Edward Tuck would become one of Dartmouth's greatest benefactors. But in 1861, Tuck was simply a Dartmouth undergraduate joining his classmates in taking stock of America's looming

Civil War.

In letters to his father excerpted in Brown's *Dartmouth Reader*, Tuck wrote of the beginning of the Civil War and its impact on him and his classmates. "This noon the Telegraph confirmed last night's rumor that Fort Sumter had been unconditionally surrendered," he wrote from Hanover on April 14, 1861. "...Everybody talks of war, 9 out of 10 profess willingness to 'go down and fight' and I've no doubt a majority of these talkers would really go if things came to the worst."

A week later, he wrote that with the term almost over the professors "are driving us very hard." At the same time, he wrote of his desire to join a student-only battalion being formed. "I wish you would give me permission."

By June of that year, though, Tuck wrote to his sister that the "war spirit has entirely evaporated at Dartmouth, leaving in its stead a spirit of destruction & devilry." One piece of evidence came courtesy of what was then Dartmouth's only graduate school:

"Last night a skeleton was stolen from the Medical College and suspended from the ceiling in the Chapel, directly over the Student's seats," he wrote. "Unluckily for the perpetrators of the deed, it was discovered before Prayers & removed, but it had to be cut to pieces, some of which remained in the Chapel, together with a large hole through which a rope had been let down, fastened to the beast and pulled up again."

"I have procured, fortunately, a collarbone to preserve as a trophy. It will be very hard for those who are found out, if any there are, as the skeleton, an immense one, was worth $50 to say the least and has hung for a long time in the Lecture Room at the Med. Coll. building and will be missed for that reason."[31]

New schools for farmers and engineers

Under Asa Dodge Smith, who took over as Dartmouth president in 1863, the "small college" seemed to be striding toward university status. The medical school had been joined by the Chandler School, and soon a federal act and a generous general would add two more "associated schools" to the mix.

Chandler averaged about 72 students in the years following the Civil War. Despite that modest success, though, its stock did not rise among Hanover's academic elite. Students attended classes in "the ugliest building in Hanover." A proposal to change its name to the "Chandler Scientific Department" met with scorn from the college's liberal arts faculty, who agreed Chandler "could not properly be called a *department* of the college; its aims were absolutely dissimilar and its scholastic requirements and standards definitely lower."

Just as unwelcome was a new agricultural school, created courtesy of the federal Morrill Act of 1862, which established land-grant institutions of higher education in every state. For a time, New Hampshire's resided in Hanover, where Dartmouth agreed to host it. The New Hampshire College of Agriculture and Mechanic Arts opened in 1868 and offered undergraduate students the chance to combine book- and hands-on learning in facilities that included an experimental farm.

While Dartmouth operated in farm country, animosity toward the agricultural college festered on campus much as it had with the Chandler School. A column in The Dartmouth student newspaper in April 1876 sniffed that the ag school's admission standards were "superficial" and its requirements for graduation "beneath contempt," Richardson wrote.

Receiving a warmer welcome was a new "associated school" that — unlike the Chandler and agricultural schools — was designed to be primarily a graduate program. In July 1867, General Sylvaneous Thayer made the first of a series of gifts to establish what became the Thayer School of Civil Engineering.

Sylvanus Thayer was valedictorian of his class at Dartmouth College, 1807, but he left Hanover three months before graduation to enroll as a cadet at West Point. He finished in one year, fought in the War of 1812 and then went on to become superintendent of West Point from 1817-1833, earning the moniker "father of West Point."[32]

Thayer revered Napoleon and had initially wanted to enter the new United States Military Academy, but there was no room when he finished high school. So at age 18, he enrolled at his second choice, Dartmouth. When he arrived at West Point as a cadet four years later, the military school was barely five years old. "It was a sorry institution. There were no physical or mental requirements for entrance. Class attendance was not required," William Phelps

Kimball — who served as Thayer dean from 1945-61 — wrote in his 1971 account of the school's first century. "Discipline was a word unknown in the school's vocabulary."[33]

Thayer changed that, laying the groundwork for West Point to become the institution it is today. After a career leading the military academy and the Army Corps of Engineers, Thayer approached President Smith with the idea for creating an engineering school at Dartmouth that would offer a technical education with a base in the liberal arts.

Thayer was in his eighties but still had plenty of energy, ideas and fondness for his alma mater. He also had wealth. To get the school off the ground, General Thayer gave the school gifts totalling $70,000 and threw in a library full of manuscripts, books and engineering plates from Europe and the United States.

The school began small, with one faculty member/director and a handful of students. Thayer and Smith set a high standard for that pioneering teacher and administrator, and they found him in the form of another West Point man, 23-year-old Lt. Robert Fletcher.

Thayer and Smith considered at least a dozen candidates before settling on Fletcher. While they had hopes for Fletcher, their offer to him was provisional. His diary entry for July 9, 1870, said Thayer "wishes me to take charge of [the school] until it shall appear whether or not I am competent." Once he got the job, Fletcher earned a healthy paycheck. His $2,500 annual salary was $1,000 more than other Dartmouth professors at the time.[34]

Thayer and Smith agreed that the school should be controlled by a board of overseers that included the college president and professionals from outside Dartmouth. The board began meeting in 1873, with the power to hire and fire faculty members, set tuition and admission standards, and make sure students had proven themselves worthy of a degree.

Thayer wanted his school to be selective and "train only men having a high order of scientific ability." He advised Fletcher to use entrance exams to be sure students demonstrated a strong grounding in not only mathematics and the sciences but also in grammar, history and surveying. Fifteen of the first 100 students "had no college education at all," but most did — largely at Dartmouth.[35]

Thayer's original gift called for a "School of Architecture and Civil Engineering." But after Smith noted that some might see "architecture" as a fine art, they agreed on Thayer School of Civil Engineering — the label it bore for 72 years when, in 1941, the word "Civil" was dropped.

The school opened in the fall of 1871, just a year before Thayer died. By 1879, Fletcher had shaped the curriculum that would remain at the core of Thayer until 1918, with courses in surveying, mechanics, resistance of materials, properties of construction materials, materials and structural elements, bridges and roofs, hydraulic works, heat and heat-engines, sanitary engineering, rivers and harbors, rockwork, tunneling, mining, masonry and foundations.

At the beginning, engineering classes were "a moveable feast" as Fletcher provided instruction in a variety of rooms in Reed, Wentworth and Thornton halls. At one point, the college allowed Thayer students to use a basement workshop in Culver Hall, "on the condition that the engineering students were to apply their mechanical skills to such projects as minor repairs for the College."

Fletcher made clear from the beginning that he was aiming to mold not narrow specialists, but engineers who had "a broad and accurate (although it may be, at first, a somewhat superficial) knowledge of each of the principal branches of the science." At the heart of learning, Fletcher impressed upon his charges, was toil. "One course conducted at Thayer school cannot be found listed in College catalogs," one former graduate recalled. "It should be called the Theory of Hard Work."[36]

Fletcher didn't exempt himself from that requirement, Kimball wrote. He was a strong teacher "who considered it his duty to mold character as well as intellect." During the first academic year (1871-72), he taught 14 different courses, a number that rose to 36 the following year, along with handling all the administrative chores. Even for a man with a strong work ethic, it was a heavy load. Two years in, he asked overseers for some help. In a missive to the board, he wrote he wanted to lead the school "faithfully and well" but could no longer "do the work which should be divided at least among two or three or, better, among four."

The overseers wanted to hire some help for Fletcher, but money was tight. While Thayer had intended his engineering school to operate independently of Dartmouth, it was clear from the start that the general's endowment wouldn't cover even the school's modest expenses.

It was another three years before the board hired another full-time professor. Thayer's endowment barely covered Fletcher's paycheck and the class averaged only five students until 1894, meaning tuition revenue remained barely a trickle.

In the 1872-73 academic year, tuition revenues totaled $108 — three percent of the school's operating costs that year. (Nearly a century later, in 1968-69, the $256,000 in tuition revenue would cover nearly 20 percent of the operating costs, with research income and a college subsidy closing the gap.)[37]

In 1891, Fletcher quietly launched the school's first capital campaign, asking overseers to solicit "friends and patrons of the higher technical education" to contribute cash for books, instruments and teaching help, according to a brief institutional history produced by the school. The fundraising effort sought $50,000 to cover, among other things, a pay increase for the school's second professor.[38]

It wasn't all toil for Fletcher. When he arrived from West Point to begin his 50 years at Thayer, Hill wrote, "he found much to entertain him." He rented a room in the house of Professor John Proctor on the west side of the Green, played croquet, attended reading parties, went on picnics with the college's banker and, in 1871, became engaged to the banker's daughter, Ellen Huntington.

The newlyweds moved into a house on College Street, where there was wood to be gathered, coal to be carried, six fires to be stoked, prayers to be said, "sanitary and recreative" exercise to be had, letters to be written, and, of course, a school to run. "Methodical, as befitted an engineer, he arose at six and retired at nine-thirty," Stearns Morse wrote in the 1964 *College on the Hill*.[39]

Fletcher kept a diary rich with details not only of his daily routines but also of Hanover's increasingly lively social scene, in which the engineering school leader and his wife played a central role. They hosted ice cream and cake parties, attended lectures by such notables as Siberian adventurer George Kennan and literary theorist Matthew Arnold, and went to the theater. "In 1879, Mrs. Fletcher went to a performance of *Pinafore* given there by the students," Morse wrote, "though her husband could not think it consistent with Christian profession to attend."

Medical school moves toward independence

From the start, Putnam recounted in her 2004 history of the medical school, professors knew it would be difficult to train doctors without the cadavers — euphemistically called "subjects" — on which students could learn, dissecting instruments in hand, human anatomy.

In a town as small as Hanover, the inventory was small. Putnam wrote that one of the reasons the school's founder departed for Yale was his hope that New Haven would provide a steadier supply of corpses. Those he left behind in Hanover, however, had to fend for themselves — not infrequently by making illicit midnight scavenger runs to local graveyards.

Dartmouth students were not the only ones who turned to grave-robbing, Putnam wrote. "At all medical institutions, 'body snatching' was an issue." Even a student who would become one of Dartmouth's most beloved professors had soil on his hands. When Dixi Crosby arrived on campus, "he brought with him a body for dissection, doubtless obtained in a questionable manner."

The problem persisted deep into the 19th century. In his address at the college's centennial in 1869, longtime surgery professor Dr. Phineas Conner called on New Hampshire to help. "If Dartmouth is to give proper fundamental training, she must have and continue to have the right of legitimately securing ample anatomical material," he declared. "Let the State, let the town, let the Judiciary decide which it prefers, educated physicians in whose hands may rest the life or death of the best beloved … or half civilized worship of the decaying body."[40]

While all these weighty matters were unfolding, students were doing what students do - studying, socializing and, for some at least, making regular trips to the college gym. Dr. Crosby applauded those sweaty sessions in a commentary published in the 1867-68 college catalog:

> Since the opening of the Gymnasium I have taken the occasion to witness frequently the exercises, and the results have more than equaled my expectations. There has been no case of severe illness in the college during that time and there have been fewer instances of slight indisposition than I have ever know in the

same length of time before. Dyspepsia, debility and similar affections incident to a sedentary life, and which have hitherto been frequent in the change of seasons from winter to spring, have, during the present season, been unknown. There has been a manifest improvement in the physical tone of the college, and the increasing muscular power and agility of the young men have forced themselves on the attention even of unpracticed eyes. I am fully satisfied that these exercises have greatly subserved the general health of the students.[41]

The medical school had its first unofficial dean in Dr. Carleton P. Frost, who received his M.D. from Dartmouth in 1857, served in the Civil War and practiced in small Vermont cities before returning to Hanover in 1870 to introduce what Morse called "much-needed, newer methods of teaching medicine." Described as looking like "Michelangelo's painting of God in the Sistine Chapel, with his flowing white beard and great dignity," Frost was known in Hanover as a skilled and sympathetic, but direct, physician. His manner "sometimes disturbed those who preferred bread pills to plain truth."[42]

Dr. Dixi's Hospital closed when its namesake retired in 1870. In 1885, Dr. Frost helped start the "Dartmouth Hospital Association." The association started a small building fund, secured a tract of land at the village's northern end and helped persuade Frost's good friend, hotel magnate Hiram Hitchcock, to devote some of his considerable wealth to founding a hospital in the memory of his wife. The Mary Hitchcock Memorial Hospital was dedicated in 1893.

Like the Crosbys, the Frosts built a family tradition in medicine. Dr. Frost's son, Gilman, taught at the medical school for nearly a half-century before retiring in 1937. He was another colorful character, with a stethoscope tethered to his vest, "his black tie askew, his thin sharply chiseled face often gray with pain and weariness from his migraine headaches." Nonetheless, "he grilled and tantalized [students] with masterly Socratic questions calculated to make them think beyond the textbook facts," Stearns Morse wrote in *The College on the Hill*.[43]

The student population was growing. In 1855, the school had 58 students enrolled; by 1875, that number had grown to 79, Putnam wrote. The age range had also expanded, with students ranging from 18 to 33 years old in 1855 to students as old as 40 two decades later. Most, however, were in their early 20s; the 40-year-old had already spent ten years in practice during an era when many physicians still gained a good portion of their skills through apprenticeship.

The 1876-77 catalog details the advantages of a medical education at Dartmouth, including "the quiet of a country village," the "inexpensiveness of living" and the "resources of the college." Around that time, entrance requirements were made more specific; any students not already doing their undergraduate work at Dartmouth or graduates of another reputable school had to pass an entrance examination.

Throughout the 19th century, the relationship between the Medical School — or Medical Department, as it was often called — was "undeniably a confused affair." From the start, the medical faculty had operated with substantial independence from the college, collecting its own fees and charting its own course with a blend of classroom instruction and clinical practice. But it wasn't until 1873 that the Medical School would have its own real leader, Putnam notes, adding that "the Medical School was increasingly being recognized as an entity in its own right, which might very well have problems peculiar to it."[44]

While Nathan Smith had been pleased with "the room No. 6 in the lower storey in the College" provided by Dartmouth trustees for his early lectures, subsequent generations of professors had delivered their instruction in the "New Medical House" Nathan Smith had secured state funding to build. Six decades later, the first major renovation to the structure added, among other things, the cupola that would become the school's visual signature.[45]

A centennial tribute

On July 21, 1869, college dignitaries, alumni, faculty and students gathered to celebrate Dartmouth's first 100 years. According to a collection of the speeches given that day, President Smith welcomed the crowd, noting that "It is well that our Centennial occurs on the very year in which the Continent is first spanned with bands of iron."[46]

Samuel Brown gave the historical address, remembering Eleazar Wheelock as "an eloquent and powerful preacher" who set for himself a mission of "Christianizing and educating those wandering, untamable races, whose cunning, ferocity, and cold blooded cruelty had made them such formidable enemies to the colonists." Carved out of the wilderness beside the gently flowing Connecticut River, Brown said, "Here grew up a little community, cultivated, intelligent, refined, learned and religious."

It included not just a college for Indigenous and English undergraduate students, but also for graduate students training to be physicians. "Dr. Nathan Smith was a man of remarkable medical insight" and founded the school "which has done such thorough work for the science and art of healing." Brown also spoke of the recently established Chandler, Agricultural and Thayer schools. "The means of education now concentrated at Hanover are such as to meet the wants of almost every person who may seek knowledge or culture."

James W. Patterson added to the praise of the associated schools, adding an endorsement of those who not only taught science but also contributed to its body of knowledge. "In every zone and climate they are pushing their researches beneath the depths of the sea and into the thick crust of the earth; with unwearied curiosity they watch the movements of nature to discover her hidden laws; obstacles and dangers, pestilence and disease allure them to their generous task."

Dr. Jabez B. Upham spoke of Dartmouth's contribution to medical training. "Ours has been aptly called the quiet profession. Its workings are for the most part silent and unseen, — its dealings are with

the secrets of diseased and suffering humanity,"
he began. Into this realm stepped Smith to found
Dartmouth's medical school, from which more than
1,200 had graduated by the time of the Dartmouth
centennial, having built their success on "a systematic early education."

Thayer School students with surveying equipment, 1876.
Image courtesy of Dartmouth Engineering.

Chapter Four
Presidents Debate "College v. University"

President Smith had welcomed Dartmouth's expansion from educating undergraduates in the classics to offering lessons in the practical sciences at both the undergraduate and graduate levels. If Smith's successors had extended a similar embrace, Richardson wrote in his 1932 history, "there is not doubt that Dartmouth today would, in name at least, be reckoned as a university."[47]

Not so fast, said Samuel Bartlett, who took over the Dartmouth presidency in 1877 and held it for the next 15 years. A New Hampshire native and 1836 Dartmouth grad, Bartlett was (like his predecessors) a minister. He came to the post after serving as a professor of biblical literature at the Chicago Theological Seminary.

A man whose manner was described as "sharp,

brusque and even overbearing," he emerged from an examination of Dartmouth's finances with the conclusion that the Chandler School was not pulling its weight. While President Smith had treated the associated schools with a measure of leniency as he tried to build his university, Bartlett had no such inclination. In his view, the schools risked becoming "parasites upon the real college," Richardson wrote.

Prompted by Bartlett, college trustees cut Chandler professor pay and generally made the school feel like an unappreciated relation. Bartlett didn't stop there; he also picked a fight with the Agriculture College. At a commencement ceremony designed to celebrate the college and its graduates, Bartlett boasted of the value of the classical course of study available elsewhere at Dartmouth while asserting that the agricultural curriculum was suited for "highway surveyors, selectmen and, perhaps, members of the legislature."

"By 1881," Richardson wrote, "the faculty of that institution was almost as disaffected toward the head of the college as was that of the Chandler School."

Bartlett's sharp tongue won him a growing list of enemies. In April of that year, the trustees received a missive signed not only by professors at the Agricultural and Chandler Schools but also by the medical school's resident faculty and half the professors in the academic department, all of whom called for the president's resignation. A delegation from the Alumni Association of New York chimed in that Bartlett was alienating "the Alumni whose co-operation and assistance are so needed." And shortly after their graduation, 44 of the 61 members of the Class of 1881 joined the petition mob — perhaps less for reasons of curricular emphasis than out of resentment at the discipline Bartlett had meted out to misbehaving students.

College officials had hoped to keep the controversy out of the newspapers, but that proved impossible due in part to the success of Dartmouth men in the business. William E. Barrett, class of 1880, was editor of the *Boston Advertiser*. And one of the New York alumni detractors was none other than Charles R. Miller, class of 1872 and the newly minted editor of *The New York Times*. Those men devoted ample space to the revolt against Bartlett, an example followed by other outlets hungry for a juicy spectacle of academic warfare.

Trustees convened a formal trial at which Bartlett's critics pressed their charges and the president and his allies rebutted them. In the end, the trustees reached the conclusion that things in Hanover weren't so bad after all and told Bartlett he could stay on the job. They encouraged the combattants to stand down and work toward harmony. Their reluctance to force Bartlett out may have been rooted, at least in part, in his success at financial management. During the 1880-81 period in which the fight raged most hotly, the college's bank account showed a surplus for the first time in a quarter century.

Tensions did not abate between Bartlett and the state-supported Agricultural College, but in 1890 a Durham man made it a moot point. Benjamin Thompson left an estate worth more than $400,000 to the school — on the condition that it move to his hometown on the other side of the state. The legislature accepted that condition and the ag school sold its farm and other property to Dartmouth. In 1893, 25 years after its creation on the Hanover Plain, the institution now known as the University of New Hampshire took shape in Durham.

"It is difficult to imagine what the outcome would have been had it remained," Richardson wrote of the state university. "While a favorable result might have ensued, it seems likely that each institution would have hampered the other and that the growth eventually in store for both colleges could hardly have been attained by either."

Meanwhile, Dartmouth and its town grew in size and sophistication. After a century of slogging through springtime mud, permanent sidewalks began to line the roads of Hanover in the late 1800s. In 1877, *The Dartmouth* reported "the long wished-for telephone is working at last." An electrical lighting system arrived in 1892, along with the beginnings of a sewer system.

As the 20th century neared, it was clear the "college v. university" question was not going away. By the late 19th century, Harvard, Yale and Johns Hopkins had formed robust and growing graduate schools, while Dartmouth's offerings remained limited. At Dartmouth, Morse wrote, the questions echoed through the halls: When does a college become a university? What is the proper blend of attention to graduates and undergraduates? The proper balance of teaching and research?

"It is a truism that curiosity and a love of learning, unless inborn in a student, cannot be stimulated in him by a teacher who has not himself a curious and inquiring mind," wrote Morse. "It also seems true that a teacher, unless he is a genius, loses his creative fire if he has no contact with colleagues who are also explorers."[48]

A new president and "a new Dartmouth"

In 1892, trustees elected one of their own to replace Bartlett, who had decided at age 75 to give up the wars and retire. The Rev. William Jewett Tucker was a Dartmouth graduate and professor at Andover Theological Seminary. While Bartlett had rubbed many wrong, he had proven a skilled financial steward — meaning Tucker was the first president besides its founder who "did not find himself confronted by an acute financial crisis" upon taking the job, Richardson wrote.[49]

At first, Tucker wasn't sure he wanted the position. He had served as a Dartmouth trustee for a decade and a half when his fellow board members in 1892 urged him to take on the presidency. He at first demurred, but when the college's search for a leader remained fruitless the next year, he accepted the challenge.

Upon his inauguration in 1893, Tucker plunged right in, seeking to restore the vigor not only of the college's spiritual life but also of its institutional growth. Bartlett's conflict-ridden tenure had taken its toll, and college leaders were eager for the infusion of energy and optimism Tucker brought, Robert French Leavens and Arthur Hardy Lord wrote in their 1965 book, *Dr. Tucker's Dartmouth.*

"The election of Dr. Tucker as president brought

a sense of relief and an outburst of enthusiasm," wrote Leavens and Lord. "(T)he trustees, after more than ten years of controversy, discord, and waning vitality in the life of the college, plus a full year of fruitless effort to fill the vacant presidency" had finally ended in appointing a "competent educator."[50]

During Tucker's 16 years, college enrollment ballooned and a construction boom expanded Dartmouth's collection of dormitories and other buildings. "Few were the daylight hours, except on Sundays, during the Tucker years when saws and hammers were not to be heard," wrote Hill.[51] Some of that growth involved the professional schools — including a graduate school in business that Tucker would help to create.

While Bartlett had been an "avowed foe of associated schools," they had become an increasingly visible presence at Dartmouth, accounting for roughly half the 458-member total student body. In the 1892-93 academic year, the undergraduate college led the way with 238 students, followed by the medical school, Chandler School of Science and the Arts (77), New Hampshire College of Agriculture and the Mechanic Arts (27) and Thayer School (8).[52]

During Tucker's first year, he cheerfully bade farewell to the Agricultural College when the state moved it to Durham. He also "resolved the problems of the Chandler School, which for years had occupied the position of an unwanted stepchild" by ending its standalone status and blending its science courses with those of the college, Hill wrote.

Thinning the ranks of associated schools reduced the college's overall undergraduate population, but it didn't erase the "college vs. university" question. Tucker made it his business to fully engage that question in a way that was more nuanced and constructive than his predecessor's. In his 1919 autobiography, *My Generation,* Tucker explained his views.

Colleges associated with Dartmouth in its early history — Harvard, Yale and Princeton — had taken clear steps to define themselves as universities, Tucker wrote. Not Dartmouth. "No alumnus of Dartmouth cherished the desire to see the College become a university."[53]

The reason was partly the lingering bad taste of the attempted state takeover resolved by the Dartmouth Case, partly the limitations on such growth imposed by Hanover's geographic isolation. But it went beyond those issues, to the shared sense of remaining true to the college's original purpose. "Dartmouth was in a peculiar sense an historic college. Its history was its great asset, both moral and material," he wrote, adding the Dartmouth and those who love it want to foster "the creation of a high college sentiment, not mere college spirit."

And what of the goal of preparing people for professions and the fear that this emphasis would overly narrow the curriculum? "Dartmouth has always kept faith with the professions, and never more strictly than in support of the recent efforts for advancement of professional standards," Tucker wrote in his book. But he warned against the risks of the "university idea," which might cause "minor professional schools" to proliferate.

Those words must have stung those taking pride

53

in the educations offered at the medical and engineering schools. Tucker didn't do much to ease that sting — or to hide his disdain for predecessors who had embraced the idea of a growing university on the Hanover Plain.

"Even so sane a mind as President Lord was at one time seriously infected with the university idea," he wrote. He turned next to President Smith, for whom he said the "university idea" held an even stronger appeal. The evidence: his embrace of the state agriculture college and establishing the Thayer school "practically on the basis of a graduate school." Happily, he said, the agriculture school's removal to Durham "closed the door on further efforts in behalf of a university based on state needs or resources."

In keeping itself primarily a small college focused on providing the highest quality education in the liberal arts and a carefully curated group of graduate programs, he suggested, Dartmouth actually served the needs of the professions which Dartmouth men would enter.

The college avoided "becoming the danger to the professions which the small university, with its inferior facilities for reaching the higher professional standards, presents." He repeated with pride the praise of Yale President Arthur Twining Hadley, who had noted that Dartmouth's success in holding the ground too many of its peers had ceded, saying, "where so many institutions claim to do more than they actually accomplish, Dartmouth accomplished more than she claims."

College trustees embraced the continued emphasis on preserving Dartmouth's historic mission as an institution dedicated primarily to undergraduate excellence. Even as undergraduate enrollment grew, they stated, "the numerical growth of the college is in no sense inconsistent with the definite policy of developing the college as a college, rather than with a fear of its becoming a university."

Dartmouth did take small steps toward awarding graduate degrees — ones that finally meant something. In 1893, the college stopped granting master's degrees, as it had previously, "to any graduate of three years' standing who applied for it." From then on, at least a year of graduate work and passing a "suitable examination" would be required to earn the distinction. In 1895, the college established requirements for the PhD, though it was rarely pursued in the years that followed. "Very few of the degrees were awarded, and the college was saved from the danger of setting up a full-fledged graduate school in a place not geographically adapted to that type of work and with inadequate financial support," Richardson sniffed in the early 20th century.[54]

However limited, Dartmouth's first steps into graduate study in the arts and sciences also carried the school a tiny step toward coeducation. In 1894, a faculty query prompted the trustees' legal committee to conclude that the phrase "English youths and others" in the 1769 charter meant the college "has the power to confer degrees upon females and to admit them to the advantages of the college."

As a result, Katherine M. Quint enrolled as a graduate student and received her Master of Arts in 1896, the first woman ever to carry home a Dartmouth degree. It was hardly the start of a revolution, however. Over the three decades that followed, only a handful of women followed Quint's lead, none of them undergrads.[55] That breakthrough would not come until the 1970s.

The college in that era produced only a trickle of PhDs, including one awarded to Leland "Doc" Griggs. Doc got his undergraduate degree in 1902 and his doctorate in 1907 before going on to teach for four decades in the zoology department. Tall and round-shouldered, Griggs was popular not only for his teaching but also for his work as advisor to the Outing and Canoe clubs, the roast pig and strawberry shortcake he served at cabin parties, his impressive collection of lantern slides on spider webs, and the cage behind his house filled with live bear, timber wolf, hawks and owls.

"His aim was not merely to teach zoology but to open the eyes and minds of his students to the whole picture of nature," Morse wrote. "He was famous for his taciturnity, but when he did speak it was with a humorous twinkle and in an absolute monotone."[56]

Chapter Five
A New Century Brings an American Original

On the eve of the 20th century, President Tucker got a letter from his Dartmouth roommate, Edward Tuck, class of 1862, who had gone on to become a wealthy Paris financier. He invited Tucker to take a holiday in France. "I see by the papers that the Dartmouth Trustees have long urged you to take a leave of absence in which to get needed rest and recuperation," Tuck wrote in a letter dated October 21, 1898.

Saying he wanted to "do something for Dartmouth," Tuck enclosed a check for $1,000, saying he hoped Tucker and his wife would use it to help cover the cost of traveling to France. "I would very much like to see you, for many reasons." Tucker sailed for France and the old classmates had a lovely visit. Tucker also returned with something for Dartmouth — $300,000 worth of stock in the Great Northern Railway Company, Tuck professor and school historian Wayne Broehl recounted in his 1999 history of the school's founding and early years.[57]

The money came at an opportune time, as Tucker pursued his ambition of shaping what he envisioned as a "New Dartmouth." The college's facilities were increasingly inadequate to the task of educating a growing student body and the college was "altogether in educational crisis," in his view. "Tucker wanted to plan not just for the next ten years but for the next fifty," Broehl wrote in *Tuck & Tucker: the origin of the graduate business school*.

But Tuck didn't want his money used for just anything. Instead, he wanted it used to support teaching in the undergraduate college — and, intriguingly, "post-graduate departments." In the latter category, Tucker had an inspiration. Students of the day were increasingly preparing not only for medicine, ministry, engineering and other professions, but also for careers in business. With that in mind, Tucker proposed to tap Tuck's generosity to establish a new graduate school of business at Dartmouth — the first of its kind in the United States.

Tuck enthusiastically agreed, as did Dartmouth trustees. "The trustees were in hearty agreement and by drawing upon the experience which the College had had in operating the Thayer School to train engineers they undertook plans for a similar school to train men for business," wrote Leavens and Lord.[58]

Tuck put his money where his alma mater's hopes were. He would follow his initial gift of

$300,000 with $100,000 to construct the first Tuck Hall (now McNutt Hall) and another $575,000 in 1929 to create the Tuck Hall complex.

Edward Tuck was an 1862 graduate of Dartmouth who was one of the college's best wrestlers, graduated second in his class and went on to serve as an financial advisor to the global elite.

"International banking turned out to be the ideal field for him, for he had an uncanny sense of issues involving the gold and silver markets, currency regulations, and foreign exchange," said his biographer, Franklin Brooks. Tuck quickly rose to leadership positions in a succession of financial institutions: Munroe & Company (which merged with Morgan Bank), Chase National Bank of New York, and First National Bank (now Citicorp), according to a 1990 institutional history complied by professor Mary Munter.[59]

Tuck did so well that by 1880 — not even two decades after graduation — he was able to retire from his career working for other people. Instead, he turned to managing his own investments and living a life of generous proportions at homes in Paris, Monte Carlo and the "Vert Mont" chateau outside of Paris.

Tuck didn't just spend money on himself. He and his wife, Julie Stell, an orphaned heiress, shared their family riches with a variety of charitable causes. They supported French war relief efforts during World War I and helped underwrite military hospitals and refugee shelters, Munter wrote. They donated a new gallery and their impressive art collection to the Petit Palais museum in Paris. In New

Hampshire, they gave large gifts to Phillips Exeter Academy, the New Hampshire Historical Society and, of course, Dartmouth.

Tuck's father, Amos, an 1835 graduate, had also lived a remarkable public life — as a lawyer, congressman, Dartmouth trustee and a politician who mobilized antislavery votes in New Hampshire to form a new Republican party. Abraham Lincoln "would never have realized his goals if his old friend, Amos Tucker of Exeter, New Hampshire … had not played such an influential role in helping him to secure the Republican party's presidential nomination in 1860," said Dartmouth historian Frank Smallwood. Tuck asked that the new business school be named after his father.[60]

Like his predecessors, Tucker was devoted to preserving Dartmouth's commitment to liberal arts education and worried about "the perplexing tendency" to lose touch with that purpose by evolving into a university, Hill wrote. At the same time, he wanted to avoid the fate of liberal arts colleges that in his view were "failing to make a responsible connection, through the lack of a proper intervening training, with the world of affairs."[61]

While business schools are today a common sight in American higher education, establishing a graduate program in business in that era "was a courageous venture into the untried."[62] It also came at the right time, as the century turned and the United States experienced a period of robust economic growth and, with it, a healthy demand for college graduates who could handle increasingly complex responsibilities.

"I have noticed the growth in numbers of our graduates who go into business," Tucker wrote to two of his confidants on the Dartmouth faculty. "Can we give then a better training commensurate with the larger meaning of business as it is now understood?"[63]

In 1901, far from Wall Street, Dartmouth welcomed the first students to the Amos Tuck School of Administration and Finance. Its purpose was stated as thus:

> This school is established in the interests of college graduates who desire to engage in affairs rather than enter the professions. It is the aim of the school to prepare men in those fundamental principles which determine the conduct of affairs and to give specific instruction in the laws pertaining to property, in the management of trusts and investments, in the problems of taxation and currency, in the methods of corporate and municipal administration, and in subjects connected with the civil and consular services. The attempt will be made to follow the increasing number of college graduates who have in view administrative or financial careers with a preparation equivalent in its purpose to that obtained in the professional and technical schools. The training of the school is not designed to take the place of an apprenticeship in any given business, but it is believed that the same amount of academic training is called for, under the enlarging demands of business, as for the professions or the productive industries.[64]

The school's establishment garnered widespread attention and applause, including from its benefactor. "It will be recognized as filling a gap in modern education which may have grown to be conscious of, but which you are the first to define," Tuck wrote to Tucker. "You are likely to have imitators, but you will always be honored as the pioneer in this most important and progressive step." [65]

In an article for *The Dartmouth,* President Tucker wrote that while some believed "commercial education" should be woven into undergraduate studies, he thought that more specialized training should come in graduate school — after a solid liberal arts foundation had been laid in the undergraduate years. The goal, he said, should be "a broad-minded man interested in business."[66]

A handful of students paid the $100 tuition and became the Class of 1901, including four — Henry Teague, Walter Blair, Oliver Foster and William Edwards — who had arrived with enough education to move directly into the second year course of study. The pioneering class attended lectures in the Old Hubbard House, formerly known as the "Pest House" because it once provided a temporary home for students suffering from contagious diseases.[67]

First-year courses were taught by Dartmouth professors with a background in such liberal arts staples as English composition and speaking, modern history, political science, economics, sociology and foreign languages. One course carried this intriguing name: "Ethnology with reference to the present race question."

In their second year, students progressed to

62

subjects with more particular application to domestic and foreign commerce, including diplomacy, finance, transportation, insurance, law and demography. At this level, the instructors were often outside professionals, including an insurance company president, an export merchant, a lawyer and an accountant.

The lineup of instructors pleased Edward Tuck, who wrote to Tucker in 1902 to say, "I am glad that it will be the aim of the School to bring students in touch with practical businessmen."

For the first two years, the school did not grant degrees, as college trustees said they did not "consider it wise at present to confer an academic degree upon graduates of this School, because no existing degree adequately expresses the character of the work done." By the time of the school's third commencement in 1903, however, trustees had found a fitting degree: Master of Commercial Science.

Tuck graduated three students in 1901, four in 1902 and nine in 1903. The momentum slipped in 1904, when only one man earned a degree, but then picked back up. Edward Tuck's continuing generosity quickly allowed the school to construct its own building and employ its own dedicated faculty.

In 1904, the new Tuck School building (which became McNutt when the school moved to its current location in 1930) was dedicated. His wife's ill health prevented Tuck from making the trip, but he crafted a letter to Tucker laying out a set of principles for Tuck students, including "absolute devotion" to one's career and employer, an unflagging dedication to excellence, and "the strictest honesty and honor."

Tuck's words were memorialized on a brass plaque placed at the entrance to the school. It concluded with his hope that Tuck graduates would go out into the world not just to do well but also to do good: "Altruism," Tuck averred in the statement, "is the highest and best form of egoism."

True to Tuck's prediction, other business schools followed. In 1908, Harvard opened its Graduate School of Business Administration, an event that did not go unremarked in Hanover. "Clearly, a strong business school shepherded by formidable Harvard and located just over the border in Massachusetts, the state so important to Dartmouth in terms of enrollment, was likely to be a challenge."

But the Tuck School strode forward, attracting a growing number of students despite the growing competition. Dartmouth's approach remained distinctive, steering clear of providing a narrowly technical education in favor of one that drew on the liberal arts and instilled graduates with a sense of business's social impact.

From the start, Tuck graduates succeeded. Men who graduated in the school's first five classes went on to lead companies including Gulf Oil and United Fruit and government bodies such as the New England Planning Commission. They took executive positions as far away as Japan and China and as quirky as New Hampshire's Mt. Washington Railroad.

Schools that had begun with a narrowly practical focus soon saw the value of Tuck's broader approach. By the end of World War I, the "Tuck

Pattern" served as a beacon of thoughtful commercial education. Years later, the Carnegie Corporation would observe, "The Tuck School probably went further than any other institution in the pre-war period in putting its work on a demanding intellectual level."

Tuck set the tone in other ways. In 1911, Dean Harlow Person and the faculty invited Frederick Taylor and 300 "leading men and women of industry" to a national conference on the then-new concept of scientific management, an event that is now widely viewed as the coming-out party for the new movement. The conference led to the formation of Society for the Advancement of Management, which became the world's largest professional business association.

As Richardson wrote, "It soon became apparent that the school was to serve a real demand."[68]

Establishing the Tuck School raised anew questions about whether Dartmouth was becoming a university. "Dr. Tucker," wrote Leavens and Lord, "answered an emphatic 'No.' "[69]

In his report to trustees in the 1900-01 academic year, Tucker said that Dartmouth's collection of professional schools didn't make it a university — in part because undergraduates hoping to pursue master's degrees at Tuck and Thayer could begin their advanced education during their senior year in college. Thus, it was an "extension of the liberal arts program rather than the beginning of a graduate program," the authors wrote.

While his words came at a time when "the

glamor of the university idea was capturing men's imaginations," Tucker proudly placed Dartmouth in a different class: the "large college." Such a college, he said, could offer students the best of both worlds — the intimacy of close contact with professors paired with the kinds of broad educational opportunities found on campuses with graduate programs.

How can Dartmouth serve not only its students but also the broader world of higher education, Tucker asked in an report to trustees. "My answer is — that it has become the duty, as it seems to be the honor of Dartmouth, to lead the way, in public opinion, in the recognition of the place of the large college in our American educational life."

An engineering school powered by Yankee thrift

In 1893, at the beginning of his administration, President Tucker threw the Thayer School a lifeline. He supported allowing Dartmouth students to take courses at Thayer during their senior year and then tack on a fifth year to graduate with an engineering degree — a smaller commitment than the six years of total undergraduate and graduate study heretofore required for the degree.

As a result, enrollment climbed, from classes of about five students before 1894 to three times that many a decade later. The new policy also had the effect of making Thayer a school that served primarily Dartmouth graduates. Before the shift, nearly half of Thayer students came from other institutions. But for the next 70 years, most of them started their college careers at Dartmouth.[70]

The overseers kept a close eye, and Fletcher

accommodated them at their first meeting with a report so lengthy that the board passed a resolution "that the Professor be recommended to reduce his official writing to the least volume necessary to keep a correct general account of his department." The board also took seriously its duty to interrogate, in person, each degree candidate — "a duty which members of the Board probably enjoyed more than did the candidates" — and which endured until World War II.

Students were generally fond of Fletcher, their "one-man faculty." His interest in them extended beyond the classroom, as he warned against drinking alcohol and helped students work through personal problems. He told one class: "Gentlemen, remember that the body is like a steam boiler. Feed it regularly and rake out the clinkers and you will always be able to get up to steam."

The reviews were not all appreciative, though. One alumnus recalled Fletcher as a "didactic fuss-budget who early each winter would get us all together on a Sunday afternoon and instruct us in what underwear to use for winter." However, he added, "he was a fine teacher."

The students could see for themselves that Fletcher's knowledge came not just from books. When he wasn't teaching classes or managing administrative tasks, he was designing and overseeing construction of steel bridges across the Connecticut and White Rivers, serving as consulting engineer for the waterworks of Lebanon, New Hampshire, and serving as president and engineer of the Hanover Water Company, among other duties. Commenting on Fletcher's technical instruction, one student said, "He socked us with mechanics till it ran out of our ears."

In 1907, the ongoing cash shortage got the attention of a new overseer, Otis E. Hovey '89. Hovey approached for help none other than industrialist and philanthropist Andrew Carnegie but — after a long lobbying campaign — reported back that Carnegie "had decided against assisting the Thayer School in any manner." Carnegie said the school's rural location worked against its success and said that because Dartmouth was a college rather than a university, it should not offer "any other courses than the old-fashioned College courses." Denied a savior, Fletcher kept the school solvent with a blend of Yankee frugality and smaller donations from alumni.

Fletcher's students, and prospective students, could be just as resourceful. In 1906, a young man entered Dartmouth as a freshman bent on earning his engineering degree at Thayer.[71]

Whitney Haskins Eastman came to Dartmouth from Fort Ann, New York, following his brother Frank, who graduated in June 1906. "I thought it would be great fun to see him graduate, but I did not have enough money to pay the railroad fare," he wrote six decades later in a typescript autobiography, *The Advantage of Being Born Poor*. "An old friend of the family who was a railroad mail clerk took me as a guest in the mail car as far as Bellows Falls, Vermont. In Bellows Falls I made friends with a brakeman on a B&M train bound for Hanover, New Hampshire, and he took me as a guest in the caboose. I landed in Hanover with twenty-five cents."

Eastman had hoped his brother would front him the fare to return home but, after having worked his way through college, the recent graduate claimed poverty. He did, however, help Eastman land a position with the family of Dartmouth French professor Louis Dow that earned him 14.5 cents an hour plus "a cozy little room and three wonderful meals a day."

At the professor's urging, Eastman applied for, and won, admission to Dartmouth for the fall term of 1906. "My brother Frank was elated and wanted me to take the necessary courses so that I could enter Thayer School, a postgraduate school in Civil Engineering."

Picking up on the interdisciplinary spirit that has long animated Thayer, Eastman made sure to take a course in public speaking as part of his undergraduate preparation. "I felt public speaking was essential because my brother Frank convinced me that there were many brilliant engineers who could not sell a good idea to their superior corporate officers."

Medical school looks to its second century

As the 19th century drew to a close and the medical school approached its 100th anniversary, change was afoot at Dartmouth and well beyond. The Mary Hitchcock Memorial Hospital had been operating since 1893, with 36 beds for patients and Dartmouth Medical School faculty members providing care.

Local residents didn't exactly flock to the hospital in the beginning, Putnam wrote, owing to the "prevailing view of hospitals at the time that they were places where the destitute went to die." But over time, the hospital would come to be known as a place where patients could find first-class care and where Dartmouth medical students could acquire crucial clinical experience.[72]

Attendance at the medical school rose to its highest-ever level — 161 students — in 1895-96. Dr. Carlton P. Frost had acted as the medical school's de facto dean, and in 1896 the faculty made it official by naming one of their colleagues, Dr. William Thayer Smith, as the first official dean — just in time for the school to celebrate its 100th birthday in 1897.

At that time, a movement was sweeping the nation to require a set period of time — four years of medical school studies, with a curriculum that would allow graduates to be licensed in any state — for the M.D. degree. Dartmouth joined in that shift, with a deadline set by an 1897 New Hampshire law requiring the four-year program. The new approach began in the 1898-99 academic year.

In the 1899-1900 year, first-year students had to attend classes 20 hours a week, with their time divided between the foundational sciences (biology, chemistry and physics) and anatomy. That time commitment jumped in their second year, with 34 hours of class time unfolding across six days of the week. Only Sunday was free for rest, recreation and, presumably, study before the demanding week to come.

In 1902, college trustees scrapped the practice of having students pay their tuition fees directly to the faculty, Richardson wrote. At the same time, entrance requirements were toughened, with at least two years of undergraduate study required before admission to the 4-year medical program. Perhaps as a result, the number of students in the medical school declined sharply, to around sixty.[73]

On a less momentous note, the presence of medical students on the college football team had created a stir as the 19th century came to a close. Not unlike today, the drive to win was fierce as the college vied for dominance in the "triangular league" of Dartmouth, Amherst and Williams. The rival schools protested the fielding of Dartmouth medical students, arguing that they were older, faced different admissions standards than undergraduates and that had plenty of time to develop their athletic skills given that — in the view of critics — "the requirements for actual work during the year might be practically *nil*."

The matter went to a formal vote by the league in 1893, and Dartmouth's opponents pushed through a ban on medical student players. That sparked outrage among Dartmouth students and corresponding outrage from students at the other schools. In the end, the controversy cooled down, although it was years before it went away. A majority of Dartmouth undergrads clung to their view that their medical school classmates should be allowed to play, "and the agitation for their reinstatement was continued as late as 1902" — to no avail.[74]

As the 19th century gave way to the 20th, Johns Hopkins University pioneered an approach to medical education that would soon become the national

model. And Dartmouth? Its medical educators —
along with those at other schools — were soon to
receive a rude awakening.

Public confidence in the quality of medical
care had begun to flag late in the 19th century, as a
hodgepodge of educational approaches and a pleth-
ora of for-profit medical schools sent physicians
into practice with skills that were uneven at best.
Such worries drove laws such as New Hampshire's
requiring four years of rigorous training. And the
large number of American physicians-to-be who ac-
quired their training in Europe returned "increasingly disturbed by low-grade education and by the lack
of effective licensing" back home, Putnam wrote.[75]

A decade into the new century, the Carnegie
Foundation for the Advancement of Teaching com-
missioned a comprehensive review of American
medical education. Its author, Carnegie Foundation
President Henry S. Pritchett, minced no words in introducing the report's findings. For a quarter century,
he said, the nation had suffered from an "enormous
overproduction of uneducated and ill trained medical practitioners." The for-profit schools were the
chief villains, but the report also identified shortcomings at respected non-profit schools in hopes
that "this publication may serve as a starting-point
both for the intelligent citizen and for the medical
professional in a new national effort to strengthen
the medical profession."

The report's chief investigator was Abraham
Flexner, an educator and medical layman who certainly did his homework — paying personal visits
to all 155 medical schools in the United States and

Canada, including Dartmouth. At every one, he compared what he found to the widely respected example of the medical school at his alma mater, Johns Hopkins.

Flexner described Johns Hopkins as "the first medical school in America of genuine university type, with something approaching adequate endowment, well equipped laboratories conducted by modern teachers, devoting themselves unreservedly to medical investigation and instruction, and with its own hospital, in which the training of physicians and the healing of the sick harmoniously combine to the infinite advantage of both," Putnam wrote.

After visiting Hanover, Flexner pronounced himself pleased with the classroom and laboratory lessons given to students. But when it came to opportunities for the full range of clinical experience, he found that Dartmouth — located as it was in a sparsely populated region with a resulting scarcity of sick patients — fell short.

The clinical facilities are "very limited," consisting of a 40-bed hospital and no outpatient clinic. "The development of its clinical work presents a serious difficulty. The village is rather inaccessible; the surrounding country is thinly populated … Surgical cases are attracted easily enough. Can medical cases be attracted too? Certainly not without a very large outlay in the form of professional salaries and hospital expense," his report stated. "That the school cannot much longer continue in its present stage is clear."

Dartmouth's misery had company, as Flexner took stock of institutional offerings and patient demand and concluded that only two New England schools — Harvard and Yale — should continue in present form. "A thoroughly wretched institution, like the College of Physicians and Surgeons of Boston, would at once be wiped out. The clinical departments of Dartmouth, Bowdoin and the University of Vermont would certainly be lopped off," he wrote.

Flexner's finding was clear: While Dartmouth provided a solid education in the first two, largely nonclinical, years of study, the education it offered beyond that was substandard and, thus, unsustainable. The Carnegie report sent waves of shock, anger — and, ultimately, deep reflection — through Dartmouth and other institutions.

Flexner made no apologies. "The improvement of medical education cannot … be resisted on the ground that it will destroy schools and restrict output; that is precisely what is needed," he wrote. What the nation needs, he said, is "fewer and better doctors."

Compounding miseries, in early 1910 President Nichols received a letter from N.P. Colwell of the national Council on Medical Education, saying that, "owing to the extremely limited clinical and hospital facilities, we cannot list as satisfactory the last two or clinical years" of the Dartmouth medical curriculum. Noting that Hanover's small population made it unlikely that this situation would much improve, Colwell added, "if the money at present expended toward the work of the last two years were used to further develop the work of the first two, it would enable you to strengthen to a great extent that portion of the medical course."

Dartmouth officials publicly pooh-poohed such criticisms. In 1911, the year after getting hammered by Flexner and the Council, Dean John M. Gile wrote a piece for Dartmouth's alumni magazine dismissing declining enrollment and extolling such advances as an "entirely remodelled" operation room, the strong job placements of graduates and concluding that in "steadily raising the standard of admission and curriculum the faculty and trustees have taken the step that they believe the future of medical education demands." Some of the push-back bordered on the melodramatic, with one professor saying that giving up the final two clinical years in Hanover would amount to "a crime."

On campus, however, medical school officials had been making efforts to modernize. Inspired by the Johns Hopkins example, Dartmouth offered third- and fourth-year students increased oppor-tunities for clinical work as early as the 1905-06 academic year. And after Flexner called for shutting down substandard medical schools and scaling back ones like Dartmouth to a focus on the foundational first two years, officials considered steps including sending students to Boston hospitals for clinical rotations.

Ultimately, Dartmouth found its hand forced. The Council on Medical Education dropped the medical school's rating from A to B, and the New York State Board of Regents announced it would bar future Dartmouth graduates from practicing in that state. In the end, offered little more than "a coun-sel of despair," President Nichols recommended to trustees "that after the year 1914, instruction in the last two or clinical years be suspended for the present."

Six students graduated in 1914, the last year Dartmouth Medical School would award an M.D. degree until 1973. The school reported that it had awarded more than 2,100 M.D. degrees in the pre-ceeding century.

After trustees endorsed the plan to shift to two years, medical school professors turned their attention to finding 4-year schools where Dartmouth students could complete their educations. Then they focused on making the best of the situation.

Colin S. Stewart, secretary of the school and the faculty member who had earlier said it would be "a crime" to become a two-year school, wrote a magazine article expressing a rosier view. "Dartmouth Medical School is in a particularly favored position to offer the courses in the fundamental sciences of the two pre-clinical years in Medicine," he wrote. "With classes of such a size that the men are always under the direct supervision of the instructor in charge of the course, with ample equipment for the work, and with a freedom from distracting interests not found in large medical centers, we believe that we are able to turn out a type of man whose training will be a guarantee of later success."

What college officials described as a shift "for the present" would continue for nearly six decades, as Dartmouth medical graduates left Hanover with two years of solid science training and a bachelor of medicine degree they took to leading four-year schools, often Harvard.

Chapter Six
World Wars Bring Dramatic Change

In 1909, Ernest Fox Nichols took over the Dartmouth presidency from Tucker and continued his emphasis on the historic mission of the college. "Dartmouth seeks to grow only as a college," he told the *Boston Evening Transcript* newspaper four years into his administration.[76]

"It is the function of the college, he believes, to teach and of the university to investigate; of the college to give general culture and of the university to specialize; of the college to interpret and of the university to interpret," the newspaper summarized in 1913. "The college rewards its great teachers; the university rewards its productive scholars."

That emphasis on teaching rather than research permeated not only Dartmouth's undergraduate program, but also its professional schools. At Tuck,

Operating the Navy's largest V-12 College Training Program, Thayer School shifts to year-round operation and accelerated engineering degrees. Specialized V-12 courses include naval organization, law, history, and strategy. *Image courtesy of Dartmouth Engineering.*

Thayer and the medical school, "the chief instructors are so busily engaged with instruction that they have but little leisure for research," the journalist wrote.

Nichols defended the pure pursuit of knowledge, saying it needed to come before any professional application. "The lad who comes to college to learn the details of any of the bread-earning arts is sure to be disappointed," Nichols told the interviewer. "Let us then put aside shallow and illusive considerations of practicality, and recognize unreservedly in each subject of study what its vigorous pursuit may yield to mind and spirit."

Nichols was succeeded by Ernest Martin Hopkins, who became president on Aug. 1, 1916 and would hold the position until 1945. Except for the founder's son, John Wheelock, all presidents of the college from 1769-1909 had come from the ministry. Hopkins' predecessor had broken that pattern, arriving as a world-renowned physicist at a time when scholar-presidents were on the rise.

Hopkins was a Dartmouth graduate, but neither minister nor scholar. He was a businessman. "He is not even an educator," one faculty member sneered. Hopkins was just 38 when he took over and his choice by trustees signaled "a closer drawing together of the college world and the world of affairs," Charles E. Widmayer wrote in his 1977 biography, *Hopkins of Dartmouth*.[77]

His appointment drew national attention. The *Seattle Times* wrote: "He is essentially a businessman and his administration may reveal to Dartmouth and other institutions of learning a way to render a better and broader and more effective service in their relations to the practical side of life. At any rate, his selection is a frank recognition not only of the fact that the administration of a college has become a business proposition, but of the fact also that the institutions of higher learning must get closer to the business, commercial, and industrial problems of man."

A New Hampshire native and son of a Baptist minister, Hopkins arrived as a freshman in Hanover in 1897 and told the dean that he couldn't accept a scholarship that required him to sign a statement pledging never to swear, drink or smoke. Happily, he was able to obtain a partial scholarship without making the pledge, and he supplemented his meager income by working as editor of the college yearbook and, later, *The Dartmouth* student newspaper.

After graduation, he took a job with Western Electric, the first of a series of increasingly responsible positions in the business world. He gained national stature as a personnel manager and lectured on that subject at business schools across the nation. He retained ties to Dartmouth, founding the Dartmouth Alumni Council and, in the process, catching the eye of trustees who were looking to replace President Nichols after he decided to leave the post.

If observers expected that Hopkins' background in business would lead him to move Dartmouth toward becoming more of a professionally oriented university with extensive graduate school offerings, he proved them wrong.

Throughout his tenure, Hopkins affirmed again and again his determination not to take Dartmouth "down the University road," wrote Widmayer. He was well aware that he and Dartmouth were bucking a trend. "With the growth of the great universities and the professional schools, many said that the liberal college as an independent, self-contained unit no longer had a viable place in the system of American higher education."[78]

Hopkins rejected that notion.

On Dartmouth's 150th anniversary, President Ernest Martin Hopkins delivered an address in Webster Hall in which President Ernest Martin Hopkins reflected on the college's purpose.

"The function of the privately endowed, traditional college may conceivably be a far different function from that of the modern, publicly supported, state college," Hopkins said on Oct. 20, 1919. "The function of the historic college … is certainly distinct from that of the college which is maintained as the undergraduate department and feeder for the university."[79]

While not ignoring the importance of original research by graduate students and faculty members, Hopkins warned against falling prey to the "great delusion which has pervaded the college world" — that research trumps teaching.

"Research is important, yes; production is important, yes; teaching ability is important, most emphatically yes," he told the crowd. "But if it be conceded that all three are not indispensable in the individual, let us be honest enough to acknowledge that teaching ability is not the first to be sacrificed."

In a 1930 speech, Hopkins said, "I have been calling particular attention to what should be the central aim of the liberal arts college — to develop a habit of mind rather than to impart a given content of knowledge," according to Widmayer.[80]

He recognized the value of practical knowledge and specialized scholarship, Widmayer wrote, but wanted to keep them in their proper place — at the latter end of the undergraduate years and, beyond, in graduate and professional schools.

At one point, the University of Chicago tried to lure him away, a prospect that may have been tempting given that faculty members were pushing to "humanize graduate education to a radical extent and to bring professional scholarship into closer relationship to men and life." But Hopkins turned the job down, saying he wanted to stay at Dartmouth and "devote himself to the mission of the undergraduate liberal college."[81]

Even as he repeatedly emphasized the primacy of undergraduate education, he did imagine ways to weave the liberal arts into graduate studies. One idea he mentioned in letters to alumni and friends was "a Master's degree concerned with the unity of knowledge and with the relationships among diverse fields."[82] Roughly a half century before the creation of Dartmouth's Master of Arts in Liberal Studies (MALS) program, Hopkins had envisioned an interdisciplinary graduate program that would be the first of its kind in American higher education.

In his book, Widmayer goes on at length, sometimes breathlessly, about Hopkins' devotion to undergraduate education. While all of that is accurate, his account might make it seem almost as if the medical, engineering and business schools did not exist and strive during his three momentous decades at the Dartmouth helm. But, of course, they did.

In times of war, professional schools are key

As Hopkins was beginning his tenure in the 1916-17 academic year, Widmayer wrote, the "clouds of war hung over the land" and Dartmouth faced an exodus of its all-male student body into military service during the First World War.[83] Even as students left in droves, Dartmouth's professional schools played a growing role in training military forces.

The Tuck School of Business Administration hosted a military stores school, where professors trained 500 men from a wide variety of colleges for work in the Ordnance Division of the War Department. At Thayer, meanwhile, an Army training detachment learned from engineering professors about telephone work, construction techniques, motor and radio repair.

Hopkins himself left campus for a time, being named in 1918 to the job of assistant Secretary of War responsible for managing labor relations in the important system of war supplies. When he returned, he made clear that he did not share the doubts some were voicing about the value of the liberal arts. Emphasizing "the worth and unique contributions of colleges such as Dartmouth," Widmayer wrote, Hopkins "gradually came to be the country's foremost spokesman for the liberal college."[84]

When World War II broke out, Dartmouth

stepped up again. In December 1942, the government announced it planned to lodge specialized Army and Navy training units, known as V-12 units, at American colleges and universities. Hopkins expressed his strong preference for a navy unit, given that branch's emphasis on shaping officers with solid liberal arts training as well as the more specialized knowledge of military topics. Hopkins told trustees he "would rather take no military unit at all than have Dartmouth's existence as a liberal college interrupted," his biographer wrote.[85]

At Dartmouth, professors of engineering, science and mathematics were joined by humanities specialists who volunteered to be "retooled" into wartime teachers. In April 1943, it was announced that Dartmouth would not only get a Navy V-12 unit, but would host the nation's largest — 2,000 trainees.

Before the unit arrived, Hopkins in a speech said Dartmouth provided an example of how to adapt to the needs of a nation at war without sacrificing principles that would endure past the final shot, Widmayer wrote. "He defended the liberal college against those who said that the success of technology in war argued for practical accelerated education ... He disapproved of acceleration and streamlining as a permanent thing, and he looked forward to the leisurely acquisition of learning after the war."

Roughly halfway through Hopkins' tenure, in 1932, the alumni magazine published a talk given by James Weber Linn, head of the English department at the University of Chicago, to a group of Dartmouth alumni living in the Windy City.[86]

"We used to believe, in the Middle West, that Dartmouth was determinedly, not to say crudely, 'athletic,' " he told the group. But over time,that respect broadened to include the college's clear intellectual successes. "Though athletic victories continued to be blazoned on her banners, one began to suspect the existence of laboratories, and even of class rooms, among her dormitories and beside her playing fields," he said, tongue planted in cheek.

The key to Dartmouth's reputation, he went on more seriously, was its clear commitment to remaining a college rather than striving for the status of a university. "The outsider sees Princeton become a university, Yale become a university. The outsider sees Amherst, Williams, Knox, Grinnell and many others remaining small colleges, beautiful, endearing to the spirit, the gift shops of culture as the universities are its department stores."

Dartmouth, by contrast, had positioned itself beauti-fully, offering students the best of both without compro-mising either. Credit was due chiefly, he said, to President Hopkins, "one of the great college administrators of Amer-ica, openly placing emphasis on scholarship and intellec-tual practice — Hopkins, a product of the very time [he had graduated in 1901 and was college president 1916-45] when Dartmouth's reputation for scholarship and intellec-tual practice and been, among us, at its lowest."

"The outsider," he concluded, "sees Dartmouth as the great American college; vivid, the one Rubens in our collection."

Thayer School struggles with its "Sword of Damacles"

At the Thayer School, Dean Fletcher was in no hurry to retire, but he ran up against the college's mandatory retirement age in 1918 when he turned 70. Even after stepping down, Fletcher continued to teach and serve on the board of overseers until his death 18 years later. In all, he had devoted 47 years to the Thayer School.[87]

He was replaced by Charles A. Holden, who began teaching during his last year as an engineering student in 1900 and took over as dean in 1918. He was well-known to students as a teacher whose attention was upon them inside the classroom and out. "A familiar sight in Hanover was Professor Holden scooting down one hill and up another on a bicycle in order to keep touch with various survey parties and their instructors," one alumnus recalled. But his vigilance came with a sense of fair play; "he always wore a fiery red and white shirt that gave warning of his approach."[88]

While electrical, industrial and mechanical engineering programs were becoming popular at other schools, Holden kept Thayer's focus on civil engineering, an emphasis that increasingly limited the school's appeal. He did, however, innovate in one important way, arranging with the Tuck School to allow Thayer students to take business courses there. In Holden's view, engineers should "be the arbiter between capital and labor."[89]

Like his predecessor, Holden struggled with a small financial endowment and enrollment that declined as World War I broke out and young men flocked to military service.

Various fundraising efforts over the early decades helped ease the financial pinch, but Dartmouth College was still carrying the burden of an annual Thayer deficit as a temporary loan. When it became clear the debt might not be so temporary, trustees began to fret. In 1923, President Hopkins wrote the president of the Thayer Society of Engineers to say trustees worried they could not "go on continuously maintaining the Thayer School from college funds … without some signs of a very largely increased endowment for the Thayer School work." College leaders set an expectation for Thayer to become self-sufficient in no more than four years.

Raymond Robb Marsden graduated from the Thayer School in 1909, went into the business world and returned in 1919 as a professor of civil engineering. When he succeeded Holden as dean in 1925, the school was small — enrollment stood at eight first-year and four second-year students — and getting smaller. When Marsden took over, Kimball wrote, a "reasonable facsimile of a sword of Damocles" hung over his head.

Nonetheless, Marsden was not one to break from tradition, keeping civil engineering as the sole focus throughout his tenure, which ended in 1933. While he was no curricular pioneer, Marsden did strengthen Thayer's relationship with Dartmouth by aligning the school calendar with the college's. That made it more appealing to Dartmouth seniors, who didn't want to miss out on the chance to participate in their final round of undergraduate social and athletic activities.

In 1933, the nation was between world wars and in the throes of the Great Depression. Frank Warren Garran, a graduate of Norwich University in Vermont, took over as dean at a time when the number of engineering jobs — and therefore demand for engineering education — was low. There were only 15 students at Thayer at the time.

Garran saw Thayer as an institution that existed primarily to serve Dartmouth undergraduates who wanted to build a career in engineering. In that thinking, he was not alone. "The associated schools were expected to serve Dartmouth students rather than to attract graduates of other institutions. Professional education in medicine, engineering, and business, based on and integrated with the College's undergraduate program was acceptable. Out-and-out graduate study was not," Kimball wrote.

Garran began moving Thayer toward offering a broader array of courses, even as college President Hopkins envisioned a way to secure Thayer's future by tying it more closely with Tuck. That hope would soon grow into the Tuck-Thayer program, which allowed students to combine three years of liberal arts study at Dartmouth College with two years of engineering and business fundamentals at Thayer and Tuck.

Thanks to a generous gift, the engineering school had a new building in which to redefine itself. In 1938, the cornerstone was laid for the school's new home, Cummings Hall. The building came courtesy of a bequest from the widow of Horace S. Cummings, an 1862 graduate. It was located next to the Tuck School, a physical expression of Hopkins' plan for a closer collaboration between the two schools.

For the first time, course offerings at Thayer extended beyond civil engineering to include electrical and mechanical engineering. In 1941, the word "Civil" was removed from the school's name. And Garren exhorted faculty members to communicate the excitement of engineering and its real-world applications in their lessons. "Engineering is alive and real," he told them. "We should make it that way in our teaching.

World War II brought with it a surge of activity. As the United States entered the conflict, Thayer played a significant role by offering training for servicemen, a pilot training program for civilians planning to join the war effort, and off-campus courses in mathematics, engineering, drawing and surveying for government and defense industry workers.

Garren had to employ some creative imagination when bidding for the V-12 assignment. The Navy negotiating officer asked if Thayer could accommodate as many as 200 men per term in its heat power laboratories. Without missing a beat, Garran said "yes" — even though, "at that moment, the School had no such laboratory nor any equipment to furnish it." When Dartmouth got word it had landed the V-12 deal, that changed in a hurry.

Once the Navy trainees arrived, Thayer shifted to year-round operation. Students woke up to reveille at 6 a.m. and went to bed with taps at 10 p.m. as the school began to operate like the naval station it had become.

Tuck consolidates and grows above Connecticut River

After World War I, both President Hopkins and Tuck Dean Bill Gray wanted to address a problem: Tuck students taking classes together but living in dorm rooms scattered across the Dartmouth campus. Hopkins said, "the values of the School and the advantages of association with it would be greatly increased if the men could live and work together," Guest wrote.[90]

Hopkins saw an additional benefit: With the Tuck School in its own location, the central campus would consist only of undergraduate buildings. In 1928, he wrote to Edward Tuck to seek his approval. Tuck, then 85, didn't just endorse the idea. He made it a reality by donating 600 shares of Chase National Bank stock valued at nearly $570,000, which Dartmouth used to build a new Tuck Hall and two dormitories, which were named after Dartmouth graduates and U.S. Supreme Court justices Salmon P. Chase and Levi Woodbury. The dining facility was named after Edward Tuck's wife, Julia Stell.[91]

The complex rose up at the western edge of campus, perched above the slow-flowing Connecticut River. While the classroom building was officially named Edward Tuck Hall, the frieze in front simply bore the name "Tuck" to avoid confusion with the benefactor's nephew, whose name was Edward Tuck Hall.

"The new set of adjoining buildings had a profound effect on life at Tuck," wrote Guest. "Their classes were together. They lived together in a stimulating interactive environment not only to enjoy its social benefits but also, as many alumni can remember, to wrestle with the tough assignments, cases and problems given to them by their instructors."[92]

Edward Tuck was generous not only with his wealth but also with his financial advice. It was in search of such advice that President Hopkins traveled to Paris to seek Tuck's advice on a question raging among Dartmouth trustees about whether to invest the college's money in stocks or bonds.

Arriving at Tuck's estate outside Paris, Hopkins strolled through the manicured gardens and into the marble halls, where he found a short, elegant man with a handlebar mustache and a frank manner, Hill wrote. When Hopkins voiced the question he came to discuss, Tuck settled the matter quickly. He declared, "Never owned a damned bond in my life!"[93]

With that settled, the two men talked pleasantly, mostly about the college, "but rapport was not really established until" Tuck asked the president what he'd like to do that evening. Tuck might logically have expected Hopkins to opt for a sophisticated evening at the legendary Paris Opera, but Hopkins replied, "I would rather like to see the Folies Bergere." Delighted, Tuck called for his car, instructing the driver to stop by the Opera to pick up two programs before proceeding to the saucy cabaret. Returning home that evening, Tuck placed the opera programs — rumpled to suggest careful study — in a visible spot on a table in the foyer, wrote Hill.

Once they arrived at the Folies, Hopkins and Tuck found some Dartmouth men in the balcony, who called out a hearty hello, Widmayer added in his biography. They weren't the only ones. Tuck was as famous in Paris as he was in Hanover and "as one scantily clad demoiselle swung out over the orchestra seats on a wire, she tickled [Tuck] with her foot and exclaimed, "Eddie, where have you been keeping yourself? I've missed you!"[94]

Thus began a long friendship between the two men. By the time Tuck died in 1938 at age 95, Dartmouth had received more than $4.5 million. While Tuck had ideas on how his money was to be used, he didn't micromanage. When a group of alumni appealed to him in the 1930s to join their fight against what they perceived as a disturbing move on campus toward liberalism, he replied that "all the money he had given had been to uphold the policies of the College, not to dictate what they should be," wrote Hill.[95]

In the late 1930s, Tuck Dean Herluf Olsen teamed up with his counterpart at the Thayer School to create the Tuck-Thayer program equipping engineers to handle the business elements of their future career. The move was part of a broader effort to equip future business leaders to operate their enterprises in an increasingly complex world.

"The function of schools of business on the collegiate level has generally been conceived as being that of preparing young men and women for careers in business on the managerial, executive or administrative level," Olsen said, according to a 1945 *Dartmouth Alumni Magazine* article. "However, in the last decade or so it has become increasingly clear that this narrow concept does not at all meet the needs of our modern business economic system."[96]

Like other parts of Dartmouth, Tuck was deeply affected by World War II, as students shipped off to serve, arrived for military officer training, and after the last shot was fired, returned to campus with an adult seriousness of purpose.

During the war, Tuck professors joined with others in equipping hundreds of Navy officer candidates with the business skills needed to manage the massive supply systems gearing up in the war effort, as well as a broader education that would serve them after hostilities ceased.

As part of an oral history project, "The War Years at Dartmouth," a number of veterans with Tuck connections recounted their experience to interviewer Mary Donin. One, Robert Fieldsteel '43, recalled that fateful Sunday — Dec. 7, 1941— when the Japanese launched a surprise attack on Pearl Harbor.

Fieldsteel was an undergraduate English major studying for an exam in one of the carrels in the Tower Room of Baker Library. "I went down to get a book and met a friend on the way. And he said to me, 'You've got to do something about your roommate … He's down there telling everybody that we're at war,'" he said in the 2007 interview.[97]

The college immediately shifted into a 12-month accelerated schedule, which allowed Fieldsteel and his classmates to graduate in December 1942. Like many of them, he then immediately joined the military, serving as an Army combat infantryman. After returning, he enrolled at Tuck.

Robert Levinson '46 came to Hanover as an officer trainee in the Navy's V-12 program. A "very poor student" from a public high school in Baltimore, Levinson told Donin in a 2010 interview that he was thrilled to get the chance to study at Dartmouth, where he earned both his bachelor's degree from the college and master's in business from Tuck.[98]

When he first entered the Navy, he recalled, his superiors "discovered I had flunked trigonometry twice and I couldn't draw a straight line … They had two choices, I guess: to send me back to the ranks as a seaman" or to send him to Dartmouth. Happily, he was sent to Hanover in February 1944. "I would have had no opportunity under normal circumstances to be admitted to Dartmouth."

There, he enjoyed learning from some inspiring professors, including one who enlightened him about the important role women play in society. After graduation, he helped to found the First Women's Bank in New York. "When we started that bank, a woman could not go into a bank and easily get a loan if she didn't have a husband to guarantee the loan, even if she may have been working and earning a very good salary."

The V-12 program brought a wide range of students to campus, including Black Americans and people of different religious and economic backgrounds. "I probably would not have met the type of people who would never have been there without the Navy," he recalled. "It was an interesting mix — it was really America."

Allen Bildner '47 T'48 graduated from high school in 1944 and, at age 17, entered the Navy's officer training program. While the V-12 officers shared a campus with regular Dartmouth students, he told Donin in 2008, their routines were quite different.

"We were under the command of Captain Cummings, of Navy captain rank, and a one-eyed colonel who led the Marine unit. We were up at 6 a.m.; that's when reveille sounded," he said in a 2008 oral history interview. "Out front, we fell into our place with each of the battalions out there. We did calisthenics regardless of the weather. The civilians on the campus were so upset with being awakened every morning that every night at taps time ... they would deliberately play Benny Goodman's "Swing, Swing, Swing" on loudspeakers to keep the rest of us up."[99]

Some of their training took place in the Spaulding swimming pool, where their superiors would have them climb on a cargo net above the water, then flood the surface with light oil that was set ablaze. "We would jump in and then learn how to swim in the flaming water to survive in the event of a shipwreck," he recalled.

Harry Carey was a member of the Class of 1944, whose studies were interrupted by the war. He served in a Coast Guard anti-artillery unit operating out of Iceland, then returned to celebrate VJ-Day with his childhood sweetheart, Patricia. After the war, they married and returned to Dartmouth, where they joined a bevy of other married student couples.

Harry was completing his combined degrees at the undergraduate college and Tuck when Patricia became pregnant, she recalled in a 2008 oral history interview. Their daughter, Susan, arrived on May 17, 1946 at Mary Hitchcock Hospital — the first baby born to the returning veterans living in their dorm at

Middle Fayerweather.

"She has a plaque, a miniature certificate of welcome from Dartmouth College signed by President Dickey," she said.[100]

Her husband would go on to success in business, eventually becoming CEO of his own bank. But their time at Dartmouth had its own kind of thrill. "Well, I just felt it was so exciting. We had more fun. Nobody knew how to cook … We had refrigerators on the windowsill, which were orange crates from Tansi's. And we'd buy our food and come home and put it out there, and the milk would freeze and pop the top of the Hood bottles. And there would be the cat sitting on top of the frozen cream."

Medical school gets another wake-up call

In 1923, nearly a decade after the shift to a two-year curriculum, Professor Frederic P. Lord led a medical school committee charged with reporting to trustees on the state of the school. Lord's report noted that Flexner's call for fewer M.D.-granting schools had been so successful that national authorities were "calling for an increase in the number of medical schools."[101]

Discussion then turned to whether to restore the four-year M.D. curriculum at Dartmouth, with college trustees calling such a move "desirable." Lord's report recognized the ongoing need for more clinical experience for medical students but said this need could be met by creating a medical center that would draw more patients.

After their seeming endorsement of the four-year plan, the trustees went silent and the idea did not publicly reemerge for years, Putnam wrote. However, a Dartmouth graduate took steps toward filling the clinical need by founding the Hitchcock Clinic. John Pollard Bowler had graduated from Dartmouth College in 1915, did his first two years of medical training there and then got his M.D. from Harvard. In 1927, he returned to become dean of Dartmouth Medical School, staying in that role until 1945.

Dr. Bowler arrived knowing that the shift to a two-year program had made Dartmouth a less attractive place for the physician-professors who wanted to both treat patients and train students. With those students completing their studies elsewhere, a "brain drain" of faculty talent had ensued.

To help fill the gap, Bowler teamed up with other doctors in 1927 to create an interdisciplinary group practice, the Hitchcock Clinic. In an era when most doctors practiced solo, their collaboration was an unusual arrangement. And for Dartmouth, it laid a foundation for what would eventually become a thriving regional medical center.

"Without the Hitchcock Clinic, there seems little doubt that the trickling away from Hanover of doctors would not have stopped when it did," Putnam wrote. The clinic made Hanover a more appealing destination and "provided the primary missing element" for a four-year medical school. The Clinic also pioneered the practice of paying all its members the same wage regardless of specialty, a "highly unusual" practice that remained in place until 1979.

At the 1927 commencement, Widmayer wrote,

the college dedicated an important and poignant addition to its medical complex. Dick's House was a gift from the parents of Richard Drew Hall, a member of the class of 1927 who had died in his sophomore year. The Halls wanted to make Dick's House an infirmary that "Dartmouth boys, when ill, would look upon as second only to their own homes for comfort, care and cheerful atmosphere." One book in the 40-bed infirmary's library came from President Calvin Coolidge, who dedicated it to Dick Hall and "my son, who have the privilege by the grace of God to be boys through all eternity."[102]

Graduates of Dartmouth's two-year program had little trouble moving to top-ranked schools, Putnam wrote. A 1927 report found that 60 percent of graduates had gone on to earn their MDs at Harvard, Columbia or Pennsylvania. Nonetheless, in 1935, another cloud passed over when a letter from the Council on Medical Education and Hospitals arrived to say that, as of 1938, it would no longer publish a list of approved two-year medical schools. Having worked for 20 years to make Dartmouth the best of those schools, the faculty and its dean were nonplussed.

Bowler wrote to the Council that, "if we read the implications of your notification correctly," the Dartmouth Medical School could respond by "locking the doors on July 1, 1938, after taking the portrait of Nathan Smith over to the Library to repose in perpetuity beside the Seal of the College on which the inscription reads, 'Vox Clamantis in Deserto.' "[103]

The pointed message apparently produced its

intended result, when the Council reversed field and announced that it would consider two-year schools individually rather than collectively. It became clear the battle was not completely won, however, when a subsequent Council inspection team report found Dartmouth to be "unique" among American medical schools but still lacking in clinical opportunities and suffering from "an inbred, provincial and relatively unproductive small faculty; an inbred and consequently provincial student body" and teaching that was too often "didactic, academic and uninspiring."

Despite the sometimes harsh assessments of outsiders, Dartmouth students continued to do well as they moved onto four-year programs and into building their own practices. Looking back at their years in Hanover, they recalled some professors with particular fondness. Dr. Frederic Lord was one of them.

The great-grandson of past college President Nathan Lord, he was one of the longest-serving faculty members, teaching anatomy from 1911-1946. He would often use a cowbell to summon students to class, leaning out the classroom window to summon his charges in from a mid-morning game of touch football. It was apparently worth the trip inside; one student said "spending a year studying anatomy with Lord was simply one of the beautiful things in life."[104]

Another legend was Ralph English Miller, a 1924 Dartmouth graduate who served as the county medical examiner and eagerly invited students to learn pathology at his side. "Dr. Miller's fetish was to be in the autopsy laboratory before the ink had dried on the permission certificate," one student recalled. Even formal dinners didn't get in the way; Miller once performed an autopsy while still dressed in his tuxedo.

Speaking of cadavers, the difficulties of obtaining them persisted well into the 1930s, when records show the school paying $40 for embalming and shipping bodies from the county poor house. In 1937, a letter to Dean Bowler from Lord began: "The cadaver situation in the Department of Anatomy has, since the first of this year, reached such a condition that I feel myself unable to carry any longer the responsibility for the proper teaching of anatomy."

Another anatomy professor (and, eventually, dean), Rolf Syvertsen, added a measure of ceremony to the disposal of corpses. Students were inducted into "the ancient and honorable Secret Society of Sextants," charged with delivering cadavers to a collective grave with a measure of respect after the students had learned anatomy from them.

Dr. Syvertson — or "Sy" as everyone knew him — steeped the process in ritual, including sending a letter to students invited to the society, conducting burial services with "appropriate prayers and readings" and then celebrating with a lobster dinner at the Hanover Inn. The bodies tended to belong to paupers and prisoners; the sextants did their work late at night, one would later recall, "to keep New Hampshire citizens unaware 'out of staters' were dissecting the remains of their neighbors."

When World War II brought the Naval officer training unit to campus, one student recalled, "Sy escorted some navy brass around, and I think their stomachs rolled when they saw us in gross anatomy dissecting with one hand and eating lunch with the other."

Alumni reported from the fields of war that their Dartmouth training had served them well. "I believe I've had a fracture or comp. fract. of almost every bone in the body & have dug out shrapnel or bullets from every conceivable locality," college and medical school graduate Dr. John Feltner reported from North Africa. "Dr. Lord's anatomy teaching never proved sounder than here for me."

With the war ending, returning soldiers and their wives brought a baby boom to Mary Hitchcock Memorial Hospital, with 557 births in 1946 — a 41 percent increase over the previous year.[105]

Meanwhile, women began to make inroads in the all-male Dartmouth medical community. In 1950, Dr. Agnes Bartlett became the first woman to complete a full residency at the hospital. Three years after that, Dr. Marian Bosien became the first woman on the medical school faculty.[106]

But in that era, men still led the way. Sy was a fixture, joining the faculty in 1921 and rising through the ranks until he became dean in 1946, a post he held for a decade and in which he exerted a strong influence. "Sy's boys" remembered him with unalloyed fondness, but his record as a leader was mixed. While other American medical schools were evolving rapidly in the period leading up to and out of World War II, particularly when it came to expanding research activity, Dartmouth was — unbeknownst to most in Hanover — lagging behind.

Again, it was outside evaluators who sounded the alarm, with the AMA's Council on Medical Education and the American Association of Medical Colleges combining to deliver "an extremely negative report" after a 1956 site visit. Wrote Putnam, "The report distressed and embarrassed everyone who cared about the venerable school," wrote Putnam.[107]

Dartmouth's small size was its great strength — allowing students generous opportunities to build a community with professors and each other. But it was also a weakness; with an enrollment of 46 in 1951, it was the smallest of the nation's seven two-year medical schools, with no obvious ambitions to get bigger or do more.

One student noted that the anatomy lab work shared by all students was memorable due not only to the learning but also to "the wonderful coffee and donuts that we enjoyed out on the rocks." Coffee is good, but it apparently did not awaken administrators, professors and students in Hanover to a "postwar explosion of physical and biological knowledge." Instead, one observer said the school existed "in a not so splendid isolation."

————————

A U.S. Surgeon General's Dartmouth journey

Dr. C. Everett Koop graduated from Dartmouth in 1937, served as U.S. Surgeon General from 1981-89 and published his autobiography, *Koop: The Memoirs of America's Family Doctor*, in 1991. The book, excerpted in Shribman's anthology, included a chapter on Koop's college years in Hanover.[108]

Koop wrote that he had chosen Dartmouth over

Princeton for his undergraduate studies because Princeton didn't have a medical school, while Dartmouth did. Additionally, Dartmouth offered would-be physicians the opportunity to condense four years of college and two years of medical school into a 5-year program. His years in Hanover shaped him as a physician, as surgeon general and as a man, he wrote.

"As we drove up the hill to the campus, the stately beauty of the brick Georgian buildings, the elm-ringed green, and the gleaming white buildings of Dartmouth Row gave me a thrill," he wrote six decades later. "They still do."

His classmates decided he needed a nickname and they dubbed him "Chick," a moniker he took with him through life. He was a key player on the football team, a fact that for a time loomed large in his self-regard. "One night during the second week of spring practice I walked down Main Street to get my usual toasted cheese sandwich and chocolate milk shake" when the team's coaches saw him and called out a hearty, "Hello, Chick!" Officially a big man on campus, Koop wrote, "I was in seventh heaven."

That perspective shifted after, in a scrimmage, he was knocked out cold and found that his vision had suffered serious damage. At the Dartmouth Eye Clinic, a professor asked him what his major was. Koop replied, "I'm premed."

"You're premed and you play this foolish game of football?" said Dr. Alfred Bielschowsky, whom Koop described as "perhaps the most knowledge-able person in the world at that time" on the eye's extraocular muscles. "Let me see your hands."

Koop obliged and the professor went on. "They're beautiful. They're surgeon's hands. So you not only risk your sight and maybe your life, but your hands and your career," he sighed. "Such foolishness."

Koop quit the team. And while the coach dismissed him as a "coward," Koop said his decision was "one of the hardest and wisest choices I made at Dartmouth." He fell into a studious group of other premed students, replacing his loss of football scholarship money by washing dishes and running a laundry service. And as a research assistant, he got to work alongside a professor in experimenting on lens transplants in the eyes of *Amblystoma notatum*, a small amphibious vertebrate. From another professor, Dr. Norman Arnold, he learned not only embryology but also teaching. "In his soft, persuasive, unhurried manner, he went to all lengths to explain the very complicated field of embryology."

Another mishap at Dartmouth added to Koop's sense of the kind of doctor he wanted to be, and the kind he did *not* want to be. After crash-landing during an icy intramural ski-jumping competition, Koop landed in the college infirmary, partially paralyzed and terrified that he would remain so. "No one discussed my condition with me. I plunged into a deep depression, feeling for sure that surgical aspirations and perhaps even a normal life were no longer in my future."

The condition turned out to be temporary, but Koop came away from the experience with a lasting commitment. "I learned what it was like to lie alone and afraid in a hospital bed," he wrote. "I resolved that when I finally became a doctor, I would not let my patients lie in fear caused by an inattentive physician."

There was one more close call, this time involving biology and Betty Flanagan, a "Vassar girl" who would soon become Koop's wife. Their love arrived quickly one night on Green Key Weekend, when Koop made a then-forbidden trip to visit Betty in her room on the third floor of the old Hanover Inn and didn't emerge until dawn.

"Not only was I in a forbidden place; I had been there all night," he wrote. "If I had been caught, I could have been expelled. It was another time my medical career hung by a thread." Luckily for the future surgeon general of the United States, the desk clerk was asleep on the job and Chick was able to sprint back to his room in the thin light of dawn, ace an exam and emerge with a clear sense of his future. "By the end of Green Key weekend, Betty and I knew we were headed for life together."

———————

Book Two

Thayer Professor James Browning '44, who invented the plasma torch, conducts experiments. Courtesy Dartmouth Engineering.

In 1966, women were allowed to take graduate courses at Thayer School, although Dartmouth was not yet coeducational. Courtesy Dartmouth Engineering.

John Kemeny teaching in 1972. Courtesy of Dartmouth College Photographic Files.

Chapter Seven
An Era of Reinvigoration and "Refounding"

John Sloan Dickey took over the Dartmouth presidency from Hopkins in 1945, a position he would hold until 1970. A 1929 Dartmouth graduate, Dickey had graduated from Harvard Law School and worked in a variety of roles at the State Department before returning to Hanover. His experience in foreign policy helped imbue him with a sense that students needed to see the connections between nations, and between academic disciplines, to be fully educated citizens.

Overall, Dickey sensed that all three of Dartmouth's "associated schools" needed to improve their work not only in their own disciplines but also in relation to the broader work of the college, rather than "just tagging along in their isolated ways," Widmayer wrote in his 1991 biography, *John Sloan*

109

Dickey: A Chronicle of his Presidency at Dartmouth College.[109]

Topping the list was the medical school. In 1954, nearly a decade into his tenure, Dickey realized the college had to make a momentous choice about the school: Shut it down, or create it anew?

The school had for years operated in a state of benign neglect from college leaders occupied with other challenges. The top-level inattention was per-haps reflected in the fact that the alumni magazine's "Associated Schools" column made no mention of the medical school from 1949-56, Putnam noted. By the mid-50s, however, Dickey "was no longer able to ignore the problems or simply accept Dean Syvertsen's assurances that all was well." [110]

While it held the distinction of being the na-tion's fourth-oldest medical school, Dartmouth Medical School's facilities were outdated, it had only six full-time faculty members, and the college had to provide a $150,000 annual subsidy to make up for the tuition shortfall caused by small enroll-ment. The "research v. teaching" question didn't really apply; there was "virtually no research being done" to enliven the teaching or draw outside sourc-es of funding.[111]

As it had since 1914, the medical school offered future physicians a two-year program in the basic medical sciences, after which students transferred to four-year schools to gain clinical experience and earn their MDs. But increasingly, the school's reputation was in jeopardy. "The consensus ... was that Dartmouth either should get out of the medi-cal-school business completely or should make an all-out effort to rebuild the School," wrote Widmayer.

In assessing the medical school, Dartmouth trustees turned to outside experts, particularly Alan Gregg of the Rockefeller Foundation. When Dr. Gregg visited campus in January 1955, he met not only with medical school officials but the entire second-year class. The students were as anxious as professors and administrators, with one later remarking, "Everyone in the class recognized the school was in trouble."[112] Given that Dartmouth's two-year program required them to go to another institution to complete their MDs, the students wanted to be sure they weren't compromising their future prospects by staying at Dartmouth.

While Gregg shared the concerns about the school's shortcomings, he also applauded the quality of the education it provided and saw the value in positioning it to help address the nation's shortage of physicians by offering a program that — especially when students combined their final year of undergraduate study with their first year of medical school — could cut the time required to become a doctor. "In this sense," he said, "Dartmouth may accomplish something of national significance."

Dartmouth trustees decided not to abandon their medical school, but instead to "refound" it in a way that secured its future, Widmayer wrote. They resolved to expand the school's physical footprint, double its student body, increase its research capacity and tighten its tie to the college's biological sciences program. To lead the refounding effort and its related fundraising, Dr. S. Marsh Tenney, a 1944 college graduate, was recruited back from the University of Rochester and given a mandate to lead the school into a new era.[113]

Even as college officials were beginning their reform effort, external evaluators sent yet another shot across the bow. In March 1956, the joint accreditation committee of the AMA's Council on Medical Education and the American Association of Medical Colleges paid a visit to Hanover. It was a routine visit and, Putnam reports, "no one at Dartmouth appears to have been particularly concerned," according to Putnam.[114]

Syvertsen did not inform college leaders of the visit. Nor, apparently, did he alert medical school faculty members and students to be at their best. Accreditation committee members were met with "blank faces" from the faculty and had to "shoulder their way through" a group of students pitching pennies and blocking the entrance, Putnam wrote. "Hardly the way to make a good impression on outsiders."

Of greater concern than the reception the visitors received was the educational approach they found. Three months after their visit, the accrediting bodies informed Dickey that Dartmouth's medical school was being placed on "confidential probation" for two years.

Adding to the sting was the sense that Dartmouth had already begun a substantial improvement effort, Putnam wrote. "Couldn't the investigating team *see* that Dartmouth was hard at work? Couldn't they give credit where credit was due? Couldn't they have waited to see the outcome of the efforts in progress?"

Despite their initial chagrin, Dartmouth officials acknowledged the problems and resolved to put them in the past. They secured from the accrediting bodies a pledge to make a follow-up visit in one year instead of two. And Tenney — the medical school's new cheerleader-in-chief — got to work. Even as memories of the Flexner report a half-century earlier returned to haunt those with a sense of history, an assessment led by Tenney pointed out that the clinical training once found lacking at Dartmouth was now a decided strength, with the hospital and Hitchcock Clinic providing "ample clinical material for teaching and for clinical research."

There was some conversation about restoring the 4-year MD degree, but college leaders decided to put that off — at least temporarily — to focus on the already ambitious mission of making Dartmouth "a much-needed prototype for similar two-year medical schools," Widmayer wrote.[115]

In 1957, trustees announced an "intensive" three-year fundraising campaign. If it failed, they warned, "the Medical School should be discontinued and the College funds thereby released and devoted to the strengthening of the undergraduate pre-medical and science programs." As the fundraising effort got underway, the accrediting agencies provided a morale boost by returning to campus, pronouncing themselves pleased with the progress and removing Dartmouth from probation.[116]

By June 1958, $4.3 million in capital funds had been raised, enough to make plans for a 7-story medical sciences building that would create a hub for the revitalized school, Widmayer wrote. The new central building was situated close to Mary Hitchcock Memorial Hospital and provided one floor each to the school's six departments — anatomy, biochemistry, microbiology, pathology, pharmacology, physiology — along with a top floor for animal operating rooms. The building's design deliberately wove together teaching and research, and it would soon bustle with a dramatically expanded faculty, and an enrollment of medical students that doubled to to nearly 100, along with 30 research fellows and 75 residents and interns.

With the expansion of research opportunities came a boost in outside funding, with $600,000 financing forty research projects by 1959-60. The expansion also helped Dartmouth attract nationally known research scholars such as Dr. Shinya Inoue, who won a major grant to study the submicroscopic structure of living cells.

As the medical school grew, its leaders also recognized the need to move beyond the tradition of drawing students largely from the ranks of Dartmouth undergraduates, Widmayer wrote. While Dartmouth students continued to make up a significant portion of the incoming classes (some took advantage of the opportunity to begin medical training during their senior year), students who had received their bachelor's degrees elsewhere began vying for the chance to begin their medical careers in Hanover.

Construction crews broke ground on the new Medical Science Building in the summer of 1959. As the capital campaign grew, so did the list of new structures, including the Dana Biomedical Library, the Charles Gilman Life Sciences Laboratory and the Kellogg Medical Auditorium. Widmayer wrote that the new facilities were seen as a "means of strengthening the close working relationship between the medical scientists of the Medical School and the life scientists of the College."[117]

The "refounded" medical school hosted a conference in September 1960 on "The Great Issues of Conscience in Modern Medicine." Among those in attendance were microbiologist Rene Dubos, author Aldous Huxley, former World Health Organization chief Brock Chisholm, and Nobel Prize winner Hermann J. Muller. The event drew wide media attention and touched on such subjects as environmental threats, new techniques in human reproduction, the risks of overpopulation and the ethical issues of using drugs and psychiatric procedures to control people's behavior.

That same year, Syvertsen died in a car accident and Tenney was named dean. By then, Dartmouth had hired its first full-time women faculty members and, in 1960, the medical school admitted its first female student, Valerie Leval.

Leval's admission to the medical school came eight years before a woman was admitted to the Tuck School of Business, 10 years before the Thayer School of Engineering and 12 years before the undergraduate division. In an interview with *Dartmouth Medicine* a half-century later, Leval — who had married and become Dr. Valerie Leval Graham — said the breakthrough came in a hurry.[118]

Graham had been a standout student, graduating

115

from Radcliffe with a fine arts degree and completing her premed requirements at Harvard. "I loved the idea of having a community of patients in a practice," she told magazine writer Rosemary Lunardini. But being a female pioneer "never crossed my mind."

It did, however, cross the mind of medical school Associate Dean Dr. Harry Savage, who had found himself with a vacancy in the first-year class and reached out to Radcliffe in search of a strong candidate. Graham had applied to ten schools and, in the midst of her interview at Dartmouth, got a call from her father saying that she had been admitted to Boston University but would have to start the next day.

Upon hearing that news, one of the Dartmouth interviewers, Dr. Heinz Valtin, said, "Come back at three o'clock and we'll have an answer for you." The answer — from both school and future doctor — was yes.

Her 23 male classmates were at first skeptical, wondering why the new recruit wasn't like them: a Dartmouth man. But it wasn't long before they embraced her, going so far as to invite her to join their fraternity, Alpha Kappa Kappa — an invitation the national organization rejected.

After completing her two-year degree at Dartmouth, Graham joined most of her classmates in going on to Harvard for the MD. She spent much of her career teaching medical and nursing students at the University of Vermont, taking pride in helping the next generation of healers.

Meanwhile, Dr. Tenney in 1962 stepped down

from the deanship to return to a quieter life of teaching and research. Or so he thought

Amid the ribbon-cuttings and celebrations of growth, a fight had been quietly brewing between those who wanted an even faster expansion of research activities and those who fretted, as usual, that the quality of student instruction would suffer. The tensions boiled over when a group of research professors protested what they saw as a lack of top-level support for developing a graduate program in molecular biology. Other faculty members countered that "an increased emphasis on graduate and post-doctoral work would destroy the School's institutional balance and would go against its primary purpose — the education of medical students," Widmayer wrote.

Dartmouth Provost John W. Masland would eventually weigh in to assert that the priorities didn't need to be cast as a question of either/or. "This is a professional school and the graduate and medical programs go together," he said. "You also cannot have one at the expense of the other." [119]

But such conciliatory thoughts didn't bridge the divide between physician-professors and their indignant research-oriented colleagues. And the large number of newcomers on the faculty meant that the collegiality that tends to develop over time was in scarce supply. Before long, Tenney's replacement in the dean's office, Dr. Gilbert H. Mudge, had a war on his hands.

Fretting over "a major breakdown in communication within the medical school," Dickey in 1963 sent a letter to Mudge asking whether he thought he could "contribute positively to both the School and the larger bio-medical community." Mudge decided to stay on the job, at least for the time being.[120]

Viewed from the outside, the new molecular biology graduate program seemed to be gaining momentum. The program's first PhD was awarded in 1964. The medical school added a second PhD track — in physiology and pharmacology — that reflected a growing role for research in an institution heretofore dedicated primarily to training physicians.

But behind the scenes, molecular biology faculty members complained of being thwarted as they tried to secure external and internal funding for expansion. The flames were further fanned in 1964 when a trustees' committee endorsed the value of research but "nevertheless generally agreed that the primary mission of this Medical School is medical education."

Frustrated by his inability to make peace, Mudge resigned effective September 1965 — but not before complaining openly of "an academic Junta" and a "sea of snarling wolves." By the following April, newspaper headlines were reporting that 11 professors had resigned. Quoting one of the departing professors, the *New York Times* reported: "Dartmouth has 'done the impossible' by recruiting a strong faculty and rebuilding a medical school 'but it has failed to do the possible — keep it together.' "

Tenney returned temporarily to the deanship to help manage the conflict. Then, in September 1966, he handed the reins to a new permanent dean. By all accounts, Dr. Carleton Chapman did a remarkable

118

job of smoothing feathers, making the frustrated faculty members who had remained feel heard, and allowing the brouhaha to end "not with a bang, but with something closer to a whimper."

Still, scars remained. The resignations crippled the medical school's first ambitious graduate research program in its infancy, at a time when the field was at the heart of a "burst of discovery" about the nature of the gene. But it's also important to remember the context of the time; "refounding" the school as a first-rate training ground for future physicians took considerable money and energy, Putnam observed. Building a world-class graduate program at the same time would have required not just collegiality, but also large sums of cash. While it would eventually be clear that both ambitions were possible, their fulfillment would have to wait.

"In the 1960s, DMS could have been a major leader in genetics," one of the departing professors would later tell Putnam. Instead, as scientists found positions elsewhere, "it seeded a lot of places that saw a good opportunity and took it."

With the molecular biology crisis settling out, college leaders returned to the question of whether to return to having Dartmouth offer future doctors the opportunity to get their MD degrees in Hanover rather than moving on at the two-year mark.

Committed though they were to making Dartmouth the nation's leading two-year school, college leaders also came to see that the school was among the last of a dying breed. By the 1966-67 academic year, just three of the nation's 89 active medical schools offered a two-year program: Dartmouth and the state universities of North and South Dakota. That, Putnam notes, was "not the company Dartmouth was used to keeping."

In 1966, trustees gave preliminary approval to a medical school expansion plan that included "an experimental tutorial program leading to the MD degree." Chapman, the new dean, took the lead and with a series of faculty retreats in 1968 came up with an innovative approach that came to be known as "The Dartmouth Plan." Rather than spending four years working toward an MD, students would go to school 11 months a year and complete their studies in three years — in keeping with the school's emphasis on getting physicians into the field as quickly as possible.

In February 1970, Dartmouth began accepting students into the new program and heralded it as one "designed to serve as a test model for shortening and modernizing medical education as one means of meeting the nation's need for increased numbers of physicians."

With these and other changes, Widmayer observed, the Dartmouth medical school "was scarcely recognizable" to those who remembered the time — just a decade and a half before — when there was serious talk about shuttering the school. "(E)ven before the MD program began in the fall of 1970, the Medical School was truly and solidly refounded, to be counted as among the major achievements of the Dickey administration."[121]

Innovation and growth at Thayer

The years after World War II were also a time of rapid change at the Thayer School. Looking ahead to the 100th anniversary of its founding, the school and its leaders worked to make the education match a world that was transforming itself politically, socially and, of course, technologically.

William P. Kimball, '29, served as dean from 1945-61, during what proved to be an era of reinvention at Thayer. After clinging to a curriculum focused on civil engineering, the school by 1946 had added courses in mechanical and electrical engineering, the dean recalled in his book. The shop-training classes created to teach Industrial Revolution skills — welding, forging, metal cutting and the like — were replaced with big-picture examinations of manufacturing processes.[122]

Scientists and mathematicians returning to American campuses from World War II took great pride in their achievements — including the atomic bomb and the computer — while tending to look down on engineering. Writing in the *The First Hundred Years of the Thayer School,* Professor Joseph John Ermenc observed that this "put engineering educators on the defensive and stimulated a reform movement" at Dartmouth and other schools. That meant putting an increased accent on the scientific and mathematical aspects of engineering, while de-emphasizing what many professors saw as the "art of engineering"— the design component that had been central to Thayer's approach.[123]

As they had with the medical school, Dartmouth trustees and administrators decided to "refound" the school, bringing its offerings in line with modern needs and, they hoped, building enrollment and financial stability. Dickey assembled a committee made up of Thayer professors, alumni and experts from M.I.T., Cornell and Westinghouse Electric, who recommended an approach that would cross traditional disciplinary lines.

"Dartmouth has a golden opportunity to do two things at once," the committee said, according to Widmayer. "The first is to train well-rounded men, and the second is to give them a training in the physical sciences that will qualify them for the kind of engineering competence that will have the greatest social value."[124]

The committee's four-year study led, in the late 1950s, to a bold move — creating an engineering science major within the science division of Dartmouth College. Rather than spending three years pursuing a broad liberal arts program in the undergraduate college and then an additional two years in Thayer's engineering program ("3-2"), future engineers would now spend a full four years in the liberal arts college majoring in engineering science and then one year at Thayer ("4-1").

The young engineers would acquire a solid grounding in the liberal arts; students were required to take about 40 percent of their undergraduate coursework in the humanities and social sciences. "This adherence to the liberal arts as the foundation for professional studies was a reaffirmation of the educational philosophy that had made Thayer distinctive among engineering schools since its founding in 1870," wrote Widmayer.[125]

The engineering science coursework was demanding, with extra helpings of mathematics, physics and chemistry. But as the 1960s approached, Thayer's engineering curriculum also "began to assert more confidently its differences from science," asking students to complete their education by synthesizing discreet areas of knowledge in ways that would help them solve real-world problems through — again — engineering design.[126]

While keeping a healthy focus on classroom teaching, Thayer professors also began to branch out into original research. Credit for the first significant breakthrough goes to civil engineering professor John Minnich, '29, who won a contract in the 1947-48 academic year to create an innovative highway bridge design, the prototype of which was used to span the Monogahela River in Pittsburgh. In 1957, in the first of what would be many Thayer start-ups, Profs. James Browning and Merle Thorpe founded Thermal Dynamics Corp. to market plasma-cutting technologies they first developed in school labs.

That enterprising spirit drew another professor to Thayer who wanted Thayer to build bridges — literally and figuratively — between academic learning and the engineering challenges of industry, Ermenc wrote. Robert Dean "saw professional engineering as analogous to medical internship." Like Browning, he brought an entrepreneurial spirit that served to launch new companies — including Creare Corporation, which he founded in 1961 and which still thrives a short distance from campus — and to connect students with learning and employment opportunities at firms run by others.[127]

"There's a tremendous chasm between people who are oriented toward real-world results and those who are knowledge builders," Dean would later say. "What got me excited about Thayer School was the effort we initiated in the 1960s to span this chasm, to produce engineers who could stand with one foot in each world, who would be technological entrepreneurs."

"A really bright guy," is how Carl Long, dean of Thayer in the 1970s, described Dean in a 2001 oral history interview. "His philosophy was, 'It's going to get into the market, and if the market rejects it, then the work wasn't as good as it should have been. Then do it over.' "[128]

In 1960, Dartmouth trustees decided that the best way to secure the Thayer School's future was to move it from the status of an "associated school" to that of a full-fledged graduate school (albeit one with a strong connection to the undergraduate college) that offered master's and doctoral degrees. Leading the way into this new chapter was Myron Tribus, who succeeded Kimball as dean in 1961 and led the school until 1969.

Coming from UCLA, Tribus was a leading researcher in fluid dynamics, thermodynamics and heat transfer who had developed ice protection equipment for American fighting planes in World War II, worked as a NATO consultant and hosted a CBS television series on science and society. "A dynamic, hard-driving personality, he was just the man to make things happen at Thayer School," Widmayer wrote.[129]

Tribus said he wanted to make Thayer "a pilot plant for modern engineering education" by requiring grad students to demonstrate the ability to use their creative powers to blend engineering, economic and management tools into their work. He famously declared, "Knowledge without know-how is sterile."

As part of their effort to give students a hands-on lesson in translating theory to real-world results through the use of engineering design, Tribus and profs. Russell Stearns and Robert Dean revamped the foundational engineering course, Engineering Sciences 21, to make it a hands-on experience in solving a problem. The first challenge for students: develop a bicycle that stores energy on its way downhill for the return trip back up.

The course "provided students with something that some engineers never learn even in graduate school — a systematic approach to problem solving," Annelise Hansen wrote in *Knowledge with Know-How.*[130] And they got it as undergraduates in their sophomore year.

It didn't take long for students to capitalize on their ES 21 projects. In 1962, some of them found ways to make brackish water drinkable, leading students Chris Miller and Dean Spatz to go on to found reverse-osmosis companies.

The ice studies conducted at Thayer helped persuade federal officials to open the new federal Cold Regions Research and Engineering Laboratory (CRREL) at a site north of the Dartmouth campus, Widmayer wrote. At the facility, scientists would study the properties of snow, ice and permafrost in an effort to improve arctic construction techniques, among other challenges. The $3.2 million facility opened in 1972, promising to host leading scholars and support 170 people on staff, bringing 80 families and a boost to the local economy.[131]

Thayer graduated its first PhD, Michael Turner, in 1964, followed by its first Doctors of Engineering, Thomas Black and Andrew Porteous, in 1965. Of the 265 students who earned Thayer degrees during Tribus's tenure, 66 received master's degrees and 17 doctorates. Outside research funding also swelled, from $186,000 in 1961 to $595,000 in 1969. Generous unrestricted grants from the Sloan Foundation ($250,000) and Ford Foundation ($150,000) helped the school hire faculty, expand facilities and boost enrollment.

Thayer also helped itself by beginning the Educational Partnership and Thayer Associates Program, which invited private sector companies to get involved with the school in a variety of ways — sending guest lecturers, inviting students to contribute original ideas, and making contributions that yielded $700,000 in unrestricted income from 1966-71. The partnerships gave students a meaningful experience of professional accomplishments, while providing companies a steady flow of ideas, "some of which have proven commercially attractive," Professor Alvin Omar Converse wrote in Kimball's book.[132]

The innovations produced results, as evidenced by the school's continued expansion during the Tribus years. By the time the Sixties drew to a close, the number of courses at Thayer had leapt from 48 to 119, the faculty had grown from 18 to 34, and the annual budget had risen from $410,000 to $1.4 million.

Tuck recruits top professors to enliven curriculum

Dartmouth is unusual in the amount of land it owns far north of Hanover, including the Second College Grant, 27,000 acres of woodland given to Dartmouth by the state of New Hampshire in 1807 and currently used for timber harvesting and recreation. During the early part of Dickey's administration, the college inherited a more unusual outdoor property: the summit of New England's tallest peak, Mt. Washington.

Col. Henry N. Teague had graduated from Dartmouth in 1900 and Tuck in 1901, one of three members of the business school's first class. When Teague died in 1951, he left his alma mater not only the mountain summit but also the hotel atop it and the cog railway carrying passengers up to a splendid vista. The college eventually sold the properties, the proceeds of which were used — per Col. Teague's will — to acquire a painting of Daniel Webster arguing the Dartmouth College case before the Supreme Court and to set up a loan fund for students at Tuck.[133]

At the colonel's alma mater, meanwhile, Tuck in 1953 changed its degree from the Master of Commercial Science (MCS) to the now universally recognized Master of Business Administration (MBA). In a series of speeches to American business leaders, Dean Arthur Upgren talked up the value of business education.

Like its sister professional schools, Tuck for the first part of its history served mostly Dartmouth students. Most of them pursued a 3/2 plan, entering Tuck after their junior year at the college. But Upgren and Karl Hill, who served as dean from 1953-57 and 1957-68, respectively, had a broader ambition — to make Tuck a national force.

Beginning with Upgren and continuing with Hill, the school took advantage of the retirements of older faculty members to recruit younger PhD's trained at the nation's leading universities. Those included such familiar names at Ken Davis, John Hennessey, Robert Macdonald, Bob Guest, Dick Bower, Peter Williamson, Fred Webster and Vic McGee, Guest wrote in his history.[134]

Also in that crop of new professors was Wayne Broehl, who arrived in 1954 and created a course that became a national model for expanding a business education beyond commercial skills to a deep consideration of its ethical, environmental and social impacts. In Broehl's "Business and Society Course," students looked at — among other things — the question of Dartmouth's investments in apartheid-era South Africa.

"And as we got into some of that student tension in the later 60s here at Dartmouth and finally culminating in the taking of Parkhurst [student occupation of the college's administration building in 1969], the issue of South Africa was very big on the minds of the people who were challenging the college," Broehl, whom The Dartmouth had dubbed "the moral conscience of Dartmouth," recalled in a 1998 oral history interview.[135]

Then there was James Brian Quinn, who arrived in 1957 having earned an MBA from Harvard and (in 1958) his PhD from Columbia. An authority in the fields of strategic planning, managing techno-logical change and entrepreneurship, Quinn spent the next three decades forging a reputation for being kind and demanding in equal measures.

"There was never a student willing to enter his Business Policy class unprepared," Jack Tankersley T'74 would recall decades later in an article by Tuck writer Alexandra Hall. "For two reasons: The most obvious was that all exams were unannounced; the second was that no one wanted to disappoint him."

Peter Volanakis D'77, T'82 said Quinn helped him think like a businessman steeped in real-world complexities. "He created classroom experiences that illustrated the fear, uncertainty and doubt that surround major business decisions," he said. "He helped me become comfortable with the untidiness of business."[136]

John W. Hennessey, Jr. was another young pro-fessor who arrived in 1957, attracted by an institu-tion that seemed to combine small-school intimacy with big-school ambitions. In a 1996 oral history interview, Hennessey said financial support for faculty research projects from the Alfred P. Sloan Foundation was also a draw. Under that program, professors who devoted themselves to teaching during the academic year could undertake original work during the summer months rather than having to make money by teaching classes or doing con-sulting jobs.

"The idea of developing intellectual capital for

three months of the year, and doing it a way that was generously supported, was very different from the style of the university from which I came to Tuck — the University of Washington," Hennessey told interviewer Jane Louise Carroll.[137]

He also liked the emerging idea of applying the social sciences — psychology, sociology, economics — to solving organizational issues. "I saw Tuck as an excellent small school with high promise, probably more promise than any other place at that time."

Hill also built on Tuck's tradition of making connections between the school and the world of business, in a way that tapped not only the expertise and connections of working professionals but also produced important new sources of revenue. The Tuck Associates program began in 1964, with businesses and professional associations providing contributions that within two decades would account for 10 percent of the school's budget. That program echoed one at the Thayer School of Engineering, as did a new board of overseers through which business executives and other leaders helped the school set its priorities and shape its curriculum.

Two influential reports — one each from the Ford Foundation and Carnegie Corporation — took many of the nation's business schools to task for providing an overly narrow education to students. Tuck suffered no such scolding in the new reports; instead, it won praise for the seriousness of its academics, which included coursework in emerging disciplines in the quantitative and behavioral sciences.[138]

Tuck graduates put those lessons to good work.

Three Tuckies — Chris Van Curan, Dick Perkins and Bill Butler — started a company called Lincoln Canoe shortly after graduation in 1959. Regular canoeists, the men grew wearing of lugging around long, heavy canoes and set about manufacturing a lighter one out of fiberglass and resin, reported the Fall/Winter 2014 edition of the *Tuck Today* alumni magazine. The company they built was still going strong in the 21st century.

Andy Beckstoffer, a 1966 graduate, went on to play a key role in making the Napa Valley region of California a force in the fine wine industry. Eventually head of Beckstoffer Vineyards, he was in 2017 called by Wine Spectator magazine "an audacious personality with an ample ego" and "one of the most influential people in California wine." He named one of his sons Tuck.[139]

The Tuck School's innovations in this era included inviting students to learn through a business simulation game called "Tycoon." The idea behind Tycoon, Hennessey explained in the oral history interview, was to use newly developed computer technology to have student teams compete in a two-week simulation of real business decisions — having to make choices about whether to buy or sell, to find the balance between costs and profits, under the pressure of a ticking clock.

Tuck had gotten its first computer in 1962. School historian Guest wrote that Tuck was a "special beneficiary" of the computer time-sharing system and BASIC computer language invented by a Dartmouth faculty team led by professor John

Kemeny. "Tuck was in front of many of the other business schools in exploiting the potential of this development."[140]

That's true, as far as it goes. But Kemeny, Dartmouth president from 1970-81, once recalled with a chuckle that Tuck at first wasn't so eager to participate in the time-sharing arrangement.

In a speech delivered at Class Officers Weekend on May 11, 1974, Kemeny reported that the American Federal of Information Processing Societies had just hosted its first annual Pioneers Day to honor groundbreaking efforts in computer science — and honored Dartmouth for its groundbreaking time-sharing system.

He gave credit to fellow professor Tom Kurtz, saying that he had shared with Kemeny the conviction that computers would come to have an "enormous impact on the lives of all of us, and that the very nature of a liberal arts education is to understand those major forces that will influence our lives so that we can try to control them."[141]

Among other things, he said, computers helped students and scholars process vast quantities of data in a way that yielded deep insights. Early on, though, Tuck was "the only part of" Dartmouth opposed to the time-sharing initiative.

"And therefore," he continued, "I am sure you have guessed that they became the per-student heaviest users of time-sharing at Dartmouth College." That, he said, is one of the reasons Tuck had established itself as the nation's best business school. "(T)heir students have become more sophisticated in quantitative methods (which are very important for business today) than those of any other institution."

When John Sloan Dickey promoted Hennessey from associate dean to dean in 1968, Tuck (along with Dartmouth) still accepted only male students. "One of the things I said to John was that I could not accept the deanship unless the trustees were comfortable with Tuck's commencement of coeducation. And to my pleasure, John was able to accept that," Hennessey said in the oral history interview. "And indeed the first woman, then, arrived at Tuck in September 1968, when I began my deanship." That student, Martha Fransson, went on to teach policy and marketing at the University of Hartford's business school.

As president of the college, Hennessey said, Dickey's engagement with Tuck was limited. "John Dickey did not understand or care a very great deal about Tuck in the way he deeply understood and nourished and cared for the undergraduate experience," Hennessey said in the oral history. "That's not a criticism of John Dickey. That's the way a president of Dartmouth probably had to perceive his total span, that Tuck was doing well and didn't need his attention except when problems occurred."[142]

At the same time, Dickey supported his new dean's efforts to improve the school. "(H)e really wanted me to be quite free to propose and innovate in the final stage of the transforming of Tuck from a largely Dartmouth institution to a free-standing, excellent business school in the front rank."

Hennessey didn't just push for including women; he also worked to increase the ranks of minority students. Tuck had graduated its first student of color, Herbert Kemp, in 1966, but minorities were few and far between. Hennessey sought to change that, an effort that began when he was Dean Hill's associate and the two men crossed the country to visit historically Black colleges and recruit talented students.

"Both Karl and I felt that the soul of America was on the line," Hennessey recalled in the oral history. Even as the nation was making progress in other areas at knocking down racial barriers, he said, institutions of higher education needed to do their part "in opening the doors to the professions, to people of all races."[143]

He served as the founding chairman of the Council for Opportunity in Graduate Management Education, which began in 1969 with a $100,000 Sloan Foundation grant and aimed to boost the number of students of color in MBA programs.

Hennessey was the oldest of two children who grew up in York, Pennsylvania, *Boston Globe* reporter Bryan Marquard wrote after Hennessey died at age 92 in January 2018. His father worked for York Safe & Lock Co. and his mother marched in the suffrage movement. He told the *New York Times* that feminism "is in my genes."[144]

He entered Princeton University at age 16, joined the Army during World War II, then went on to earn a master's degree at Harvard and PhD at the University of Washington. While proud of such achievements, he was troubled that the application of his wife, Jean Marie Lande, had been rejected by Harvard Law School because of her gender.

"I was wrong to be willing to go to Harvard Business School when it was all-male," he said in the oral history. "I mean, why did that happen? Well, it was America. America was slow to pick this up," he said.[145]

It proved easier to recruit female students, he said, than to attract students of color. While most female applicants were white and came from cultural backgrounds similar to traditional Tuck students, students from different ethnic backgrounds found it hard to picture themselves at Dartmouth in that era.

"It was much more difficult to recruit blacks, Native Americans, Asian Americans to Tuck than to recruit women," Hennessey said in the oral history. "To recruit women meant that we simply had to say, "The door's open. There should never have been discrimination. Our education is your education. Come and get it. And change us in the process. And we'll change with you."

That's not to say that opening Tuck's doors to women was universally popular, especially in the ranks of conservative alumni. "The major opposition to women at Dartmouth had been from the alumni," Broehl recalled in his oral history interview. "We had die-hards among Tuck alumni, too."[146]

As dean, Hennessey had an increased opportunity to shape the curriculum to include the behavioral sciences he and others thought central to a modern business school education. "Because for me that was one of the major transformation processes," he said, "... away from the historical business school that was giving a degree in commercial science to an applied behavioral science school that was interested, above all, in preparing the students for an unknowable future. Preparing them to cope with dramatic changes in their careers."

Traditionalists on the faculty weren't always so sure; nor were some of their students' future employers.

"There was a substantial amount of resistance from the business community," he said. Some of those leaders feared "we were beginning to turn out graduates who didn't fit in easily, who were ambitious to change things. Who were intellectually very sharp and not simply ready to go to work and ask no questions. It took a time for that to work its way out."[147]

The Dartmouth Medical School Class of '62, including Valerie Leval Graham and her 23 male classmates. *Image courtesy of Dartmouth Medicine.*

Chapter Eight
Moving into 1960s, Research Booms

Moving through the late 1950s and into the 1960s, questions about how best to balance undergraduate teaching and the research efforts associated with graduate study and teaching grew increasingly important at Dartmouth — and for reasons that went well beyond the philosophical.

In the early 1950s, fewer than half of Dartmouth seniors went on to graduate work; by 1963, the number had jumped to 80 percent. In addition to providing opportunities for Dartmouth undergrads to pursue advanced degrees without leaving Hanover, an expansion of graduate offerings appealed to professors who wanted to share their knowledge — and research work— not only with graduate students but also with undergrads.[148]

In 1957, at the quarter-century reunion of the

undergraduate class of '32, math professor Bancroft H. Brown talked about that question and how it affected the education not only of graduate students, but also of undergrads.

Scholars must both create knowledge and pass it along through teaching, he told the alums. "Now it is a silly and wrong oversimplification to say that colleges should teach, and graduate schools should do research. Both must do both. The problem is one of shading and balance."[149]

For some scholars, including famous ones, research is their passion and teaching a distant secondary concern, Brown observed. Among the brilliant researchers who were "flops" as teachers was one of the greatest mathematicians of all time. "Sir Isaac Newton, required to give lectures at Cambridge, delivered them to empty halls."

At Dartmouth, the emphasis had always been on strong teaching, he said, but sometimes to a fault. He said that "in the 1930s, we made a very honest mistake. We knew that the universities gave an exaggerated emphasis to research. We knew that some colleges aped them. We knew that was wrong." But then, he said, the college went too far the other way, affirming only the work done in the classroom. "We should have asked more. And so in the thirties there was a subtle slackening of the creative urge at Dartmouth. We were content with too little."

To illustrate his point, he turned to math. While some might think of mathematics as a static subject, he said, it is in fact a field in which the fundamentals change rapidly, as evidenced by the emergence of (then) new fields of symbolic logic and game theory. "A college faculty must not be static; it must continually draw in younger men, trained in different schools and in different disciplines," he said. "There must be a constant flow in and out."

To help manage that flow, President Dickey in 1956 created a new position of provost, who would serve as a top aide to the president in overseeing not just the undergraduate college but also the growing graduate programs in the arts and sciences and the professional programs at the medical school, Thayer and Tuck. Sixty-two years later, in 2018, Thayer School Dean Joe Helble would ascend to that position.

By 1964, enrollment in the graduate and professional schools had grown dramatically. Tuck led the way with 205 students, followed by the medical school (150), arts and sciences (91) and Thayer (45). During the 1961-62 academic year, trustees had approved two new PhD programs, in mathematics and molecular biology, and the faculty had unanimously adopted a resolution calling for other programs "in selected areas as a means of enhancing the educational position of the College and the recruiting and training of faculty," Widmayer wrote.

The growth in doctoral programs demonstrated that "Dartmouth College, despite its name, was increasingly fulfilling the function of a small university."

"Immediately, the question arose: What does this mean for the primacy of undergraduate, liberal arts education to which the College had adhered so strongly, even proudly, through its history?" Widmayer wrote. Dickey "took pains" to make clear that the programs were limited and "intended to strengthen the undergraduate college by attracting the sort of teacher-scholars Dartmouth wanted for its faculty."

At the same time, Widmayer wrote, Dickey averred that "Dartmouth had to get over being afraid of the word *university*." [150]

In a 1965 article for the alumni magazine, Leonard M. Rieser, dean of the faculty of arts and sciences, reflected on the history of graduate study at the college.

Even as Dartmouth was embarking on a dramatic expansion of its PhD programs, only ten doctoral degrees had been awarded in the college's history. Compared to peer institutions, it was definitely a late bloomer.

The slow beginnings a century earlier were not unique, Rieser wrote. Yale, Harvard and Johns Hopkins were leaders in bringing European-style graduate study to the United States, but not until the 1870s. Dartmouth followed suit in a limited way in 1893 in establishing the first graduate scholarships "designed particularly for those who intend to teach."[151]

Before that, three PhDs had been awarded, one in 1885 and two in 1887. One was to Owen Hamilton Gates, whose thesis title — "The Gigantomachia Among the Greeks and Romans" — would have given cheer to those who valued Dartmouth's roots in the classics.

At their 1895 meeting, college trustees took a step toward formalizing the pursuit of doctoral degrees, available at that time in biology, geology and social science. But advance study continued at a slow march, including three in the field of physiological optics through the Dartmouth Eye Institute in the late twenties and thirties.

Writing in 1965, Rieser said the pace had not quickened during the first 15 years after World War 2. Under the leadership of Dickey, Dartmouth focused largely on recruiting faculty, strengthening its undergraduate programs and "refounding" the professional schools.

Also a priority was expanding the master's level science offerings. During the 1959-60 academic year, 36 men were pursuing a master's degree in the sciences. Faculty members began discussing reigniting a doctoral program that could dovetail with a rapid growth in the size of the faculty and student body at the medical school.

At their April 1960 meeting, college trustees considered proposals to expand MA offerings in the college and develop a PhD in the medical school. "President Dickey took the opportunity during these discussions to explain the need of today's teachers to pursue scholarly activities and he emphasized at the same time Dartmouth's determination to retain its sense of purpose as a college pre-eminent in undergraduate instruction," Rieser wrote.

Trustees voted to begin developing the program. However, "It was soon evident that the PhD degree could not be offered by a professional school alone but had to come under the aegis of a body representing the entire institution and deeply committed to the philosophic tradition of the Sciences and Humanities."

In 1962, trustees created a Council on Graduate Studies, which included representatives from each of the three college divisions — sciences, social sciences and humanities — and the professional schools in medicine, engineering and business. The Council had two newly minted PhDs to add to the mix: in mathematics and molecular biology. Rieser called the mathematics PhD "perhaps the single most decisive step taken in the reestablishment of doctoral study at Dartmouth." It was launched with help from a $250,000 four-year grant from the Carnegie Corporation.

In approving the two new programs in January 1962, trustees stipulated that all candidates "receive a liberal learning experience comparable to that required of a Dartmouth undergraduate and directed that the program should not adversely affect undergraduate instruction."

By the close of the 1964-65 academic year, the number of master's degree candidates had grown from 36 in 1960 to 100. Two-thirds of those students were pursuing PhDs in subjects including molecular biology, mathematics, physics, engineering science and physiology/pharmacology.

Rieser predicted that the number of grad students in the sciences would grow to 175 in the coming five years, and that other programs might develop in the social sciences and humanities. Recalling Richardson's 1932 warning about the "danger" of establishing a full-fledged graduate school, Rieser said a careful expansion of graduate study was entirely consistent with Eleazar Wheelock's intent in founding Dartmouth. Given the need to

142

provide budding university professors with the best possible training, among other factors, he wrote, the "inclusion of doctoral candidates in appropriately selected areas … should be a source of continuing strength to the College."

An article in the April 1967 alumni magazine — "Uncle Sam at Dartmouth" — made clear that research yielded not just educational benefits for the college, but also financial ones.

Some might assume that federal funding is not a major factor in Dartmouth's revenue stream, author Charles Widmayer wrote. "But the assumption is dead wrong."[152]

While the $5 million in federal cash received by Dartmouth in 1965-66 paled in comparison to the $60 million given to M.I.T. and generous sums flowing to places like Michigan, UCLA, Stanford, Cornell and Harvard, it still made up one-quarter of the college's operating income (excluding athletics and auxiliary activities).

Most of the federal dollars went to faculty research and graduate training, with the medical school claiming the fattest share, the article reported. And the tide was rising, with federal support growing from $1.9 million in 1961-62 to more than $5 million in 1966-67.

The cash underscores the college's "contemporary characterization as a small university in everything but name," wrote Widmayer. Most of the funding went to the sciences; of the 110 faculty members of the medical school, Thayer School and college engaged in federally funded research, only ten were in the social sciences and none worked in

143

the humanities. Graduate students benefited from fellowships, including — in this Space Race era — 48 receiving NASA funding.

The article asked, without exploring the question seriously, whether the growth in federal funding might subject Dartmouth to something it had long resisted: government officials influencing its character and direction. "The danger that federally funded programs will shape the institution is perhaps greater and more subtle for unified colleges like Dartmouth than it is for huge universities that are composites of autonomous segments," Widmayer wrote. With more than a trace of boosterism, he added, "But certainly no one at the College seems alarmed in the present circumstances, and Uncle Sam is a welcome presence."

Looking ahead to the retirement plans he had just announced, President Dickey said he took pride in Dartmouth's record at attracting teacher-scholars. "That hyphen is something we look for — we want men who have outstanding abilities as teachers, who can teach with competence, but we also want them to show some scholarly interest, to have that kind of creative urge that will keep them on-going learners for the next 20 or 30 years,"[153] he said in a *Yankee Magazine* interview.

With its emphasis on undergraduate education, he said, Dartmouth is not a welcoming place for someone who wants to spend a professional life immersed only in research. On the other hand, he said, the students don't benefit from someone who simply wants to "retail other people's knowledge."

144

Dickey took pride not only in striking that balance in classrooms for undergrads, but across the campus. As the 1970s approached, he said, "Dartmouth is not a small college, but a relatively small university complex with three graduate professional schools and a growing graduate program in Arts and Sciences." He pointed with pride to the "re-founded" medical and Thayer schools and the "extensive strengthening" of the Tuck School. "We have, I think, been able to grow strong in today's terms without losing the basic qualities I inherited."

Kemeny bemoans influence of graduate schools

After Dickey ended his long tenure, Dartmouth in 1970 welcomed its new president, a math and computer whiz named John Kemeny. The college's new leader was born in Hungary in 1926, earned his PhD in mathematics from Princeton and joined the Dartmouth faculty in 1953.

On May 4, 1972, Kemeny spoke on the future of liberal education at Dartmouth in an address to the Dartmouth Student Forum and Educational Planning Committee. In it, he took aim at graduate schools for pressuring undergraduates to take courses that are narrowly aimed at winning admission to graduate programs, rather than encouraging those students to exercise their freedom to choose a broad range of liberal arts courses.

"I want to identify as the villains ... our graduate and professional schools." He didn't mention Dartmouth's schools; nor did he exclude them. Officials at such schools will say their admission requirements are "absolutcly minimal" and leave undergraduate hopefuls with great freedom, Kemeny said. "In practice, however, this is not what happens. In practice, they drop a great many hints as to what courses they would really like to have students take." As a result, "most students panic and take everything that could possibly help them be admitted."[154]

The advanced schools also make undergrads "terribly grade-conscious," he observed. "I have sometimes said to a student that getting a C- in a course is really not going to ruin the rest of his life. But the student often responds: 'Yes, but it may keep me out of medical school and that will totally change the rest of my life.'"

Such grade-consciousness tends to tamp down students' sense of intellectual adventure; they play it safe rather than exploring boldly. And that, Kemeny concluded, is the opposite of the goal of a liberal education. He cited with pride the note he had received from a former student whom Kemeny had failed in an undergraduate math course.

It was during that course, the student reported, that he had learned to overcome his aversion to math by seeing that some saw it as a "very exciting discipline." Kemeny concluded, "That a student can fail a course and yet say that it was an important part of his liberal education to me holds a key to what we should be doing rather than what graduate schools force us to do. I feel very strongly that we must not allow Dartmouth to become a preparatory school for our graduate schools."

That same year, Kemeny gave an interview to the *Boston Globe* in which he reflected on his first two years in office. Speaking in his office, with a bust of Albert Einstein — with whom he had worked — looking on, Kemeny spoke of navigating student and faculty unrest over the invasion of Cambodia, the agitation of conservative alumni in response to campus protests, and the challenges of taming a budget that would allow Dartmouth to "maintain the facilities of a large university and the intimacy of a small college."[155]

The article by *Globe* staff writer John Wood didn't provide much insight into Kemeny's hand in shaping Dartmouth's professional and other graduate programs. But it did serve up a telling quote from the Hungarian-born computer whiz as he learned his way into being president.

"I really don't know what the right preparation is for a college presidency," he said. "As I told a member of the board of trustees, the search committee asked all the wrong questions of me, and I presume of the other candidates."

He went on, "For example, none of them ever asked me, 'How are you at choosing the dean of the medical school?' which is at the moment my major problem. Four weeks ago I knew nothing about it, but by now I think I am up to date on all the possible problems."

In the summer of 1970, Dartmouth created the Master of Arts in Liberal Studies (MALS) program, which the Dartmouth Alumni Magazine described as a summer-term graduate program for secondary school teachers. "For in a world of rapidly expanding and specialized knowledge, the teacher's role must include the capacity to synthesize and relate to give to education at all levels its full meaning and import," Robert B. Graham wrote.[156]

In the decades that followed, the summer program evolved into a year-round one. While high school teachers attending in the summer months remained a core part of the MALS learning community, students from other walks of life — including recent college graduates, military officers, Wall Street executives, authors, artists, journalists and Dartmouth College staff members, with ages ranging from early 20s to mid-60s and beyond — began filling class rosters in the fall, winter and spring terms.

Literature professor Donald Pease was one of the early teachers in the MALS program, and in 1999 rose to chair the department. In a 2018 interview, he said that the Dartmouth program arose from the countercultural ferment of the late 1960s, when educators and students alike wanted to tear down walls — in this case, between traditional academic disciplines.

"There were silos … stable and impenetrable walls that walled out what was outside" the perspective of a particular graduate discipline, Pease explained. From the start, Dartmouth's MALS courses tore down those silos and gave students — and professors — the chance to see how playing one discipline against another complicates and enriches understanding.[157]

Take, for instance, an early MALS course in Cold War culture. It was taught by Pease, who trained as a literary scholar at the University of Chicago, and Martin Sherwin, a Pulitzer Prize-winning historian. Pease brought a narrative sensibility to the subject, while Sherwin's was more fact-based. Seeing the two professors combine efforts — and sometimes clash — provided a kind of "critical reflection that only an interdisciplinary classroom can enable," Pease said.

Many credit Pease with significantly broadening the program's appeal and deepening its quality. While all MALS students are expected to take courses that span a range of liberal arts subjects, they also have the opportunity to choose a focus in creative writing, globalization or cultural studies. Pease came up with the specializations in an effort to give students the chance to identify a focus — and lay the foundation for work at the doctoral level. "I wanted to encourage students to consider going on to PhDs because they had a master's degree that had all the legitimacy and authority they needed."

In the early years, MALS would not accept students right out of undergraduate programs, wanting instead learners who had spent some time in the working world, said Barbara Kreiger, a veteran MALS professor and head of the creative writing program. But Kreiger said that model tended to exclude students from less privileged backgrounds, who wanted to get their master's degree and get on track — through doctoral study or a job — for a career. Now, the program accepts everyone from new college graduates to retirees.

The program currently has roughly 130-150 students enrolled in any given term, says Wole Ojurongbe, who graduated from the program in 2008 and has been its director since 2011. While other graduate programs in liberal studies are housed in the continuing education departments of their home institutions, Dartmouth's program is unique in operating as a full member of the arts and sciences division.

The program has attracted a wide range of accomplished professionals, who come to Dartmouth to hone their craft and gain a broader base in the liberal arts. That group includes Anna Schuleit Haber, a German-born artist and McArthur "genius grant" winner; retired Air Force fighter pilot and best-selling author Dan Hampton; and Larry Olmstead, a writer who got himself blacklisted by the *Guinness Book of World Records* after demonstrating how easy it is to set oddball records. Tyné Angela Freeman is one of the younger stars, a 2017 Dartmouth graduate and musician whose fourth album, *Bridges*, was named a finalist in the 2018 Independent Music Awards as Freeman was pursuing her MALS degree.

A growing percentage of MALS students — currently 25 to 30 percent — comes from foreign countries. Students arrive from Europe, India, Pakistan, China and other Asian nations. Africa has tended to be underrepresented, Ojurongbe said, because students from there lack the financial resources to live and study abroad.

This "plurality of voices, different outlooks" enlivens classroom discussions of issues that increasingly cross national lines, he said. "American students can get the chance to see American exceptionalism" through the eyes of classmates with a sharply different perspective, said Ojurongbe, a Nigerian. "Here's 'otherness' literally coming to you."[158]

————————

Chapter Nine
Stability, Growth and Women on the Rise

As medical school dean, Chapman was credited with calming the waters of the molecular biology storm, leading the way to a restoration of the MD program, and introducing stability by awarding tenure to all faculty members from the associate professor level on up. At the same time, he could be a divisive figure, called by some "arrogant" and prone to eruptions of temper.[159]

"Faculty hated him. He was very dictatorial," medical school professor and leader Dr. Joseph O'Donnell recalled in a 2018 interview. At the same time, O'Donnell said, "he was a brilliant visionary."[160] Chapman left the post in 1972 and was replaced the next year by Dr. James P. Strickler.

A graduate of the college (1950) and medical school (1951), Strickler had earned his MD from

Cornell and returned to Hanover in 1967 as a professor and associate dean working to revive the MD program. Once he took over as dean, he "soothed bruised egos," Putnam wrote.[161] He also worked to resolve a financial crisis that presented yet another threat to the school's survival.

The school was running a $1.2 million annual deficit. In a 1976 appeal, the school told alumni that it badly needed their support. "Our fiscal situation is now more serious than at any time in the School's 180-year history," a report stated.

Over a glass of vodka, Strickler came up with part of the cure: a program in which Brown University would team up to share the education — and tuition revenue — of a large group of medical students.

The idea came at a meeting in Pensacola, Florida, where the U.S. Navy invited the deans of leading medical schools to brainstorm on ways to increase the ranks of Navy doctors, he recalled in a 2018 interview. During a cocktail hour break, Strickler heard from his counterpart at Brown that the Rhode Island school was struggling to provide its medical students with a solid grounding in basic sciences during the first half of its four-year medical program.

Strickler had an idea: What if Dartmouth took in 20 Brown students for each of the first two years of medical training, then sent them back to Brown for the final, clinical, years? The Brown dean embraced the idea, setting up Dartmouth to collect an additional $400,000 a year in tuition without having to add significant expense in Hanover.

"That was part of the fiscal salvation of the school," Strickler. When combined with increased fundraising and strategic cost-cutting, he thought, Dartmouth could wipe out the deficit.[162]

But first he had to sell Kemeny, who initially resisted the idea. Kemeny was "the brightest man I've ever known," Strickler recalled. However, "he was unenthusiastic about the Dartmouth-Brown program and I couldn't figure out why."

He scheduled a meeting, telling Kemeny's secretary, to "pick a good time. I want to catch him when he's in relatively high spirits."

At the appointed hour, Strickler walked into Kemeny's office and said, "John, I want to talk with you again about the Dartmouth-Brown program." Kemeny reached for a cigarette, signalling his reluctance. Strickler pressed on, arguing that the medical school deficit was only getting worse and that a bold move was needed.

Kemeny listened carefully, then said, "Jim, you have persuaded me."

Strickler took over in a "very turbulent time," said O'Donnell. "He really saved the medical school."

For a man who said "administration is not why I went to medical school," Strickler is credited with bringing financial stability to his alma mater during his tenure as dean, which wrapped up in 1981. While the Dartmouth-Brown program would not begin until his successor took over, it laid the groundwork for the medical school to erase its deficit and balance the budget. According to Putnam, Strickler "took hold of the administrative reins and — with some creative planning — helped stabilize DMS fiscally."[163]

Strickler also had to grapple with another issue during his time: whether the school's innovative effort to squeeze four years of medical school into three was working. A faculty assessment of the shorter program concluding that "the unrelenting inflexible 'lock-step' pressure on the students" was a major problem. In the fall of 1980, school leaders began shifting back to a traditional, 4-year program.

"When DMS returned to the MD program in the late 1960s, it adopted the shorter program to help alleviate the national physician shortage and lower the cost of a medical education," explained that year's school catalog. But the need had shifted, with the demand growing for primary care doctors in rural and inner-city areas. "The curriculum expansion will allow students more time for the study of both the basic sciences and the clinical disciplines."

Playing a key role in the students' clinical training were the doctors at the Hitchcock Clinic. Dr. Harry Bird had joined the clinic in 1964 after serving in the Navy. During the early part of his tenure, Dartmouth Medical School was still a two-year program that had graduates going elsewhere to gain clinical experience.

When Bird arrived, the clinic was a vibrant place — 53 physicians who worked as a team on providing patient care, without the usual turf battles or economic incentives to keep treatment to themselves. "No matter what the patient's problem, you quickly knew who had an interest in that, and there was no difficulty in involving that physician in the

155

patient's care," Bird recalled in a 2002 oral history interview with Daniel Daily.[164]

When the MD program returned, the landscape shifted dramatically. Suddenly, Clinic physicians became true professors, incorporating medical students and their education into their treatment routines. That impacted not just the doctors but also their patients. Bird said patients "were not accustomed to having medical students being observers or participants in their care, which both slowed it down and provided some of them with the maddening experience for them of repeating their story three or four times."

Attending to students meant doctors couldn't see as many patients and, thus, bring in as much revenue. Nonetheless, he said, "most of us loved the time we were with the students, so there was never a problem getting the physicians to do that."

Just as Dartmouth had always put students at the center of its academic priorities, so did the medical center put patients first. "The typical academic medical center may or may not do that," Bird said. At some, "patients are tolerated, barely tolerated" for the purpose of providing clinical training for students, interns and residents. "That was never to be our model here."

With the flexibility afforded by more time, Dartmouth students were able to gain clinical experience not only close to home but also at New England hospitals in Concord, New Hampshire, Brattleboro, Vermont, and Hartford, Connecticut — as well as at locations as far away as Alaska.

Dartmouth's involvement in health care didn't

stop at the walls of its medical center, Putnam wrote. Dr. Thomas Almy, who joined the faculty in 1968 and advocated making a link between the medical school and the (then) independent regional hospitals treating patients across the Upper Valley region of New Hampshire and Vermont. A 1973 report on the school had echoed that ambition, saying the school could not boast of its research and clinical successes within DHMC if it was going to "remain indifferent to the privations of medical care experienced by its rural constituency."[165]

Almy and his colleagues in the community medicine department responded to the call, inviting regional physicians to become adjunct professors, giving students the opportunity to learn in their practices and, by extension, forming a team that raised the overall quality of health care in the region. The Hitchcock Foundation also helped, providing funding to focus on "community health problems which are special to the northern areas of New England." One example of that was a deep look at hundreds of members of an extended family that suffered from a high rate of thyroid cancer.

At one point, Strickler said, "The school makes a special effort, as New Hampshire's only school of medicine, to help this state."[166] Among the visible signs of that continuing in the 21st century: the DHART (Dartmouth-Hitchcock Air Response Team) helicopters that take to the sky to transport seriously injured car crash victims to the medical center in situations where seconds count, and David's House, where the families of seriously ill children being treated at CHAD (the Children's

Hospital at Dartmouth) find a comfortable home away from home.

O'Donnell played a leadership role in the community health efforts. As an oncologist, he had seen that many illnesses resulted from behaviors such as smoking, drinking too much alcohol and eating poorly. He helped medical students learn about the social determinants of poor health by giving them opportunities to work in community outreach programs, working with low-income residents, migrant workers and school children.

And all the while, the students benefited from faculty members who took a personal interest in their careers. Referring to the popular TV program, he said, "Dartmouth Medical School became a place like 'Cheers' where everybody knows your name."[167]

Over the post World War II decades, the school's graduates took their learning into the world, becoming leading clinicians, researchers, educators and public policy advocates.

Dr. Fred Plum graduated in 1945 and, by the time Dartmouth Medicine magazine featured him during the school's bicentennial celebration in 1997, had risen to the position of professor and neurologist-in-chief at New York Hospital-Cornell Medical Center, served as the founding editor of the *Annals of Neurology*, authored the essay on headaches in *Encyclopedia Britannica*, and become a nationally recognized expert on comas sought by the media to comment on such high-profile cases as Karen Ann Quinlan and Nancy Cruzan.

In the years leading up to and including his undergraduate years at Dartmouth, Plum had explored his interests in music, literature and architecture. None seemed a career path but medicine — with its opportunity to explore science and better the lives of patients — beckoned.

He was particularly fascinated with how the brain operates. "It's how we understand the universe," he told the magazine.[168] The Dartmouth student build a small electroencephalograph — New England's first — to chart the circulatory pathways. After completing Dartmouth's two-year program, he earned his MD at Cornell, where he was inspired by neurologist Dr. Harold Wolff and found his calling.

Over time, Plum became a champion of using technology to understand the workings of the human brain. But from the start, he displayed a knack for bedside diagnosis. "He had a remarkable ability to think on his feet," said Jerome Posner, a physician who studied with him as a resident and went on to co-author with Plum the leading book on comas. "He is one of the best clinical teachers in medicine."

Dr. Karen Kramer Hein was one of only four women (along with 44 men) in the Class of 1968. While she had followed the path of her father, a 1933 graduate, she was no insider. She was, however, a pioneer. As the only female player on the Medical School baseball team, she was booed off the field by opposing players at her first game — and she was surrounded by teammates who wore t-shirts declaring them the "Virgin Surgeons," the magazine reported.[169]

In 1973, she did a postdoctoral fellowship in adolescent medicine and found a home in the cutting-edge field. "I wanted to be where I felt the action would be next," she told the magazine. She rose to become medical director at New York City's juvenile detention center, founded the nation's first adolescent AIDS program and became a key part of the team shaping the campaign for health care reform in the Clinton White House. While that effort came up short, she did not lose her faith in the potential for substantial, if incremental, change, and went on to lead the National Academy of Science's Institute of Medicine.

"I'm glad I came to Washington when I was 50," she said. "If I'd been younger, I would have been tempted to take it too seriously" when setbacks came along.

Increasingly, the medical school's graduates earned PhDs as well as MDs. When Richard Miller was pursuing his doctorate in pharmacology and toxicology at Dartmouth in the late 1960s, he and his wife had the first of their six children as he was working on a project tracing the effect of drugs on the central nervous system in rats. He began to wonder about the effect drugs might have on the development of human embryos — a question that eventually led to him becoming an authority on birth defects.

Miller got his PhD from Dartmouth in 1972 and in 1978 was named research director at the University of Rochester's obstetrics and gynecology department. There, he focused on the hazards faced by pregnant women in workplaces such as a plant where vehicles were cleaned using toxic chemicals.

Just as he had learned from professors at Dartmouth, he valued the opportunity to teach the next generation of scientists and doctors. Dartmouth Medicine noted that his CV listed not only his own professional milestones but also those of his graduate students. Said Miller, "We are just one big family."[170]

One of the most significant hires Strickler made during his time as dean was Michael Zubkoff. Zubkoff came in to chair the medical school's Department of Community and Family Medicine and his appointment raised some eyebrows because he arrived not with an MD but with a PhD in economics.

Zubkoff, in turn, hired a controversial figure: physician and health care outcomes gadfly Jack Wennberg. Wennberg had begun raising hackles in the 1970s when, while serving as director of Vermont's Regional Medical Program, he observed that doctors in neighboring communities made very different treatment decisions based not on scientific data but on personal preferences.

Looking at hospital discharge data, he learned that in one northern Vermont town, 70 percent of children had their tonsils removed, while the tonsillectomy rate for children the next town over was only 20 percent. Broadening his research, Wennberg found striking — and illogical — differences in treatment decisions nationwide and began to sound the alarm about the resulting excessive costs and medical risks, Maggie Mahar wrote in a 2007 profile of Wennberg published in Dartmouth Medicine.[171]

Strickler would later say that Wennberg confirmed with data the gut instinct he and others had felt in medical school. Strickler recalled one professor asking, "What are the indications of a tonsillectomy?" and one of his classmates responding, "A hundred dollars and a pair of tonsils."

At Dartmouth, Wennberg won over skeptics and began recruiting colleagues to support a broadening field of research. By 1984, the respected journal Health Affairs introduced an article by him by writing, "Without much attention from the profession and no public fanfare, John Wennberg … has uncovered systematic and persistent differences in the standardized rates of use for common surgical procedures and other medical services in the United States."

In 1988, Wennberg established the Center for Evaluative Clinical Services at Dartmouth, assembling an interdisciplinary group — clinician investigators, epidemiologists, economists and statisticians — to expand his research. By 1993, the center had gained enough authority to begin teaching its methods to students pursuing master's and doctoral degrees.

In 1996, the center published the first Dartmouth Atlas of Health Care, which drew national headlines for revealing "astounding" geographical variations in the distributions of medical resources — including a 33-fold difference in the rate of lumpectomies and mastectomies from one region to the next. Dr. Jack Lord of the American Hospital Association called the finding "staggering."

The findings by Wennberg and his colleagues shook the medical establishment, informed health care consumers and pointed the way to a more analytical approach to treatment decisions for students at Dartmouth and other medical schools. "In the basic sciences, you have discussion and debate," Wennberg said. "Why not in medicine? We need to be continually evaluating what we do over time."

At Thayer, research increases and women advance

After Myron Tribus left in 1969 to take a job in the administration of President Richard Nixon, David R. Ragone served briefly as dean of Thayer School before leaving to take the helm of the University of Michigan's College of Engineering. Ragone had brought an appetite for change similar to Tribus's, and the pace of transformation had left many at the school eager for a calmer period in which to absorb and build on the changes already made.

Carl Long seemed just the man for the job. An 18-year faculty member who enjoyed deep respect from his colleagues, he had seen great changes not only at Thayer, but in the world. In announcing his appointment in October 1972, the college noted that when he joined the faculty in 1954, "Space flight and moon-walking were unheard of, pollution and computers had no impact, there were no resident coeds at Dartmouth, and there were no doctoral programs" at Thayer, Doug Wilhelm wrote in *Knowledge with Know-How*.[172]

In 1971, Thayer had marked its 100th year. "Innovation coupled with the entrepreneurship necessary to spread the new gospel, so to speak, emerges as a central thrust of the Thayer School at Dartmouth as it enters its second hundred years," overseer Gordon Stanley Brown said shortly after the centennial.

When he took the job, and in the 12 years he served as dean, Long saw history speed forward. The Vietnam war drew to a close, President Richard M. Nixon resigned in disgrace after the Watergate scandal, and an energy crisis loomed as OPEC countries pushed the price of oil ever higher. Cynicism among young people about industry's impact on the environment and society led to a decline in interest in engineering school, and Thayer saw the number of students in its core 5-year Bachelor of Engineering program plummet from 20-25 students at the beginning of the 1970s to just eight in 1975.

"Engineering or technology is not a field considered desirable by very many entering Dartmouth as freshmen," school overseer Joseph A. Baute wrote in the school's magazine, The Year, in 1974. That put a squeeze on a budget that was already struggling with a small endowment, the depletion of Sloan Foundation funds, and a stubborn reliance on the $200,000 subsidy — or "subvention" — the college provided each year.

Kemeny, who had taken over as Dartmouth president in 1970, floated the idea of eliminating Thayer as a separate engineering school, but the board of overseers ejected it. "We discussed it," said board member and Thayer graduate Sam Florman, "and in the end we all said, 'Wouldn't it be a shame? We know technology is important. We know Thayer School is important to Dartmouth. We know engineering is important to the country. We're not going to close the School.'"

Fundraising had never gotten much attention at Thayer, but Long resolved to change that. "I'd guess I was spending around one quarter, maybe even one third, of my time on the road visiting alumni and foundations and making corporate visits," Long told Wilhelm. The dean recruited business people to the board of overseers and courted Thayer alumni who might otherwise have lost touch with their alma mater.

"This was a time when the [Dartmouth] Indian symbol went away, when women came to campus, when a lot of changes were taking place, many of them to the good," observed Peter Brown, who graduated from the college and Thayer in 1949. "But many of the alumni felt that Dartmouth was headed in a direction that we didn't understand. I think we felt alienated from the College. But for the engineering school grads, there was a bond that continued for life, because that was our lifetime vocation. Carl was the person who reignited that interest

"Many Dartmouth alums were upset with the college," agreed Long. "We used to tell them, 'If you give to Thayer School, you can maintain your loyalty to Dartmouth College without telling them.'"

The efforts paid off, as the school's endowment grew from $1.9 million in 1977 to $10.5 million in 1984. During Long's tenure, the annual operating budget grew from $1.4 million to $4.8 million and the faculty from 18 to 24. Sponsored research also grew, rising from one-third of the budget in 1973 (or about $60,000 per faculty member) to better than half the budget in 1979 (or nearly $84,000 per professor).

"Carl was always pushing for research," said one professor, Russell Stearns. That confirmed a cultural shift that built steadily after World War II, and it was one that Long saw as essential to securing the school's financial health.

"Thayer School in effect said to the faculty, 'If you're going to have students work with you to take your courses, then you're going to have to help pay the cost of their education,'" lest tuition bills become prohibitively high, Long recalled in a 2001 oral history interview with Chris Burns.[173] The school set a goal of a professor's research covering about one-third of a professor's employment costs, plus all the costs of the students working with them in the lab.

Thayer did its part, Long said, working with professors to identify and secure outside funding. Long also began offering three- or four-year appointments to faculty members at the beginning of their careers, offering them the chance to devote 80 percent of their time to original research and only 20 percent to teaching. The arrangement proved a win-win: Thayer increased its overall research output and the junior faculty members got the chance to carve out an area of expertise before, generally, moving on to a tenure-track position at another school.

"You could say that we instituted these appointments as a service to the profession and to young faculty," Long said in the interview.

Longer-term faculty members also benefited, Wilhelm wrote. Professor John Strohbehn said, "In a field as dynamic as engineering, it's your research that keeps you up with the field."[174] Strohbehn came to Thayer during Myron Tribus's innovative tenure as dean, then went on to do some innovation of his own, teaming up with specialists at the Dartmouth-Hitchcock Medical Center to help develop a biomedical project investigating whether cancerous tumors can be fought with microwave heat therapy or hypothermia.

Companies benefited from their investments in Thayer research, Long said in the oral history interview. Take, for instance, the work by John Colliers '72 TH '76, who found that properly engineered hip replacements could allow a patient's bone to grow into the device. "Instead of anchoring it with glue, you allowed the hip to grow into the prosthesis and provide strength enough that it would work," he said in the oral history. That work was funded by the DePuy prosethetics company, which turned his research into devices for which patients were happy to pay.

While a spirited debate unfolded over the undergraduate college's decision to admit women beginning in 1972, no such rancor existed at Thayer, where Long worked to attract talented future engineers not only from Dartmouth but also from other top-flight northeastern colleges. "We thought we could interest some predominantly women's colleges — Skidmore, Vassar, Smith — that did not offer engineering degrees," Long told Wilhelm.

Prospective students would follow a 3-2 program, taking the first three years at their home schools before spending two years at Thayer to earn their B.E. degrees. One of the pioneers was Jane Brechlin Olesin, who began at Mount Holyoke College and then came to Thayer to earn her B.E. in 1976 and master's in 1978. "Dean Long was very supportive of women coming to the school," she said.

Most of the women reported being accepted as peers. "I really felt very welcome," said Judy Geer, a 1975 Dartmouth grad who entered the B.E. program in 1980. "I just woke up one day and realized that engineering would be the perfect thing for me to do. I wondered why no one had suggested engineering for me sooner. I think people just weren't talking about engineering for women then."

Still, some couldn't help but notice the vestigial culture of an all-male institution. "They had a pretty entrenched male community there — but I'd seek out the people who were friendly to me and ignore the others," recalled Diane Knappert Clark, who earned her B.E. in 1977 before going on to become the first woman to earn a doctorate in engineering (D.E.) in 1981.[175]

In 1976, Apple introduced its first personal computer and, before long, the computer revolution had sparked a renewed interest in engineering careers among young people. Under Long, the combination of increased enrollment, aggressive fundraising and creative management of Thayer's financial relationship with the college eliminated the need for a subsidy and put Thayer on solid footing. During the 1982-83 academic year, Long won trustee approval to further increase tenure-track faculty, enrollment and a 40 percent boost in physical space. The next year, he retired.

"We owe him a great debt," said his successor, Charles E. Hutchinson. "He kept the school alive."

Tuck stays true to roots and branches out

When the student protests that swept the nation in the late 60s and early 70s arrived in full force at Dartmouth, neither Tuck students nor their dean held themselves apart. A group of Tuck students made plans to go to Wall Street for an outdoor rally of business students from Harvard, Columbia, Wharton and Tuck.

"And they asked me if I would go as the Tuck dean. And I immediately said yes. And the Harvard dean said, 'No, I'll send the associate dean.' And so did all the other deans," Hennessey recalled in the oral history. "And so in that wonderful moment in the Wall Street canyon, with thousands of people around and the press and microphones, I became the spokesman for the schools."[176]

He got an earful about it from Tuck alumni, many of whom occupied powerful positions on Wall Street. One of them threatened to have him fired, asking, "What are you, a Communist?" But Hennessey made no apologies. The best professional schools see themselves as part of a university's challenging culture, he explained. "They're not preparing students to walk into first jobs like some sort of trade school."

"There is simply no way to overstate John's impact on our institution," Matthew Slaughter, Tuck's current dean, said in a message to the school after Hennessey died in 2018. "John presided over one

169

of the most consequential periods in Tuck's history, transforming our community and campus and ushering in important changes that helped make Tuck the vibrant school it is today."

By the late 1960s, the school was bursting at its seams. A third dormitory, now known as the Buchanan Residence Hall, was completed in 1968. But the school had outgrown its available classroom, library and computer space. The limitations cramped Tuck's ability not only to educate its students but also to participate in a growing collaboration with the Thayer School and expand its continuing education program.

The answer — thanks to donations from friends, alumni and a gift from Thomas Murdough (Dartmouth Class of 1926) and his wife Grace Clark Murdough — was the Murdough Center, which opened in 1973. The wedge-shaped center provided ample additional space and provided a physical link between the Tuck and Thayer schools. The building also houses the Feldberg Library (a gift of Theodora and Stanley Feldberg, Dartmouth Class of 1946) and its extensive collection of books and electronic resources.[177]

Long had particular praise for Feldberg, which he said is "one of the better libraries around. Rather unique in its combination of business and engineering." It was, he said in the oral history interview, an important resource for students trying to bring a product from the laboratory or classroom and into the world. "You need to determine how to get your solution to market, cost, required capital, etc.," he said. "Feldberg is built beautifully for that kind of activity. You have all the references needed to do a complete job."

The 1970s also saw Tuck working hard to maintain and build its alumni network. *Tuck Today* magazine kept alumni and supporters of the school up to date on the latest doings, while also allowing former classmates to keep up with each other's professional and personal lives. Assistant Dean Robert Kimball traveled around the country to start alumni clubs.[178] The Tuck Annual Giving program began in 1971, with 27 percent of alumni contributing a total of $71,000.

In 1972, the school launched its own student loan corporation, TELCO. The brainchild of associate Dean Paul Paganucci '53, the program made wise use of the Tuck endowment and the markets to offer students loans at just above the prime interest rate — all in an effort to make the MBA program financially accessible to a broader range of students.[179]

In 1974, Tuck professor Ken Davis led the way to creation of the Tuck Executive Program. A summer program catering to executives with the potential to play top management roles, the program had Tuck professors offering participants cutting-edge information and tips for advancing their careers in a way that benefited them, their employers and society.

Four decades later, the program is still going strong. Amy Wuerch took a break from her duties as a security manager to come to Hanover and work with other mid-career leaders to reflect on approaches to leadership and learn about aspects of business outside of their wheelhouse.

In a 2011 interview with Tuck writer Kirk Kardashian, Wuerch said she particularly enjoyed learning about accounting and finance and how her work might improve Boeing's bottom line. "The faculty have been exceptional," she said. "Phillip Stocken, for example, has been able to take accounting principles and break them down and make them understandable."[180]

In his convocation address on Sept. 22, 1975, Kemeny joined the Dartmouth community in celebrating the 75th anniversary of the Tuck School by invoking the memory of William Jewett Tucker — the president who had worked to create the nation's first graduate school of business.

Kemeny told the audience he wanted to reflect anew on a question close to Tucker's heart: "Should Dartmouth be a college or a university?" That question was at the heart of Tucker's inaugural address in 1893 and, 82 years later, "is remarkably modern and relevant to our problems today."[181]

When Tucker took over at the century's turn, Daniel Webster's beloved "small college" was so small that "it was no longer possible to attract a first-rate faculty, and it was not possible to offer a modern curriculum." Under Tucker's leadership, he said, Dartmouth went in a decade in a half from being a "regional institution" to a "significant national institution." How? By, in what Kemeny said was a radical notion for the time, offering students a wide variety of electives — electives that would only be possible if the college grew in size and scope.

During Tucker's 16 years, Dartmouth's undergraduate enrollment grew from 300 students to nearly four times that many. While that allowed for significant growth in the faculty and the courses they could offer, "some became seriously worried that Daniel Webster's small college existed no longer and that Dartmouth was becoming a university."

Opening the Tuck School in 1900 rekindled those anxieties, he said, "as many critics said that adding one more professional school would push Dartmouth over the borderline and turn it into a university." But Tucker had rejected that notion, stressing that the research traditionally associated with graduate schools and teaching associated with undergraduate colleges are not mutually exclusive. Far from it.

In his inaugural address, Tucker had asserted, "I believe that discovery stimulates teaching and that teaching necessitates discovery." Kemeny said that belief lived on at Dartmouth as Tuck celebrated its 75th year. "Here research and scholarship prosper, probably better than at many universities, encouraged and supported because they are essential for good teaching."

Kemeny went on to say that Tuck had also demonstrated that a professional school could respect and advance Dartmouth's historic emphasis on the liberal arts. Noting that Tucker decided on a graduate school in commerce rather than incorporating commercial studies into the undergraduate curriculum, he said "he believed that each individual should have a firm foundation in the liberal arts before engaging upon professional education."

Alluding to the advanced degrees offered in

medicine, engineering and some liberal arts disciplines, Kemeny said, "Dartmouth has pioneered in graduate education when it felt that it had a unique contribution to make." And in all those schools, the college had prided itself on a culture of strong teaching, close relationships between professors and students and a commitment to build strong graduate schools without compromising the quality of undergraduate programs.

Kemeny said that he, like Tucker, had "advocated an intermediate position for Dartmouth between the small college and the large university." He said he had coined the phrase "small university" before reading the 1893 address, in which his predecessor had called Dartmouth a "large college." Kemeny concluded that "the words are different but the goal is the same."

Richard West took over as dean of the Tuck School in 1976 and — thanks to contributions from alumni, friends and companies in the Tuck Associates program — was able to lead the school to achieve financial independence from the college. During his tenure, aggressive hiring meant the student-faculty ratio dropped from 14-to-1 to 10-to-1 even as the number of applications soared. The goal was to keep a "firm commitment to Tuck's special distinction as a small school" wrote Guest.[182]

In 1980, West approached a junior professor, Lee Greenhalgh, to ask if he'd like to teach entrepreneurial skills to Black, Hispanic and other minority business executives in a program Tuck was just getting off the ground. The idea, which began with former Dean Hennessey, was to do something

174

to help reverse the high failure rate of minority owned businesses.

Greenhalgh embraced the opportunity, explaining in a later interview that racism had denied economic opportunity to business people of color in the decades leading up to the Civil Rights movement. But it wasn't a simple matter of putting out the economic welcome mat; minority executives didn't have the lessons passed through generations that fuel many businesses.

Minority entrepreneurs didn't enjoy "a long history of family businesses the way, for example, Cuban Americans in south Florida had, or Jewish families in the garment district of New York," Greenhalgh said in an interview for an article about the program in the Tuck alumni magazine. "Mexican Americans, for example, came to the U.S. as agricultural workers, and black people from the South were brought in as plantation workers; they didn't have an entrepreneurial history to draw on."[183]

The Tuck Minority Business Executive program aimed to change that, bringing in minority executives for intensive, week-long sessions on how to take their products or services and make them work as an ongoing enterprise — plotting strategy, managing workers, looking to the future while making the books balance in the present.

Over the decades, the program would grow to include an expanding list of underserved groups: women, Indigenous peoples, the LGBTQ community, disabled people and veterans. It became one of Tuck's most successful non-MBA programs.

"Statistically, it's about one out of every nine

175

people who has the personality to be an entrepreneur, rather than work in some safe corporation or public sector agency," Greenhalgh observed. "And that's true across racial groups and gender."

A nursing school begins and ends

From its beginning in 1893, Dartmouth's hospital had served as a clinical training ground not only for medical students, but also for nurses. The Mary Hitchcock Memorial Hospital School of Nursing operated until the evolution of nursing education led to its closure in 1980.

Over the nine decades, all but 11 of the school's graduates were women, Laura Stephenson Carter wrote in "Beyond Nightingale," a retrospective article in the Fall 2005 edition of Dartmouth Medicine.[184]

The diploma-granting nursing school offered plenty of hands-on clinical training. An early application form said "instruction will be given by lectures and recitations, at the bedside in the Hospital and in the homes of patients," adding that the nursing profession "calls for the exercise of self-denial, patience, gentleness, and good temper."

The program was initially two years, with students working 12-hour shifts with duties that ranged from making beds and stoking fireplaces to treating patients by preparing mustard plasters, applying oil of wintergreen and making home visits to care for patients suffering from typhoid fever, grippe and bone fractures. In 1905, the program shifted to three years, with increased classroom learning.

By 1920, the school had grown so much that

a building was constructed to house the student nurses. The rules were strict: no smoking, marriage "considered beyond the pale," regular chapel and uniform inspections, 12-hour shifts and to bed at a respectable hour. Students were so busy they "didn't even have time to sit down."

They learned to defer to doctors, especially in the early decades. "If you saw a doctor, you'd have to stand back against the wall and let them go by," recalled Dorothy Coutermarsh, a 1940 graduate. "They were the ones who gave the orders. They were the ones who made the decisions."

In 1955, the hospital established one of the nation's first intensive care units, providing the nurses with valuable experience. The school also formed affiliations with two large Boston hospitals, allowing students to rotate away for experience in obstetrics, pediatrics and urban medicine.

By the 1960s, nursing education leaders across the country began to debate the merits of diploma schools such as Hitchcock's versus the more academic associate and bachelor's degree programs. The recognition of the need for more sophisticated academic training led in 1980 to the Hanover school's closing. And along the way, nurses gradually came to see — and be seen for — their important role as partners in health care.

After she graduated in 1966, Rosemary Swain said nurses were still expected to stand when a physician entered the room. "There was a distance. You didn't work as part of a team," Swain recalled four decades later. "Now at DHMC, nurses are respected members of the team."

Chapter Ten
The 1980s Bring a New President
and New Challenges

Kemeny's successor as Dartmouth president had plenty of green in his veins. David T. McLaughlin was a star receiver on the Big Green football team during his undergraduate years, was voted the class of 1954 graduate possessing "the greatest promise," and passed up a chance to play for the Philadelphia Eagles to earn his MBA in 1955 at the Tuck School.

He did not, however, come from the Academy. After graduating from Tuck, McLaughlin found his success in the world of business. After serving two years as an Air Force pilot, he joined Champion Paper and rose to a senior management post, then joined the Toro Company, where he was promoted to chief executive officer and chairman before taking the Dartmouth presidency in 1981.[185]

McLaughlin took office at a time of rising tensions between alumni, faculty, students and college administrators, and he would resign after only six years at the helm. During his tenure, however, he devoted considerable energy to Dartmouth's graduate programs — particularly its medical school and related medical center.

In his autobiography, *Choices Made*, McLaughlin recalled that after taking office, he held regular meetings with former Presidents Dickey and Kemeny. But in February 1982, he got a call from Dr. John H. Turco, the college's medical services director, who said that Dickey had suffered a stroke at his home and had to be rushed to Mary Hitchcock Memorial Hospital. McLaughlin hurried there and learned Dickey might not survive. Dickey's condition stabilized, but it quickly became clear that he would not be able to return home; he could hardly speak and the left side of his body was paralyzed.

Rather than having Dickey transported to a nursing home, McLaughlin wanted to bring him to Dick's House, the college infirmary. Used primarily for treating students with short-term medical needs, Dick's House was regulated by Hanover and not supposed to house longer-term patients. McLaughlin reached out to the town manager, who said that while he could not officially waive the rules, the town would also not formally intervene. The manager said, "You won't hear a word from us."

Initially, Dickey's older daughter, Sukie, protested that her father would not want special treatment. But, McLaughlin wrote, she dropped her objection when he said, "Sukie, let's suppose that while your father was president, Mr. Hopkins had been stricken in this way." She responded, "You've got me!" Dickey lived another nine years, cared for by the college to which he had devoted the prime of his professional life. "Each visit, during the first years of his confinement, I told him about goings-on at the college, and he might respond by saying "good" or "bad," McLaughlin recalled. "The sight of students would light up his face."[186]

McLaughlin faced his own health challenge in 1982, when he had to travel to Boston to receive a then-pioneering treatment — angioplasty — after suffering a heart attack, he recalled in his memoir. Returning to Hanover, he gave up smoking, began regular sessions on a rowing machine and got to thinking that "northern New England ought to have a medical facility with a capability to perform the most modern of procedures, so that patients would not need to travel to Boston or anywhere else."

At that time, the Dartmouth-Hitchcock Medical Center was located at the northern end of campus, just below the college-owned golf course. It consisted of three entities: the medical school, the Hitchcock Clinic and, of course, Mary Hitchcock Memorial Hospital. Also part of DHMC was the Veterans Administration Hospital, located to the south in White River Junction, Vermont.

"I had been warned by both John Dickey and John Kemeny that, because the medical school's existence was tied vitally to the hospital and clinic, a good deal of my time in office would be taken up with complex medical-center matters," McLaughlin wrote. He had his doubts at first, but found "they

180

were prophetically correct."

One decision McLaughlin made early in his presidency would play a large role in the medical center's future. Shortly after his inauguration in 1981, McLaughlin heard from a local construction company owner, Jack Nelson, who wanted to sell 2,000 acres of land that began at Hanover's southern edge and extended into Lebanon. Known as the Gile Tract, it was a wooded, rolling expanse that McLaughlin suspected could come in handy for a college pushing up against its physical limits in downtown Hanover. When Nelson agreed to sell the parcel at his cost — $750 an acre — college trustees recognized a bargain and agreed to buy "the parcel as fast as the necessary paperwork could be drawn up."[187]

Meanwhile, hospital officials were making plans to build a new ambulatory care facility about three miles south of the existing medical center, on Route 120 in Lebanon. McLaughlin and other college officials resisted, fretting that this would put an important clinical facility at too great a physical remove from the medical school. At the same time, McLaughlin said he and others "certainly sympathized" with the hospital's wish to expand.

Paul Paganucci, a college vice-president and key aide, used to take long walks around Hanover with the president. One evening in 1981, the two men departed a college function and walked back toward their homes. Paganucci, who played a leading role in the 2,000-acre land purchase, stopped to ask a question.

"Do you think we could move all this?" he asked.

181

"Move what?" McLaughlin replied.

"Move the whole thing, the whole medical center," Paganucci said.

The two men discussed the possibilities deep into the night. What if, they asked themselves, they could keep the medical education and treatment complex together — but move it entirely to the vacant 2,000-acre tract? In addition to providing DHMC with almost unlimited room for expansion, it would also free up a key parcel at the northern end of a tightly packed college campus. McLaughlin recalled that "before the evening ended, we had sold ourselves on the idea."[188]

But it wouldn't come easily — or soon — to fruition. For a time in 1983, there was talk of expanding the medical center on its existing site and at Dewey Fields, the former farmland adjacent to the medical complex on campus. That had the clear virtue of keeping the medical school and its clinical facilities in close proximity, but town officials protested that it would increase traffic congestion. Other options were considered, but just as quickly shot down.

Frustrations grew. At one point, McLaughlin had a visit from the chairman of the Hitchcock Clinic and key members of the medical school faculty, saying they hoped the college could help them pave the way for expansion "in a town that seemed no longer to want either" the hospital or clinic, he recalled in his memoir. "I was told that unless it all could be resolved, the future existence of the Dartmouth Medical School, as well as of the Mary Hitchcock Memorial Hospital as a tertiary care facility, could be in jeopardy."

"I had no intention of being the president who presided over Dartmouth Medical School's demise," McLaughlin wrote. He decided it was up to the college — which owned the land, controlled the teaching appointments and generated the medical research dollars — to come up with a solution. The estimated cost of moving the entire center to the 2,000-acre tract came in at $204 million, a figure that he said "hit the Upper Valley like a bombshell." Officials with the hospital and clinic positioned themselves on different sides of the issue, with McLaughlin and his aides squarely in the middle of sometimes warring factions. He and Paganucci joked that they should each get bracelets saying, "If I require medical attention, do *not* transport me to Mary Hitchcock Memorial Hospital."

By late 1985, tensions had eased to the point where the key parties agreed to move the clinical treatment complex to the new location. Entering 1986, though, one major issue remained unresolved: Would the medical school move from the Dartmouth campus to the new site? The medical school faculty said yes, college trustees said yes, and McLaughlin said, enthusiastically, yes.

But the college's arts and sciences faculty, fearing a disconnection from the undergraduate science program, rose up in opposition. In the end, officials agreed upon a compromise, with about one-quarter of the medical school relocating south and the rest remaining cheek-to-jowl with Daniel Webster's no-longer-small college in Hanover.

As it turned out, the protracted drama over the

medical center relocation proved to be the final major act of McLaughlin's presidency. He would later write that "to my particular gratification, we held a ground-breaking ceremony for the new hospital on the day before my successor was inaugurated."[189]

Move-in day arrived on Oct. 5, 1991. "The biggest moving party in northern New England's history — the relocation of Dartmouth-Hitchcock Medical Center and 232 patients from Hanover to new quarters … three miles down the road — was held yesterday," a *Boston Globe* reporter wrote. "Thanks to two years of planning and more than 3,000 movers, the transition proceeded, in the words of a nursing director, 'slick as ice.'"[190]

From 1982-1990, the medical school was led by a new dean, Dr. Robert McCollum. Dr. McCollum first became interested in a medical career as a child growing up in Texas, when the family physician made frequent visits to the family home to treat his mother for a serious illness, he recalled in a 2002 oral history interview.

"Those were the days of house calls and he was a visitor every morning and every afternoon at the end of his day and he became sort of a hero figure to me," McCollum said.[191]

He went to medical school during World War II at Johns Hopkins. He did his residency in internal medicine at Yale, where he spent 31 years on the faculty before coming to Dartmouth. McCollum used to come skiing in Vermont and had visited Dartmouth during the Vietnam era.

However, he didn't feel a burning desire to

come to Hanover, or to Dartmouth Medical School. "It looked rural, it felt rural and that was wonderful," he said, but he didn't think Dartmouth had "a medical school of much note."

After learning more, however, McCollum took on the challenge, coming to Hanover as McLaughlin was beginning his presidency. McLaughlin didn't mince words; the medical school had an outstanding $2.1 million debt to the college, he told the new dean. "You have got to get it on a solid financial footing. We cannot support the medical school any further."

There also remained a pronounced tension between the medical school and the college's science faculty. "The faculty of arts and sciences had no interest in the medical school," he recalled in the interview with Daniel Daily. The animus was especially strong in the biology department, which was located right next door to the school and shared the Dana Library. "There was a glass bridge between the two institutions, so to speak, but no love," Mc-Collum recalled. "In fact, there was not a love/hate relationship, but a hate relationship."

McCollum wanted to ratchet up the level of original research done by members of the faculty, and to freshen up the teaching, but he faced obstacles. "We had a few faculty members who were giving lectures from the same notes that they had used perhaps ten years before — same notes and jokes," he said.

McCollum started pushing for more, using as an important yardstick the amount of money professors generated in outside research funding. Some of the underproducing professors had come during an era in which there was a lot of federal funding, but those days were over. "There were a lot of them who were not paying their freight." When he had the chance to hire, he stressed the need to create new knowledge as well as engaging with students through their teaching.

With the growth of DHMC, the clinical opportunities for students had improved. But there were still gaps, McCollum said. In a region heavy with college students and elderly residents, for instance, there weren't many babies born. "We didn't have an abundance of deliveries to take care of sixty-five medical students who had to go through obstetrics," he noted. So Dartmouth sought opportunities elsewhere, sometimes across the continent. At a California hospital, for instance, "they would deliver more babies in a week than they would have delivered in six months here."

When it came to recruiting students, the rural location and more relaxed pace of clinical work proved a drawing card. Students and prospective residents visiting Bellevue or Presbyterian hospitals in New York City would see that their emergency room rotations would be full of treating patients suffering gunshot wounds, drug addiction and AIDS. At Dartmouth, by contrast, "you wouldn't be spending your entire internship in the emergency room or on AIDS."

Students who chose Dartmouth also felt "they were part of a medical family, not part of a huge institution located out on First Avenue with everything thirty-three stories above where you were."

Thayer School: Off the ropes and into growth

In his autobiography, McLaughlin wrote that the Thayer School was "in something of a crisis" when he took office, "lacking the critical mass to continue as a world-class graduate school in its field." College officials went so far as to discuss ending its status as a graduate school, simply folding the engineering courses into the undergraduate college.

To continue as a graduate school, McLaughlin concluded, Thayer would have to expand — and it needed cash to do so. Recalling that the University of New Hampshire had at one point gotten federal funding for its engineering school, he traveled to Washington, D.C. to meet with U.S. Sen. Warren B. Rudman, a New Hampshire Republican. Over the next six months, McLaughlin and Thayer School Dean Charles E. Hutchinson made several trips to Washington to meet with the senator and his staff — and were rewarded with $18 million for Thayer.

"The money was, of course, pure 'pork,'" McLaughlin wrote, "and I must confess that I never really had believed in legislative pork-barreling until the day in 1985 when Warren called to tell me the bill had passed."

He added that — "quite unrelated to this event" — Dartmouth presented Rudman with an honorary degree the next year, at the same time his daughter received her master's degree from Tuck. "Tears ran down the senator's cheeks as his degree was conferred, and he confided to me that he had always wanted a degree from Dartmouth and that he was now proud that two Rudmans had achieved that distinction on the same day."[192]

Hutchinson had become Thayer's dean in 1984 and would lead the school through a major period of growth in the decade to come. He grew up in a blue-collar West Virginia family, served in the U.S. Navy and earned his doctorate from Stanford, where he was a classmate of Thayer stalwart John Strohbehn. When the school was looking for a new dean to replace the retiring Carl Long, Professor Strohbehn thought of his old Stanford pal.

When Dartmouth reached out, Hutchinson was at the University of Massachusetts, which he had earlier chosen over M.I.T.. "I didn't want to go to a big research house," he told Doug Wilhelm for the Thayer School history. Coming from a job in industry, he said, "If I was going to go into the academic world, I wanted to teach."[193]

When Strohbehn called, he asked Hutchinson if he had gotten a letter saying Thayer was looking for a new dean.

"Yes, I got the letter," Hutchinson replied.

"What'd you do with it?" Strohbehn said.

"I threw it away," Hutchinson recalled in the 2003 oral history interview. In the interview, he explained that he had no particular appetite for an administrative post and, besides, "when I looked at the map, Hanover was two hours colder than Amherst."

But Strohbehn persisted, and Hutchinson eventually took the post in chilly Hanover. He was attracted by Thayer's blend of liberal arts and technical training, which gives the school "a distinct market niche … and a very important one."[194]

While enamored of teaching, the new dean also

embraced research. At UMass, he had helped design microelectronic chips and video networks, taking pleasure in finding ways to connect work done on campus with customers in the business world. When Strohbehn approached him about the Thayer job, Hutchinson embraced the school's emphasis on training engineering students across traditional disciplinary lines, and he also brought a commitment to finding real-world problems for faculty and students to solve.

"If you're going to have leaders in technology, you need the liberal arts piece because they need to know how to read, write and speak," he said in the oral history. "Very few engineers can read, write and speak … and you have to have a very broad vision and context for technology; it can't be narrow. Because the one thing you know that's constant about technology is it's going to change." Quoting the school's founder, General Thayer, he said, "First you get educated and then you become an engineer."

Real-world needs weren't hard to identify. The economy was booming, computers were proliferating and the demand for young engineers was surging. Speaking at the school's 1986 investiture ceremony, Thayer graduate and author Samuel C. Florman said engineers have an impact not just on industry but on society. "If we are not technologically creative, ingenious, productive, and far-sighted," he declared, "we can say goodbye to our high standard of living and with it our dreams for a more noble society."[195]

Florman applauded the school's commitment — unmatched by any other American engineering school — to require students to earn a liberal arts A.B. before earning their B.E. "In the better engineering schools all over the country, deans and faculties are scrambling to come up with programs that deal with the demands of a new age," Florman said. "Well, the pilot program is here at Thayer School."

An ambitious $25 million fundraising campaign exceeded its goal by $1.5 million, and Hutchinson reported that "scores of corporations" — including Ford Motor Co. — were among those chipping in. Cummings Memorial Hall underwent a dramatic expansion, the sponsored research budget tripled and the endowment doubled.

Hutch — as the dean came to be known — developed a reputation for strong listening skills and a decisive manner, Wilhelm wrote in a chapter on the dean's tenure in *Knowledge with Know-How*. "He would listen to the faculty first," recalled professor Horst Richter. But when the time came for an executive decision, he didn't shrink from it. While crediting Hutch for being "democratic and egalitarian," Associate Dean Carol B. Muller said, "he would also say, 'I know who's the boss, and it's me.' "

Hutch managed on his feet, regularly looping around the school to check in with professors and students and provide a sounding board for new ideas and challenges. His style included a regular supply of chiding, which could irritate some on his faculty. But overall, his genuine interest in their work and care for their well-being engendered a fierce loyalty.

"I always feel that a dean should have his staff so committed that they would walk barefoot over hot coals for him," said Richter. "Hutch got this school united behind him. The staff loyalty was such that people from up-campus wanted to work here, because they knew that the spirit in this building was great and the collaboration was wonderful."

In the area of research, he supported fields of expertise — including biomedical engineering and space plasma physics — already going strong at Thayer, while also promoting new professors in such emerging fields as semiconductor and superconductor devices, optics and solid state physics. He set a high standard for new hires and veterans alike, insisting that they create new knowledge in their specialties, while also teaching in the school's broad, interdisciplinary tradition.

Hutch was "very Darwinian" in the way he set standards, said one professor, John Collier. "It was really survival of the fittest … It was 'You're in it — I'll give you a list of things that you need to learn how to do, and you need to learn them well.' "

When he took over, Hutch said in the oral history, Thayer had a "very good" undergraduate program, an active master's program but "no real research agenda or a PhD program agenda." As faculty members departed to take other jobs or retire, he replaced them with scholar-teachers who could increase the school's reach.

Even with the emphasis on research, Hutch made clear that teaching was job one, Wilhelm wrote. Graham Wallis, associate dean of graduate studies, said that "sometimes the faculty needed to be reminded of the importance of their teaching, and Hutch did that."

Left to right, ENGS 21 teammates Renee Foisy '88, David Lindahl '86, Christoph Mack '88, Corey Brinkema '86, Susan Smith '86, Patrick Walsh '88 with the keyboard they created for a young disabled muscian. *Image courtesy of Dartmouth Engineering.*

Dean Hutchinson (left) worked with Thayer School and Tuck School faculty to establish one of the country's first master's degree in engineering management (M.E.M.). Dean Carl Long (right).
Image courtesy of Dartmouth Engineering.

Chapter 11
A 'Liberal Arts University'

On April 13, 1987, University of Iowa President James O. Freedman was selected to succeed McLaughlin. In a get-acquainted address to faculty, he addressed head-on the question of whether Dartmouth was a college, a university or, in its unique way, both.

"I want to assure you that I begin this second presidency with the highest of hopes — and the deepest of beliefs — that Dartmouth College is on the threshold of an era of great opportunity and achievement," Freedman said. "I deeply admire the central role that Dartmouth College has always accorded to liberal education and the high importance that it has placed upon the teaching of undergraduates."[196]

The "Dartmouth experience" has inspired in its graduates an extraordinary fondness and loyalty for their alma mater, he said. But that experience and affection is not limited to those who spent their undergraduate years there, he said.

One thing that distinguishes Dartmouth is its ability to build strong graduate programs alongside undergraduate ones, he said. And here he showed how far the college, and its newest president, had come from the days when "research" was, if not a dirty word, then one that was uttered only with qualification or trepidation.

"As we seek to maintain Dartmouth's stature as a major research institution, we will want to continue to explore how, and in which new areas, the college may be able to make an enlarged and distinctive contribution to graduate education — a contribution that will be consistent with the Dartmouth tradition and will enrich the Dartmouth experience."

Nor did he shy away from the U-word. "As we assemble an outstanding student body, we must also emphasize the role that great universities should play in preparing students for the responsibilities of citizenship and leadership," he told the faculty.

Quoting Alfred North Whitehead's *The Aims of Education*, he said, " 'The task of the university is to weld together imagination and experience.' " That work begins in the classroom where scholars do not keep their research in the lab or library but instead share it with everyone from freshmen to graduate students. Quoting Whitehead again, he said, " 'Do you want your teachers to be imaginative? Then encourage them to research. Do you want your researchers to be imaginative? Then bring them into intellectual sympathy with the young.' "

Freedman concluded by sounding a note that would echo increasingly loudly in the years to come, speaking of the need to move beyond the silos of particular disciplines to see how the world's challenges often require interdisciplinary solutions. "We want our students to move to the measure of the scholar's thought — in interdisciplinary studies, as they come to appreciate that many of our most baffling problems are beyond the competence of even the most advanced thinkers in any single discipline."

The next year, in a major address to faculty on Oct. 31, 1988, Freedman made clear once and for all (or so he hoped) that Dartmouth is a "liberal arts university." Freedman told professors that it was an opportune time to think hard about where the college had been and where it might go. He explained that in a self-study report completed for for the decennial accreditation process, college leaders had identified three important areas for growth: intellectual environment, diversity and graduate education.

"Is Dartmouth a college or is it a university?" Freedman asked. Alluding to the tension that had historically greeted that question, he went on, "The degree to which that question disturbs us is a measure of its symbolic importance."[197]

But the importance wasn't just symbolic, Freedman said. The question and its answer cut to the core of important practical questions: How do the strengths of its graduate and professional programs square with the historic mission of educating undergraduates? How can the college attract and keep the best faculty? To what extent is Dartmouth's mission not only to impart knowledge but also to create it?

A visitor to Hanover would immediately see that Dartmouth was no longer the small liberal arts college of a century before, Freedman said. "It has long since become a liberal arts university."

The evidence was all around, he said: not only an arts and sciences curriculum the equal of any university but also three top-shelf professional schools: Tuck, Thayer and Dartmouth Medical School. "Each has a venerable tradition. Each, in President John Sloan Dickey's words, 'maintains an extraordinarily close, mutually rewarding relationship to the total life and work of Dartmouth.' "

There was more. As of 1988, the college offered 11 doctoral programs in the natural and social sciences, a master of arts in liberal studies and a new master's program in the humanities. The college had built a university class research library of 1.75 million volumes and "appointed a faculty of devoted scholars, nationally and internationally prominent, who are dedicated to research and to exploration of the frontiers of knowledge." The level of sponsored research had doubled in the preceeding five years, rising to $38 million in 1987-88.

The sense of a "small college" had been hard to shake, Freedman suggested. He recalled the time, a quarter-century before, when then-President Dickey spoke of people new to Dartmouth "who asked him, in some amazement, 'But then you *are* a university?' " And 13 years earlier, in 1975, President John G. Kemeny had written, "Perhaps because 'college' is a word hallowed by tradition, we sometimes overlook the fact that Dartmouth is a small university."

Freedman pronounced himself ready to remove any doubt, calling on all gathered there "to assert confidently and unambiguously that Dartmouth *is* a liberal arts university." But that didn't mean turning the school into a carbon copy of other schools that long ago embraced the university designation, he said.

"We are a liberal arts university that does not seek to become a traditional, large-scale, highly impersonal research university," he asserted. "Rather, we are a liberal arts university that seeks to become the best of what we already are."

That doesn't mean according second-class status to undergraduates, he said, but instead drawing them into a campus-wide excitement about research and teaching that as much as possible reaches across disciplinary lines. "We will insure that faculty members communicate to our students, who are among the most talented and gifted in the nation, the excitement of intellectual discovery and intellectual risk-taking, by igniting in them what Horace Judson calls 'the rage to know.' "

Declaring Dartmouth as a liberal arts university would pay many dividends, Freeman said. It would "dispel whatever ambiguity may still remain" about the college's academic purpose. It would reward faculty members who use research to develop new knowledge, often with emerging technology, in areas ranging from cognitive science to electro-acoustic music, molecular genetics to applied ethics, film studies to biomedical engineering. It would allow the college to lure and hang onto the best faculty members, rather than losing them to large research universities. It would attract the best students, offering them the chance to share in the "trials and tribulations, the wonder and joy, of discovering new truths and conveying new ways of seeing and understanding."

Finally, it would create more opportunities for cross-pollination between the faculties of the arts and sciences divisions and the professional schools, "so that the intellectual achievements and satisfactions of both faculty members and students may be truly synergistic, as well as significantly greater than the sum of the individual parts."

Defining Dartmouth as a liberal arts university would produce some concrete results and needs, he continued. The amount of sponsored research would grow, reducing "our excessively high reliance on endowment income, tuition and annual giving." It would entail adding faculty members, to spread the teaching load around and allow individual professors time and energy for research. In addition to maintaining the priority historically given to undergraduate education, it would mean developing "a unique role for graduate education, instilling the values of a liberal arts approach to the study of advanced and highly specialized subjects."

Freedman repeated his hope that an increasing percentage of Dartmouth undergraduates would aspire to doctoral degrees and careers in the academic world, the sciences and the visual and performing arts. By 1988, the number of graduate students had grown to approximately 1,000. In the professional schools of medicine, engineering and business, he said, Dartmouth had won "national distinction" for the way those programs had infused the pursuit of increasingly specialized knowledge with the broadening power of the liberal arts.

At the same time, he said, Dartmouth's doctoral programs had not always been built and operated with clear expectations of excellence. "We have never been entirely clear about whether we expect our graduate programs to be among the very strongest in the nation or merely sufficiently strong to satisfy the needs of faculty members who might leave Dartmouth if we had no such programs at all" — in other words, good enough to provide research assistants but not to urge graduate students to the highest standards.

"We have not formally stated for our graduate programs the expectations of preeminent excellence and of national recognition that we have long taken for granted for our undergraduate programs," he said. As a result, he said, graduate programs had had uneven records of success in attracting outside research funding "and are sometimes regarded, within the Dartmouth community, as subsidiary and peripheral to the larger educational enterprise, thereby causing many of our doctoral students to feel marginal and undervalued."

Freedman went on to say that the college community should undertake strategies to insure that Dartmouth had something to offer the best graduate students, but doing so with a selective set of offerings instead of "a full panoply of doctoral programs."

"Even as we proudly adhere to the right heritage

summoned up by Dartmouth's designation as a 'College,' even as we gratefully preserve our loyalty to the values that Daniel Webster and successive generations have loved so dearly, we shall succeed in further achieving Dartmouth's destiny as a commonwealth of liberal learning that enriches the lives of its students and contributes effectively to the life of the nation and the world."

Introducing Freedman's speech, editors of the alumni magazine said it was "seen by some professors and students as an academic fiat." But at a press conference after the talk, Freedman said he was simply opening a needed debate on Dartmouth's future. "It's a rule of academic life that a president has two years to get the attention of the faculty and of the community," he told reporters. The point, he said, was to "set an agenda that leads to questions."

Those questions came, sometimes in the form of sharp-elbowed criticism. Graduates young and old lit up the letters column of the alumni magazine.

Mark C. Henrie, a 1987 alum from Cambridge, Mass., called Freedman "disingenuous" in saying he simply wanted to open a debate. "You do not open a debate by announcing *a fait accompli*," Henrie wrote. "By orienting ourselves as a university, we would perhaps attract more big-name professors actively engaged in research. Dartmouth would get better press and our administrators would carry more clout in their professional organizations. But do we really want Dartmouth undergraduates taught by professors who were attracted to Dartmouth by a university 'image' and not by our traditional liberal-arts orientation?"[198]

A 1959 grad, Sigmund G. Ginsburg of New York City, was more sanguine. He called Freedman's vision "clear and compelling," saying it could secure Dartmouth's future as long as it struck a balance that improved graduate offerings without compromising undergraduate instruction. By "making sure that Dartmouth does not try to be everything to everyone and indeed strives to be a 'liberal arts university' and not a traditional research university, Dartmouth should be able to achieve the same quality in its graduate programs as it will in its undergraduate program."

Mike O'Connell, class of 1965, cut to the point: "Anyone who needs to puzzle over the question 'Is Dartmouth a college or a university?' doesn't know much about Dartmouth," he wrote from Wisconsin. "A president who dares to declare that Dartmouth College is no longer Dartmouth College is a malevolent despot. I say set this man free. Get him to a university, any university. Get him to Boston, New York, anywhere. Get him the hell out."

At the other end of the spectrum were alums such as Maxwell Field, a Florida resident who earned his bachelor's degree in 1933 before going on to earn a master's from Tuck in 1934. "It is my hope," he wrote, "that out of all the discussion and debate on this issue there will develop a united support among trustees, faculty and alumni for President Freedman's position and eventual acceptance of a Dartmouth University."

On this and other issues, controversies sometimes prompted alumni to publicly scold college

201

leaders and threaten to withhold financial support. Others chided their fellow alumni for such scorched-earth tactics.

"My support for Dartmouth remains strong," Edward Schechter, class of 1940, wrote from Pennsylvania. "My answer to those who threaten to stop their contributions to the College will be to double mine."

James G. Birney, class of 1950, wrote from Wilmington, Delaware: "It seems to me that my debt and gratitude to Dartmouth calls for more from me now that she is under fire from rude, ungrateful children who abuse their great privilege of free speech; and now that she is being deserted by alumni who wish everything could stay the same forever. I am sad that they cannot rejoice in their mother's growth and maturity."

Freedman's speech sparked a discussion that unfolded not just among alumni, but also among faculty members and college administrators. The cover story in the February 1989 edition of the *Dartmouth Alumni Magazine*, entitled "The Rise in Research," opened with an imagined scenario of how college representatives had traditionally sold Dartmouth to prospective students — and how that might change.[199]

"It's a familiar scene, played a thousand times at alumni interviews and college nights around the country about this time of year," wrote Anne Bagamery, a 1978 graduate. " 'Harvard, Berkeley, Michigan — yes, those are all very good schools,' says the Dartmouth representative to the high school senior, in best damning-with-faint-praise manner. 'But their emphasis is on research, not on undergraduates. They're, well, universities. Dartmouth' — pause for effect — 'Dartmouth is a *college*.' "

"It's a good line but, like most sales pitches, it's only partially true," concluded the author, Anne Bagamery.

Daniel Webster's 1818 Supreme Court oration helped ensure that this "small college" would keep some version of that identity alive for the centuries to follow. But the facts circa 1989 — "three professional schools, thriving graduate programs in the sciences, improved facilities and an increased emphasis on research" — had led many on campus to stop "referring to the institution as a 'college' at all."

That didn't mean it had become a big research university, Bagamery noted. "A recent study of graduate programs at Dartmouth shows that its faculty members produce fewer publications, supervise fewer graduate students, and have fewer colleagues in their departments than those of most research universities," she wrote.

Nor was it a small New England college along the lines of Williams or Middlebury. P. Bruce Pipes, dean of graduate studies and a physics professor said, "the question is no longer whether Dartmouth is a college or a university, but what kind of university Dartmouth is going to be."

The article focused on a question central to Freedman's hopes of Dartmouth being a "liberal arts university" — research programs that increased the production of original knowledge and provided students with the chance to develop it, and which

203

— no small matter — drew outside financial support that would help pay the bills and reduce the reliance on tuition and alumni giving.

In the 1987-88 fiscal year, 25 percent of Dartmouth's externally generated funds came from corporations and foundations. An impressive number, to be sure, but much lower than the 40 percent share reported by Harvard and Princeton, let alone M.I.T.'s 60 percent.

By 1988, Dartmouth faculty had landed $38 million in research awards, the largest amount ever, from sources including New England Digital Corporation, Pfizer Pharmaceuticals and the Pew Memorial Trust. Those entities weren't just donating money to a good cause, said Ken Spritz, Dartmouth's head of corporate and foundation support. They want products and services to take to market.

"With corporate America there's always a quid pro quo," he told the magazine. "Corporations want two things from academic America — our graduates and access to our research."

How to compete with the likes of M.I.T.? By emphasizing Dartmouth's areas of unique strength, Spritz said. "If M.I.T. is a department store, then Dartmouth is a boutique — fewer items but very high quality."

One corner of the boutique is found in the Dartmouth ice research labs. There, Thayer School professors Francis Kennedy and Samuel Colbeck were working with grad student Guy Warren on a project to help Rossignol skis figure out how to make their skis speed up on the snow.

Using a ski equipped with thermal sensors, the

researchers studied the way a moving Rossignol melts snow, creating a lubricant that helps the ski go faster. But they were also looking for a ski surface that wouldn't melt the snow too much, which tended to make the ski slow down, "such as one might find on a warm March afternoon," Kennedy said.

Such practical research was not a completely new thing for Dartmouth, the article noted. Ernest Fox Nichols, president from 1909-16, was "a world-renowned physicist whose plans for [research] expansion were stymied by the outbreak of World War I." His successor, Ernest Martin Hopkins, for the next three decades "deliberately played down research in favor of the small college model." When John Sloan Dickey '29 became president in 1945, he ushered in the steady growth toward an institution devoted to the "production of ideas" as well as teaching.

Balancing a full teaching load and original research isn't an easy task, especially with intensive 10-week terms. But professors who choose Dartmouth over more traditionally research-oriented universities do so because they love to teach, said Jim Poage, vice provost for computing. "They do research not because they have to but because they want to."

Not all the new generation of teacher-scholars was convinced that Dartmouth did as much as it should to support research; a 1988 survey found that only 55 percent agreed the college "provides sufficient support for scholarly development." Nor had all students embraced a research culture. A campus committee studying Dartmouth's intellectual climate warned that the faculty's research orientation "will isolate them from the students unless the students themselves move toward a greater interest in research."

Boosting Dartmouth's research activity while maintaining strong undergraduate education requires more graduate students, argued trustee Ira Michael Heyman, a 1951 graduate and chancellor of the University of California at Berkeley. But not everyone agreed, saying anything but the best graduate students could lower the classroom denominator.

"Bad graduate students just get you confirmed in bad ways," said Bernard Gert, a professor in the philosophy department, which in the early 80s had decided against a PhD program.

Even faculty members who supported expanding the graduate departments urged caution, saying existing programs should be strengthened before adding new ones. That is the hard-won wisdom of universities that grew their graduate programs without ensuring consistently high standards. "If you got all the heads of the major research universities together for a beer, they would probably confide that they'd like to shed 50 percent of their graduate programs because they're substandard and unproductive," said Pogue. Dartmouth, on the other hand, positioned itself to "do it right or not do it at all."

In 1988, the college had approved a new master's program in electronic music, but only after it was found to have satisfied four requirements: it capitalized on a unique strength (a state-of-the-art electronic music studio), taught skills that were in demand, featured a degree offered by no other

206

school, and was open to undergraduate as well as graduate students. The sense of faculty members, said music professor Jon Appleton, was that "these were the *minimum* acceptable criteria."

Would bringing more graduate students to the campus take Dartmouth away from its tradition of having professors teach most undergraduate classes? No. But faculty members argued that increasing the presence of graduate student instructors would not automatically be a bad thing. Surveys of both faculty members and students found that three-quarters or more thought their graduate students who were already teaching did a good job.

In his speech calling for Dartmouth to fulfill its "destiny" as a liberal arts university, Freedman said the size of the faculty would need to grow. That pledge drew skepticism from some quarters. "President Freedman has evoked a grand picture for which he entirely lacks the resources," said Ted Fletcher, a member of the Graduate Student Council. "It's a nice pipe dream but the reality of the vision is a long way off."

Freedman's vision provoked similarly mixed feelings among faculty members, for reasons philosophical as well as financial. Ed Bradley, chairman of the classics department, said, "I think Dartmouth should strive for greater excellence in the area of undergraduate education and not dissipate its resources in an attempt to become a pale imitation of Yale or Harvard."

"There is no question but that Dartmouth is a university," countered Dan Lynch, associate dean of the Thayer School. "But it also continues to be true that Dartmouth is a small college, and yet there are those who love it." [200]

Responding to a Dartmouth planning committee call for graduate studies to "measure up to the rest of the college," *Dartmouth Alumni Magazine* Editor Jay Heinrichs in 1991 sounded a cautionary note on breathless expansion by pointing to other schools that have done that (or the opposite) and gotten it wrong.

He cited Middlebury is an example of an institution that has remained focused exclusively on the "small college" side of the coin. Consider the science building that was planned in the 1960s to be just part of a state-of-the-art complex at Middlebury. Those plans never came to fruition, he wrote, and now "Outer doors on the second and third stories lead to nowhere; if you managed to unlock those doors you would fall straight down."[201]

The result: Even as the pace of hard science discoveries picks up at institutions able to take part, Middlebury struggled to attract grant money and teacher-scholars. "The doors leading to nowhere reflect the little college's reluctant acceptance of its role: to offer excellent, personalized instruction in the sciences, a step or two back from the frontier," he wrote. "Meanwhile, Dartmouth has started construction on a $28 million chemistry building."

At the other end of the spectrum, the large research university, the rising cost of research combined with cutbacks in federal funding had led to a wholesale slashing of programs, including those affecting undergraduates. At Syracuse University, students formed a lobbying group called "Under-graduates for a Better Education," he wrote. "At Dartmouth, at least in the present, such a group would be unthinkable."

Finally, at Harvard, the former dean of the undergraduate faculty, issued a call for better teaching at universities. "That is something Dartmouth never abandoned."

The editor seemed to embrace the committee's call to ensure that Dartmouth's graduate programs hew to the same high standards as the rest of the school. But he pointed out that, at least in the arts and sciences divisions, that had generally not been the case. "With a few glorious exceptions, the College's graduate programs have not come close to achieving the stature of the undergraduate and professional schools."

How to improve that track record? Heinrichs didn't offer a detailed prescription, only pointed out the risk of a "zero sum" approach that bolsters graduate programs at the expense of undergraduate ones. He also urged that Dartmouth have the courage to kill programs that don't hit the mark. "To prevent that academic center of gravity from shifting irretrievably away from the undergraduate, the faculty must decide which graduate studies to keep, and which to shut down."

That, it seems, is the "hard part."

Karen Wetterhahn: Tragic Pioneer

Any list of Dartmouth's Most Influential Women would include chemistry professor Karen Wetterhahn. Wetterhahn and Carol Muller, '77, then

209

assistant dean of the Thayer School, had noticed a vexing statistic: while nearly half of freshmen women indicated an interest in science, only about one in seven chose a scientific major. In 1991, they co-founded the Women in Science Project, which quickly turned those numbers around. By 1996, one in four female students at Dartmouth graduated with a science degree and 60 percent of entering first-year women indicated an interest in science. [202]

Wetterhahn was no stranger to firsts. A leading researcher on carcinogens, she was Dartmouth's first female chemistry professor and the first woman to serve as acting dean of the faculty.

She was also an intrepid researcher. Since her arrival at Dartmouth in 1976, Wetterhahn had been investigating whether, and how, chromium increases the risk of cancer for factory workers. When she began her inquiry, she had two undergraduates assisting her. Over the years, her research team had grown to include ten people, including graduate students in chemistry, biochemistry and pharmacology toxicology, the alumni magazine reported in February 1989.[203]

Nine years later, though, another alumni magazine story would provide a tragic sequel. Even as she was being lauded as one of Dartmouth's female pioneers, Wetterhahn was struggling to survive after accidentally poisoning herself in a lab experiment.

As part of her ongoing research into the role toxic metals play in causing cancer, Wetterhahn had used a syringe-like pipette to draw a small amount of dimethylmercury out of a vial and place it in a sample tube, according to an April 1998 article.

Knowing the chemical was highly toxic, she took all the precautions deemed at that time to be necessary, donning disposable latex gloves, protective lab coat and goggles, and working in a chemical fume hood that would draw away dangerous vapors.

In transferring the chemical, a "drop or two" of the mercury dripped onto her left glove. The substance didn't seem at the time to have penetrated the glove, but she still followed standard procedure and, after removing the gloves, thoroughly washed her hands before going home to her husband and two children.

"She should have gone straight to the hospital," wrote Karen Endicott in the magazine. "For the dimethylmercury that had landed on her glove had penetrated the latex and then her skin and was already beginning a slow, unseen journey into her blood and into her brain."[204]

It took five months for the symptoms of the poisoning to make themselves clear, as the "deliberate, focused, and precise scientist found herself stumbling into walls and slurring her speech." Her eyesight and hearing faded, as lab results showed she was the victim of severe mercury toxicity. An attempt to use chellation therapy — in which Wetterhahn was given a medication designed to act as a magnet and allow her body to excrete the poison — came up short. On Feb. 6, 1997, just three weeks after she suspected she was sick, one of Dartmouth's leading female researchers slipped into a coma from which she would never emerge.

As it turned out, Wetterhahn's tragic death may have carried lessons after she was no longer able to teach them, alerting researchers to the until-then-unknown risk of working with the substance. Wetterhahn wasn't exploring the role dimethylmercury plays in harming people. She was simply using a chemical that not only she but many others had seen as a useful calibrating agent in their research. By donning the latex surgeon's gloves, she had done what she and fellow scientists thought was enough.

It wasn't. As it turned out, nobody had tested the gloves for their resistance to dimethylmercury. Tests conducted after her death showed most — including the ones she had worn — were inadequate to the task. The drop or two that penetrated to Wetterhahn's body left her with 80 times the toxic level in her bloodstream.

A chemist's daughter, Wetterhahn had earned her doctorate at Columbia University in 1975 and become the first woman in the Dartmouth chemistry department the next year. Even as she established herself as a gifted classroom teacher and mentor to young scientists, she also developed a national reputation for her research. Said fellow researcher Kent Sugden, "Karen was one of the best — if not the best — in metal toxicology."

The Women in Science Project she co-founded pushed to get female students into labs from the start of their Dartmouth careers. "She wanted to captivate students at their highest level of interest — during their first year — and get them into labs," said Mary Pavone, who became the project's director. While some faculty members were skeptical about involving first-year students in serious researched, she kept pushing — and by the time of her death, 175 faculty members and researchers had invited students to assist them, making the Women in Science Project a national model.

Along the way, she became associate dean for the sciences and acting dean of the Dartmouth faculty, both times becoming the first woman to fill those roles. She used the opportunity to build bridges between disciplines and schools: the medical and engineering schools, biology, chemistry and environmental studies.

After her death, the research went on, but students and scientists at Dartmouth and beyond handled dimethylmercury with the greatest care. Michael Blayney, the college's environmental health and safety director, said, "Once in a while, you get to the trembling edge of science and something bad happens."[205]

<hr>

The Dartmouth Formula Racing car in 1996. Courtesy of Dartmouth Engineering.

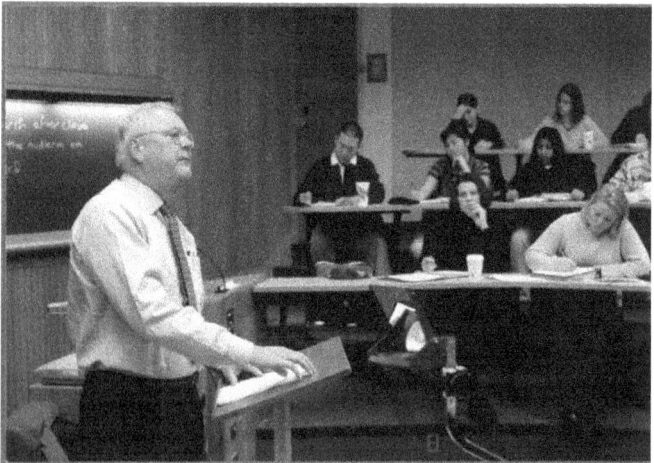

President James Wright, 1990. Courtesy of Dartmouth College Photographic Files.

Book Three

Undergraduate researchers working in Professor Robert Hill's laboratory. Courtesy of Dartmouth Biology Department.

Chapter Twelve
The Professional Schools Mature

At Thayer, Dean Hutchinson led the way to a renewed collaboration between the engineering school and the Tuck School of Business. The dual degree program had come back to life in 1988 as a way to equip future engineers with the management skills they would need to become business leaders. The program eventually came to be known as the masters in engineering management (M.E.M.).

To Hutchinson, though, the partnership felt one-sided. With Tuck's focus on the two-year MBA, Tuck Dean Colin Blaydon said his school couldn't invest much energy in another program, Hutch said in the oral history interview. As a result, he took the lead, identifying management courses that would be useful to future engineers and then hiring Tuck professors to teach them. "I said, 'Well, I'm not going to drop it. We're going to do it ourselves.' "

Earlier, Hutch had met with an investment firm chief to discuss his ambitions for positioning Thayer as an "innovation incubator" — not just creating new technology but finding ways to market those inventions. "There's a fundamental resistance to this in any academic institution, because there's a fundamental feeling that anything that makes money is evil," he told Anita Warren for a chapter in *Knowledge with Know-How*.[206]

Hutch begged to differ, saying that Thayer — along with its sister professional schools in medicine and business — were ideally positioned to do just that. "All three of the grad schools are separately endowed," he explained. "And they're small enough that they can be very nimble, without a lot of built-in bureaucracies to deal with."

Entering the 1990s, Thayer played an important role in the effort to open more opportunities for women in the sciences. "There are few fields in which the current absence of women is more notable than engineering — nationally, only 16 percent of scientists and less than 5 percent of engineers are women," Assistant Dean Muller wrote in a 1991 article.[207]

The female students who came to Thayer in increasing numbers found few role models, and a culture only slowly becoming more inclusive. Muller recalled that when she arrived in 1987, "I felt I had stepped back in time 20 years in terms of gender issues."

Communications director Lois Wood said when

she arrived in the mid-1980s, women worked mostly as support staff and were "a bit subservient and somewhat disdained by faculty." But, Wood continued, "Hutch changed that very fast, by making it clear to everyone that the only thing that mattered was that we worked hard and did our jobs."[208]

The early 90s brought a dramatic improvement in the shops where students learned to translate book theories into working devices. The school's facilities had been lagging behind, lacking an up-to-date x-ray machine, scanning-electron microscope, ultra-clean room and computer-guided machining equipment. Roger Howes, a 1972 Dartmouth graduate and longtime instructional supervisor in the machine shop, recalled students lining up for the limited available time slots.

"One morning, Hutch came into the shop and said, 'Why the hell is that girl sleeping out there in her sleeping bag?' I said, 'So she'll be the first to sign up for shop time in the morning.' " That soon changed, as Hutch made sure students got the chance to work in a new state-of-the art facility with plenty of room and both conventional and high-tech equipment.

Howes grew up on a Vermont farm and became a fixture in the basement shop, one of the last "farm-boy engineers" who had learned to fix and build machines before having the chance to learn the theory behind them. He saw the labs as being a place where students could make up for their lack of hands-on experience. "Today, if you talk about a plunger arm and bearings and castings, these very bright kids have nothing to relate that to," hc said.

218

"We have to create a lab situation where they understand these basics — and not from an equation point of view."

Like Robert Fletcher, the school's first professor and dean, Hutch was unapologetic about the need for hard work. After he left the post in 1994, a catalog of his sayings — "Hutchisms" — remained. Among them: "Stop moping around the building. You are in engineering school, for goodness sake — you should expect to be overworked and up all night."[209]

Nor did he spend much time feeling sorry for himself over what he saw as a lack of institutional support from the school's mother institution. "I mean, [in] nothing Thayer did was there any help from Dartmouth," he said during a segment of the oral history interview covering the engineering school's efforts to attract a broader array of students, including women. "The only reason it works — candidly — I would not have come here as the dean except for the fact that Thayer is separately endowed and has its own board."

In the interview, Hutch said Dartmouth ignores the value of its professional schools at its own peril. "Dartmouth is a very strong institution that exists in that open niche between Harvard and Amherst College. The only reason that Dartmouth is different … is because it has three professional schools," he said. "However, the trustees, the president and Parkhurst take the position that the professional schools do not exist. And, where they do exist, they are simply a thorn in their side. And it's sad because it is *the* differentiating factor."

219

Hutch was succeeded, but only for two years, by a woman who brought to Thayer a brilliant career in research but who struggled with the complex dynamics of leading a school.

Elsa Garmire became the school's first female dean in 1995, after having earned degrees at Harvard and M.I.T., teaching 20 years at U.C.L.A. and establishing herself as a leading innovator on laser technology. She had secured nine patents, published better than 200 papers and staged a one-woman laser art show on Sunset Boulevard in Hollywood, Wilhelm wrote in *Knowledge with Know-How*.[210]

Garmire arrived as a supporter of Thayer's inter-disciplinary approach to teaching engineering, and pushed hard from the beginning for changes she thought would improve its offerings — including centers of excellence and a costly expansion of the physical space. But would later acknowledge that she perhaps tried to move too quickly without first developing the support among the faculty and over-seers needed for bold change. "I couldn't get trac-tion," she later reflected. "I was not patient enough."

She did, however, get credit for playing a role in a successful fundraising campaign, making some first-rate hires and planting seeds for later growth. She also celebrated the first effort by a Dartmouth student team to design and drive a Formula race car in the annual student competition run by the Society of Automotive Engineers, a lab-to-road adventure that continues to this day. When Garmire left the deanship after two years, she didn't go far — be-coming a senior professor and continuing to earn her reputation as the "First Lady of Lasers."

At Dartmouth Medical School, a broadening sense of purpose

As Dartmouth Medical School approached its bicentennial in 1997, many students carried a strong sense of medicine's social mission, particularly when it came to serving patients in underserved urban and rural areas.

They got plenty of opportunity to build those skills through volunteering at the Good Neighbor Health Clinic in White River Junction, teaching health education in local schools and working with victims of domestic violence. Such efforts were coordinated by a community service committee that began in 1990 and, five years later, was given a national award for fostering the development of "socially responsible physicians," Putnam wrote in her history of the school.[211]

Also in the 1990s, students were given the opportunity to put down their stethoscopes and pick up books to gain insight into the humanity of their patients. "Literature and Medicine," a course designed by O'Donnell, aimed to "remind students there is more to people than their symptoms."

More than 130 years after rejecting the application of a woman who wanted to be the school's first female student, Dartmouth in 1985 announced that more than half of its incoming class was made up of women — the first time an American medical school not historically dedicated exclusively to educating women had done so. The school's early postgraduate programs — biochemistry, physiology-pharmacology, molecular biology (as long as it lasted) — were also doing their part, with each counting women as about one-third of their enrollment in 1979.

Female students found some role models on the faculty, although those women — particularly in the early years — had to deal with "the awkwardness, oddity, and sometimes downright discomfort of working in such an overwhelmingly male enclave," Putnam wrote. At a 1964 lunch where she and other faculty members who had been promoted to the status of full professor were to be honored, Dr. E. Lucile Smith recalled, "the other candidates (all male) assumed that I had come to serve the lunch and handed me their empty sherry glasses."

Progress had come, but slowly. Dr. Helen Pittman became the first woman on the Hitchcock Hospital staff in 1928, and later recalled with appreciation the encouragement she received after performing some appendectomies during her internship. But "it was to be another fifty years before the idea of a woman being a general surgeon was taken seriously enough at Dartmouth" for Drs. Martha McDaniel and Kathleen Kopach to win appointment "above the intern level on the general house staff."

While Dartmouth had never become the school for Indigenous peoples that Eleazar Wheelock had envisioned in the late 1700s, the medical school boasted in 1995 of having "produced in the last 20 years the highest number of Indigenous graduates of any public or private medical school in the East," Putnam wrote. Students of all backgrounds had the chance to learn from a 1979 Dartmouth College graduate, Dr. Lori Arviso Alvord, who became the nation's first Navajo woman surgeon and pledged herself to creating "a synthesis of the very best elements of all types of medicine."

Even as the school continually refined its classroom and laboratory offerings, faculty members did an increasing amount of research. Under Dr. Marsh Tenney, the physiology department was a "hotbed" of respiratory advances, including in preventing Sudden Infant Death Syndrome. Professor Frances McCann did "elegant electrophysiological studies" on the moth heart. And the Norris Cancer Center, established in 1972 and named after the senator who secured its funding, became the first comprehensive cancer research and treatment center established in an American rural area.

As their counterparts did at Dartmouth's engineering and business schools, medical school faculty members found ways to link research and commercial applications. One, described as the medical school's first effort of the kind, also led to controversy. Using advances they had made in the treatment of a form of leukemia, three Dartmouth researchers in 1987 formed a company called Medarex and took it public through a stock offering, winning praise for the school's "first effort in the world of corporate-academic partnerships."

But a shadow fell over the project in 1992 when the author of an anonymous letter alleged business and scientific wrongdoing. While investigations showed the charges to be baseless, Putnam wrote, the Dartmouth administration initially responded "in a ponderous, insensitive and legalistic way that seemed designed primarily to spare the institution from damage and left the bewildered targets of the accusations in limbo for some time."[212]

The best-known research endeavor of the late 20th century was the Dartmouth Atlas of Health Care, which in 1996 began giving health care consumers and providers the first nationwide guide to health care costs and outcomes. The Atlas — which continues to this day — was produced by Dr. Jack Wennberg and his colleagues at another Dartmouth creation, the Center for the Evaluative Clinical Sciences. In 1993, CECS began the nation's first graduate program in the evaluation of clinical health care costs and outcomes, offering master's and doctoral degrees.[213]

The medical school founded by Nathan Smith entered its third century in 1997, an event that prompted Putnam's book and her look back at the achievements and transformations along the way.

She noted that research activity had picked up considerable steam toward the end of the school's 200 years. In the 1988-89 funding year, sponsored research brought in a record high of $25 million; but that record fell just a year later when the outside grants and contracts totaled $34 million. She and others also celebrated the discoveries and innovations that had begun long before.

In 1820, for instance, Dr. Lyman Spalding authored the first U.S. pharmacopoeia, Putnam wrote. On Feb. 4, 1896, a team made up of an enterprising Hanover photographer, members of the Dartmouth physics department faculty and the medical school combined forces to take the nation's first clinical x-ray for diagnostic purposes — barely a week after the New York *Sun* broke the story of William Conrad Roentgen's discovery of x-rays.

Then there was Dr. William T. Mosenthal's work to open one of the nation's first intensive care units at Mary Hitchcock Hospital in 1955; Dr. Radford Tanzer's development of what became the standard technique for total ear reconstruction in 1957; Dr. Edward Ball in 1983 performing the nation's first autologous bone marrow transplant on a patient with acute myeloid leukemia; the first NIH study of the ethical use of genetic information — part of the human genome project — beginning in 1990 with Dartmouth doctors, biologists and ethicists; and toward the end of the first 200 years, the medical school and New Hampshire crafting a first-in-the nation program for providing mental health treatment for patients across the state.[214]

For their 1997 issue commemorating the school's first 200 years, the editors of *Dartmouth Medicine* asked Dr. Andrew Wallace — who took over as dean in 1990 — to take stock of the medical school's past, present and future.

Dartmouth tries to attract would-be physicians and researchers who have an aptitude for medicine and a commitment to using it for the public good, Wallace said, and who are "continuous learners, capable of adapting to change."

"When I went to medical school, for example, there was no medication to lower blood pressure, no open heart surgery, and no transplantation," he continued. Because polio was rampant at the time, this hospital had 30 iron lung machines when he began his clerkship in internal medicine. Clearly, much had changed since that era, and medical students need to be prepared for change, "which, in all likelihood, will come even faster in the next 40 years than in the last 40."

Echoing the comments of his predecessor, Dean McCollum, he said Dartmouth tended to attract students more interested in learning medicine in a small, community oriented teaching and clinical setting rather than in the "intense, trauma-oriented" world of big city schools. They find a school that emphasizes a collaborative approach to treatment. In the past, medicine "attracted people who were very self-confident and most comfortable working in an autonomous mode," he said. "Today we look at the practice of medicine as a team effort, at research as a team effort."

Wallace said the school was shifting its curriculum to reduce "the amount of sit-there-and-listen lecturing" and provide more opportunity for students to learn on their own and in small groups. Professors were also weaving more themes — such as ethics and genetics — into the fabric of ongoing courses rather than doing short, break-out courses.

As the earnings of physicians declined and the financial pressures on health care increased, Wallace said, "we are attracting a different kind of person than we were." The number of women had increased dramatically, older students were applying, and students who hadn't majored in the biological sciences were finding their way into medicine. "They are more liberally educated, more socially conscious. They are less driven by a desire for income … So I think the pendulum has swung back a bit in the direction that it should."[215]

Tuck looks toward its second century

The growth at the Tuck School of Business continued during the administration of Dean Colin Blaydon, who led the school from 1983 to 1990. With Edward Tuck and his largesse now a chapter in the school's early 20th century history, Dean Blaydon launched Tuck's first capital campaign in 1986, eventually exceeding the $15 million goal with help from a $3 million gift from the Byrne family, the largest in the school's history. The campaign led to construction of a new academic building, the first constructed in two decades, named Byrne Hall, according to Munter's school history.[216]

Tuck's reputation, meanwhile, continued to grow. In a 1988 *Business Week* survey, the school won the highest approval rating in the nation among alumni. By the end of the 1980s, applications for admission had reached an all-time high, including a rising number of international students — 20 percent of the Class of 1991, with students hailing from 20 foreign nations.

Entering the final decade of Tuck's first century, Edward Fox became the school's eighth dean in 1990. After building the Student Loan Marketing Association (Sallie Mae) into the 39th largest corporation in the nation, Fox arrived with ambitions to lead Tuck into what he described as "a new era in graduate business education — an era in which it's important that the Tuck School participate in the dialogues which will determine what graduate education will look like, that the school remain a leader rather than a follower, and that the school continue to be on the cutting edge."

227

As its centennial approached, Munter took a look back at numbers that gave a sense of the school's growth over the 20th century. Among them:

- Number of Tuck-specific faculty members in 1900: Zero. 1990: 36 full-time teacher-scholars.
- Students: 1900: 4; 1990: 330, representing more than 145 different colleges and 25 foreign countries.
- Selectivity: 1900: Not an issue, given that Tuck was the first graduate business school in the nation and drew its students exclusively from Dartmouth. 1990: Second-most selective in the nation, with 13 percent of more than 2,600 applicants being offered admission.
- Alumni: 1900: Zero. 1990: 6,000-plus. In 1989, Tuck boasted 63.2 percent alumni giving, the highest in the country and worth $1.2 million.
- Average starting salary for a graduate: 1901: $518. 1989: $54,600.
- Executive programs: 1974: First program, serving 44 businesspeople. 1989: 300 enrollees in five programs, including the Minority Business Executive Program.
- Annual total number of pages in Tuck Today, the alumni magazine: 1971 (founding year): 96 pages. 1990: 234 pages, including 108 of class notes.

Fox didn't last long, resigning in 1994 after serving just one term. A "malaise" had permeated the school, professor Bob Hansen would recall years later. "We didn't really have a clear strategy. Faculty weren't happy, students weren't happy … People were looking for someone to rally around."[217]

Enter Paul Danos, a business scholar who had

learned accounting as a teenager working in his father's oil-rig servicing business in New Orleans. He became dean of Tuck in 1995.

Danos's family had moved to Louisiana from a Canadian fishing village in the 1930s. As a teenager, he showed up after school to help in any way he could, working as a deckhand and cook on tugboats and, after learning the skill from his brother, keeping the books.

Danos enjoyed the work, but decided to pursue a different path. "I set my sights on being someone who got the knowledge and skills to understand and manage the companies that wield power in the economy," he told Tuck writer Kirk Kardashian.

After earning his bachelor's degree at the University of New Orleans, Danos got a full-time accounting job with a minerals company and went to business school at night. That (nearly) around-the-clock work ethic traveled with him through a PhD, a successful stint as a professor and senior dean at the University of Michigan, and, finally, to Tuck.

His ambitions for Tuck involved recruiting the best possible faculty, said Scott Neslin, a marketing professor and associate dean when Danos arrived. "He very much stressed the increasing need for the faculty to be cutting edge," said Neslin. "The Internet, advances in information processing, and several other factors were accelerating change in the practice of management. This meant the school needed to be on top of the latest research; faculty couldn't rely on their notes from five years ago."

Hiring top talent takes money, of course, and Danos says his early training in accounting helped him manage the books in an efficient way. "Most people don't get that," he said. "They understand the concepts but they don't really have it deep in their psyche like I do. It was a visceral part of what I did as a teenager."[218]

In 1997, applications to the school topped 3,000 for the first time. Tuck formed its Global Alliance with the HEC School of Management in France and Oxford University's Templeton College. And Danos extended Tuck's reach beyond the MBA students enrolled there full-time.

Begun in 1997, the Tuck Business Bridge Program provided an immersion course in business skills to recent graduates of undergraduate programs with an ambition to build careers in business. Two decades later, some 5,000 students had completed the program, with many crediting it with equipping them for success. "On Day 1, I pulled my car up to Tuck, knowing no one on campus and nothing about the material," said Claire O'Brien, who attended Bridge in 2016. "Four weeks later I was presenting a company valuation with a team of four in front of high-level professionals."

Some of the "Bridgers" found their way back to Tuck's MBA program. The Tuck class of 2018 counted 17 Bridge alumni in it ranks.[219]

President James Wright on university question
The sixteenth president in the Wheelock Succession was no stranger to Dartmouth or the nearly two-centuries-old debate about whether it was a college or a university. James Wright was a former mineworker, United States Marine and 30-year

history professor and leader at the college when trustees gave him the top job in April 1998.

The next day, he — like President Freedman before him — clearly signaled his position on the college v. university question. For Wright, there was no question at all.

"My vision of Dartmouth is of a research community that is committed to attracting and retaining the very best faculty and recruiting and engaging the very best students," Wright told the crowd assembled in Alumni Hall at the Hopkins Center. "A place marked by learning rather than teaching, learning in which students are full participants rather than passive observers."[220]

"Research in the academy is not a pastime that competes with teaching, but a critical activity that informs the best teaching," he continued. "The American research university is the most successful in the world, and we should never forget the importance of this to our national well-being."

"Dartmouth is a research university in all but name," he asserted, adding that this created "full opportunities for interdisciplinary work bridging not only arts and sciences departments, but also including the strong programs we have developed in the professional schools."

Wright did not speak of "associated schools," but instead made clear that the medical, engineering and business schools would participate as full partners in an era of innovation. "We have the potential here to develop new models of academic medicine and of health-care delivery, to strengthen engineering as a professional field while enriching its ties to the liberal arts, and to build upon Tuck's position as a residential business school committed to new models of business education and research," he said. "Dartmouth's venerable professional schools and her impressive graduate programs are fundamental to the special character of this College."

Wright was the furthest thing from a rarified ivory tower dweller. He had grown up in the struggling mining town of Galena, Illinois, played center on the football team and, because college didn't seem to be an option, joined the Marines at age 17. Neither of his grandfathers had finished eighth grade, and his father was a bartender who dropped out of college during the first semester, Wright said in that early speech, "because the Depression blunted his aspirations."

Wright had the opportunity to aim higher. Military service brought him to California, Hawaii and Japan. Returning home, he enrolled at the University of Wisconsin, Platteville, with an ambition to turn his love of history into a high school teaching job. He married and "worked like hell" as a janitor, bartender, cheese factory employee and deep-mine powderman to pay the $160-per-semester tuition, he told Dartmouth Alumni Magazine editor Jim Collins. Wright's professors saw his spark and, with their encouragement, he won a Danforth fellowship and earned his PhD in history at the University of Wisconsin.[221]

In Wright's inauguration speech, he returned to the college v. university question. "What was true in President Dickey's day is even more true today," he said. "If neither of the descriptive labels — college or university — fits us easily, that is eminently acceptable, because we are comfortable with what we are and what we aspire to be. Typically colleges are primarily concerned with undergraduate education and teaching. Universities are primarily engaged in graduate education and also place a greater emphasis on faculty research. We at Dartmouth are proud to call ourselves a college that has many of the best characteristics of a university. We are a university in terms of our activities and our programs, but one that remains a college in name and in its basic values and purposes. In this paradox, in this tension, lies our identity and our strength."[222]

At an institution that remained small but had big ambitions, he said, there exists an opportunity to break down barriers not only between disciplines but also between undergraduate and graduate study. "Interdisciplinary work is strong here because of our size and we will make it stronger," Wright said. "We need to build upon our core distinction in the Arts and Sciences. The professional schools can serve as a greater resource to the College even as the College can be a greater resource for them."

In an interview a decade after he ended his tenure, Wright said he took office knowing that his predecessor had stirred considerable debate about whether the increasing emphasis on research and graduate study was compromising Dartmouth's traditional commitment to undergraduate education and the liberal arts. "I wanted to be clear right up front," he said. "Dartmouth has been a university in all but name for many years."[223]

As the 21st century began, Dartmouth's steadily

increasing emphasis on graduate programs became central to a war waged by dissident alumni. In 2007, leaders of an alumni-run Committee to Save Dartmouth College said they planned to invest $300,000 in a national advertising campaign to stir opposition to college plans it said were aimed at diluting the strength of alumni voices on the Board of Trustees.

"The energy of the place, the resources, the focus, was always on undergraduate education," Stephen Smith, a 1988 graduate and University of Virginia law professor who had won a seat on the board, told *Valley News* reporter Peter Jamison. "I think that made Dartmouth distinctive. I think it gave it a niche in the field of higher education. A lot of alumni, judging from the recent [trustee] election results, fear that distinctiveness is being lost."[224]

Wright and other college leaders, along with no small number of alumni, saw such complaints as presenting a false dichotomy. "I don't think we should try to polarize these things," Wright said in the 2018 interview. "It's possible to do both of these things well, and I think we're doing it."

Chapter Thirteen
Entering a New Century

As Tuck prepared to celebrate its 100th birthday, students began participating in a new program that put their founder's credo — "Altruism is the highest and best form of egoism" — into action. The community surrounding Dartmouth extends from the tony neighborhoods of Hanover to places like White River Junction, where many live paycheck to paycheck and struggle for basics like healthy food and affordable health care.

Beginning in 1999, an annual community outreach day has sent first-year students to a variety of nonprofits hungry for management advice. How can a group that provides legal services to vulnerable immigrants build public understanding and support? How can the Children's Hospital at Dartmouth-Hitchcock raise money to serve patients and their families?

"Partnering with Tuck allows us to tap into a community of extremely professional, talented and driven individuals who are not typically from this region. We gained a lot of insight from that diversity," CHaD marketing manager Benjamin Hall said.

"It confirmed for me that my business skills translate directly into social impact," said Eric Giles T'16. "It helped reaffirm that if we're going to solve the pressing issues of our generation, business skills have to come into play."[225]

At the school's centennial and the dawn of the 21st century, Danos reflected on where Tuck had been and where it needed to go. He noted the "paradoxical quality of our school's distinguishing characteristics:" While it was America's first graduate business school, it remained the smallest of the top ten. While enjoying an international reputation and sending graduates into top leadership roles in urban centers, it operates in a place that remains a rural idyll. While the emphasis remains on high-quality teaching, the faculty "conduct groundbreaking research and publish widely and frequently."[226]

Even as Tuck aimed to remain a place where students would enjoy plenty of one-on-one interaction with professors and peers, Danos told alumni that the school would expand the size of its entering MBA class from 185 to a maximum of 240 in coming years. To ensure the intimate quality of the program, the faculty would also expand from 40 to 50.

Danos said growth was needed in an era of "fierce competition" among schools for tomorrow's business leaders. But, he stressed, it needed to be thoughtful. In speaking with his counterparts at other American schools, he said, a recurring theme is "the temptation to maximize growth at the expense of focus." While Tuck would continue to offer other short-term programs for visiting executives and students, its core would remain the two-year residential MBA.

Students would learn from professors doing cutting edge research, a goal advanced by the newly established "centers of excellence" devoted to the study of corporate governance, private equity and emerging economies.

"The initiatives we have undertaken to effect managed growth, sustain competitive advantage, and support our faculty help to ensure that Tuck will continue to produce many of the nation's most successful managers and to provide them with an educational experience that earns their lifelong loyalty," Danos concluded.

In 2000, Tuck overhauled its MBA curriculum for the first time in a half century. While retaining many of the foundational elements of the old plan, the new approach aimed to give incoming students increased exposure to alumni experts and new skills in weaving technology into their business plans.

Recognizing that students increasingly came to Tuck with more work experience than previous generations, the new curriculum gave first-year students a wider range of electives from which to choose. And it gave each a chance to develop skills by working with professors, other students and alumni on a year-long project with real-world potential.

"Many of these projects will become real businesses," said Danos. "Until now, we have drawn a line that says, 'While you're in school you study; then you do real things later. Well, that line is going to be blurred."[227]

An important component of the new approach invited alumni not only to share their business expertise, but also to tap into the creativity of current Tuck students to help grow their enterprises. "So there will be an excellent route for an alumnus who says, 'I've got a business development issue,'" said Associate Dean Bob Hansen.

Also new was a core course in technology systems, whose goal was to prepare students to lead technological innovation efforts, including e-commerce, biotech and pharmaceuticals. Presaging the revolution that would reshape the economy in the decades to follow, Danos said, "It is just a fact of life that most high-profile startups today have some technological background."

In 2001, Tuck came out on top in a Wall Street Journal survey of international business schools. The study focused on the views of corporate recruiters, who put Tuck ahead of such powerhouses as Harvard, Stanford and Wharton. "Recruiters who rated the schools in an online survey praised Dartmouth's small, collegial MBA program for producing general managers who make loyal team players," *Journal* staff writer Ron Alsop.[228]

To be sure, the article said, other schools offer top-shelf educations. But recruiters said graduates of some of the prestigious schools "expect too much in terms of salary and position and are difficult to retain for long."

With its small class sizes and intimate atmosphere, Tuck tends to produce graduates who want to work as part of a team. "You have to get along at a small business school like Tuck; there's no place to hide," said Bill Sones, a Boston software consultant quoted in the *Journal* article. At Dartmouth and Yale, his alma mater, he said that students "aren't out for No. 1 as much."

Tuck's founding fathers wanted the school to educate business leaders not just to climb the economic ladder but also to recognize the impact business decisions have on society. In 2001, the school deepened that focus through what would become known as the Allwin Initiative for Corporate Citizenship.

The initiative began when adjunct professor John Vogel and 1995 Tuck graduate Jeffrey Halpern began talking about ways to more fully engage students in bringing business skills to not-for-profit organizations. "Students in the '90s were volunteering at Tuck," said the professor, John Vogel. "But it was like they were volunteering in spite of being at Tuck, rather than because they were here."[229]

Connecting students with non-profits became a key component of the initiative, which in 2002 received a major financial and moral boost from Tuck overseer and alumnus Jim Allwin. In its first decade, Tuck students launched such initiatives as TuckBuilds, a weeklong program in which students work with local organizations on Habitat for Humanity-style projects.

The Initiative also worked to build a stronger academic component to help students grapple with such issues as Starbucks coming under fire for exporting bottled water. Said Associate Dean Bob Hansen, "We want to study corporate responsibility, but it should be an investigative, learning-oriented approach."

To help students carry their skills into the non-profit and public sector organizations after graduation, Tuck in 2002 created the Nonprofit Fellows Program. Successful applicants could win a salary supplement of up to $20,000 per year to help them afford working at organizations that couldn't pay high wages.

"This new fellowship is part of a comprehensive program at Tuck designed to broaden the education of our MBA students and to provide the resources for them to learn about and participate in the nonprofit and public sectors," Danos said in a May 2002 announcement. "It will provide high caliber management and analytic support to organizations that could not otherwise attract such talent."

In 2007, Tuck announced that two-thirds of the school's alumni had given a financial contribution to their alma mater, far above any of its peer institutions. According to *BusinessWeek*, no other schools broke the 50 percent mark in alumni giving, and most had less than 20 percent participation.

"This extraordinary support is a testament to the real value that our alumni continue to see in their Tuck education, throughout their entire lives," said Danos.

Medical students learn by doing good

On the eve of the 21st century, Dartmouth responded to the nearly complete project to map the human genome by creating a new Department of Genetics at the medical school in 1999. While genetics had long been an area of research in Hanover, the new department — headed by internationally known geneticist Jay Dunlap — represented an attempt to advance knowledge by deepening collaboration.

"Dartmouth has a tradition of strength in genetics, scattered across many parts of the Medical School and the Faculty of Arts and Sciences, but this new department has created a formal, unified scholarly community around this burgeoning field," medical school Dean John C. Baldwin wrote in a column published in 2000.[230]

This community includes not only medical school and college researchers, but also ethicists and the business and engineering schools, Baldwin wrote. "We all recognize that this is a field so transcendent in its importance, so compelling in terms of its many ramifications throughout society, that all these aspects of the university community will have vital roles to play."

The school's global focus also found another, deeply humanitarian, expression in efforts to help rebuild Kosovo's only medical school after a protracted period of ethnic cleansing, bombing and exclusion. For a decade, Albanians had been barred from Kosovo's educational programs and hospital staffs. After peace was brokered, Dartmouth medical educators traveled to Kosovo to see how they could help refound the University of Pristina's medical school.

It was a big job at a school with little electricity and no books for students. But the Dartmouth representatives helped both by offering guidance in Kosovo, and by bringing the school's dean and a group of medical students to Hanover to learn.

Former Dartmouth Medical School Dean James Strickler led the entourage, reporting upon his return that medical education in Kosovo was still operating on a Soviet model. "Teaching was almost exclusively in the hospital, and the relationship between students and faculty was far different than it is in the United States," Strickler said. Even in 2000, "there's not the freewheeling exchange we have here."

"DMS is trying to steer a careful course," he continued. "We have said repeatedly, 'We are here to show you what we do — you have to decide what's best for Kosovo.' "[231]

Some parts of the medical school curriculum come not from administrators or faculty members, but from students. When Gary Maslow was a first-year, he felt an educational void: while he was learning plenty about the scientific aspects of being a doctor, he wanted to know more about how illness and treatment play out in the lives of patients.

"We don't spend enough time learning about how illness can develop over time, and how things change, and how chaotic or wonderful this can be," he told Dartmouth Medicine writer Katrina Mitchell. "That is something that was missing in my medical education: watching people change and develop."[232]

Maslow in 2002 led the way to launching the school's Patient Partnership program. By pairing medical students with patients undergoing treatment for a variety of illnesses, the program helped students learn about the human beings on the other end of the stethoscope.

Kathy Boisvert was one of those patients. A French teacher struggling with breast cancer, Boisvert was paired with medical student Rebecca Cogswell. Cogswell's role was not to diagnose and treat, but instead to accompany Boisvert on her journey through treatment, hope and struggle.

"Rebecca came into my life as a medical student but now has become a friend who happens to be in medical school," Boisvert told the magazine.

In 2002, cinema verite filmmaker Richard Kahn introduced a documentary film, *In Our Midst*, that showed in poignant detail a year in the life of a family whose four children had all spent the first months of their lives in DHMC's neonatal intensive care unit.

Neonatologist and medical school professor Dr. George Little founded the unit in the early 1970s and, by the time the film came out, had overseen the treatment of 12,000 babies struggling to survive. But he said the film — which he and Dartmouth ethicist Ronald M. Green helped to produce — opened his eyes to the challenges faced by parents such as Karen, the mother portrayed in the documentary.

The film aimed "to make those of us who work in the NICU — doctors and nurses and all the health-care providers — take a moment and think

243

about what happens afterwards," he told *Dartmouth Medicine* writer Laura Stephenson Carter. "It made me think very seriously about whether I could do what Karen does."[233]

In Our Midst was a follow-up to an earlier documentary Kahn filmed in the Dartmouth NICU in the 1990s, *Dreams and Dilemmas*, in which two premature twin brothers struggled to live as health care providers and their parents made difficult decisions at every step. For the new film, producers wanted to answer the question many viewers had: what happens after the babies who survive leave the hospital?

The answer can be a challenge that lasts for years, if not a lifetime. Three of Karen's four children (the film only identifies the family by their first names) deal with health issues remaining from their premature births: Andrew has learning and emotional problems; Allison suffers from cerebral palsy and frequent seizures; Aiden is legally blind, hearing-impaired and is fed largely through a stomach tube.

In scenes captured over the course of a year, Karen is shown as a fierce advocate for her children and an ever-patient, loving mother who prepares special foods, administers tube feedings, makes regular trips to the doctor, and still finds time to play games and bake brownies with them. Her husband is shown working long hours to support his family, then pitching in as best he can when he gets home. There's plenty of work, and plenty of joy, in the home.

"As doctors and nurses, we are taught to be

scientific. We're taught to look at things objective-
ly," Little told Carter. "Part of the process of being
a healthcare provider and taking care of babies and
families is to truly be able to empathize and understand what is going on in that family."

The first years of the new century brought a rapid succession of deans, as medical professors took
turns at the helm. Dr. Ethan Dmitrovsky, chair of
pharmacology and toxicology, served as acting dean
from 2002-03, succeeding Baldwin. In July 2003,
the school reached outside of Hanover for its new
leader, pediatrician and pharmacologist Stephen
Spielberg.

Dr. Spielberg had since 1997 served as vice
president for pediatric drug development at Johnson
& Johnson, where he was a leader in developing
new medicines for children and in assuring high
ethical standards in clinical investigations.

Having worked both as a clinician and an industry executive, Spielberg said he came to Dartmouth
with a keen sense of the role a medical school can
play in addressing a "dearth of well-trained clinical
investigators and translational scientists." He said
Dartmouth featured the "kinds of people who have
a vision of what medical school, medical education,
research and health care should be."[234]

In 2004, the medical school brought a new
method of quantification to the question of how
professor-clinicians strike the balance between
treating patients and educating the next generation
of doctors.

"Every physician is expected to contribute some

portion of their effort to" teaching, said Dr. Blair Brooks, associate professor of medicine. "But there has been no accounting for that time."[235]

Brooks teamed up with Jennifer Friend, business manager in the Department of Medicine, to devise a system for professors to track how many hours they spend in educational activities, ranging from leading a small-group discussion of medical students to mentoring students in the lab or residents making hospital rounds.

"The metrics for clinical research are crowding out other things," Brook observed. "This is a way to help individuals get credit for the teaching that is getting done."

Year after year, Dartmouth researchers make discoveries and reach conclusions that reverberate far beyond the medical school campus. Professors Brenda Sirovich and H. Gilbert Welch analyzed data and concluded that nearly half of the 21 million American women who had undergone hysterectomies went on to get unnecessary Pap testing.

The problem, the researchers concluded, is that doctors and insurance companies kept pushing for Pap tests even though many of their patients had undergone hysterectomies for reasons other than cancer — meaning they were at little risk of testing positive for the disease. The result: needless cost and, for patients, anxiety.

After publishing their findings in 2004 in the *Journal of the American Medical Association*, the researchers were flooded with interview requests from media outlets, *Dartmouth Medicine* reported. "We can be a little optimistic," Sirovich said, "that the publicity will make a difference."[236]

In 2005, researchers from the medical school and Norris Cotton Cancer Center also drew wide attention with a study showing that children who see characters smoking in movies are more likely to light up themselves. Citing the Dartmouth research, attorneys general in 32 states put movie studios on notice that they should provide anti-smoking public service announcements on copies of movies that show smoking.

"Part of the reason that exposure to smoking in the movies has such a considerable impact on adolescent smoking is because it is a very strong social influence on kids ages 10 to 14," said pediatrics professor and study author Dr. James Sargent. "Its impact on this age group outweighs whether peers or parents smoke or whether the child is involved in other activities, like sports."[237]

The study involved interviews with 6,500 children in that age group, finding that those with most exposure to smoking in films were 2.6 times more likely to take up the habit than those with the least exposure.

In 2006, *Dartmouth Medicine* featured the work of Dartmouth medical faculty and students in addressing the high rates of HIV and AIDS in Tanzania through the DarDar Clinic in Dar es Salaam.

The clinic — whose name is drawn from the first syllables of the school and the eastern Tanzanian city — began as a single clinical trial to test an experimental vaccine for tuberculosis, a common result of contracting HIV.

But from there, the project grew to include a

primary care clinic for patients enrolled in the trial, a pediatric clinic for their children and an exchange program that allowed professors from Tanzania to earn degrees at Dartmouth, and Dartmouth professors and students to work in Dar es Salaam.

Cara A. Mathews spent six weeks working in Tanzania while a Dartmouth medical student. Despite the challenges of living in a country where one can't take for granted the basics of transportation, nutrition and health care, she returned with an ambition to start a clinic in an underserved nation and train local people to run it.

"Upon my return to DMS, I began drafting classmates to volunteer in my still-hypothetical clinic," she recalled. "A future orthopaedic surgeon, two pediatricians, a plastic surgeon, two internists, and one emergency room physician have already signed up."[238]

Harkening back to Nathan Smith's call to provide medical care for people living around Dartmouth, medical students in 2003 began running a free clinic for uninsured residents of working class towns along the Mascoma River in New Hampshire. In 2007, the Mascoma Free Clinic was given the college's Martin Luther King, Jr. Social Justice Award for student organizations.

Better than half of all second-year students volunteered at the clinic, with a number of students from other classes joining in. The work not only helps patients who couldn't otherwise afford care but provides an early opportunity for students to put their classroom learning to work.

"Students do not have the same time constraints

as do full-fledged doctors, enabling them to have longer interactions with patients," said student Matthew Laquer. The experience also gives students a sense of the harsh reality of managing chronic conditions such as diabetes, high blood pressure and elevated cholesterol, Danielle Thomas wrote in *Dartmouth Medicine*.

"One pill can be so expensive that it wipes out an entire month's income," said Theodore Yuo, who has also helped raise cash to support the clinic. He added that students learn "there are other ways of treating these illnesses than the most expensive."[239]

At Thayer, putting know-how to work in the world

Lewis Duncan, a soft-spoken radiophysicist, became dean in 1998 and led Thayer into the 21st century in a six-year tenure that saw the school grow at a dramatic clip. Like Hutch (who had returned as interim dean for a year after Garmire shifted to a faculty post), Duncan grew up in rural West Virginia and brought a practical orientation to the job.

Educated at Rice University in Texas, Duncan had taught physics and astronomy at Clemson and worked for a time at the Los Alamos National Laboratory. He was chosen along with Sally Ride, the first American woman in space, as a mid-career Carnegie Science fellow at Stanford.

Arriving in Hanover at a time when the Internet and globalization were transforming the technological, economic and political landscape, Duncan was determined to keep Thayer on the cutting edge of emerging technologies, Wilhelm wrote in a chapter about the dean in *Knowledge with Know-How*.[240]

During his time, sponsored research tripled from $6.3 million in 1998 to $18.5 million in 2004. The school that operated in its early decades with a handful of faculty members brought in 60 research scientists, and its total operating budget ballooned from $14 million to $32 million.

Duncan was able to coalesce support for the "centers of excellence" idea initiated by Garmire. The idea of bringing together independent but related research efforts into such centers was at first a tough sell, but Duncan moved the project forward by securing large federal earmarks — a.k.a. "pork" — with help from U.S. Sen. Judd Gregg of New Hampshire. "The metaphor that we used in our strategic planning was that the tenure-track faculty were basically 27 individual points of light, many of them stars in their own discipline," Duncan told Wilhelm. "We talked about trying to build constellations."

One important example of such a constellation was the Institute for Security Technology Studies, which began in 2000 as a collaborative effort involving Thayer, Dartmouth Medical School and Dartmouth's computer science department. Fueled by a federal grant, the center worked on solutions to cybersecurity risks and — particularly in the wake of the 9/11 terror attacks. Another collaborative effort that began at Thayer but reached across campus was the Alternative Breast Cancer Imaging Modalities project, begun with a $6.5 million federal grant.

"This was something that I felt the need to accomplish," Duncan said of such teamwork. "I spent a lot of time building bridges to the other professional schools, and especially to the arts and sciences."

Duncan also worked to raise money for the school's expansion, particularly for what came to be known as the MacLean Engineering Sciences Center. Seeded by a $15 million commitment from 1961 Thayer graduate and longtime overseer Barry MacLean, the center was designed to not only provide expanded space for Thayer professors and students but also to allow visitors walking through a clear view of the working laboratories of tomorrow's engineers.

For all the looking forward, Duncan also had a clear sense of what came before: the commitment to a smart blend of the liberal arts and the advanced engineering sciences. "Dartmouth's breadth of liberal education is the best deal going right now," Duncan said shortly after taking over as dean. And the benefits of engineering education didn't just apply to those who major in it, he continued. "A graduate of college today who doesn't have some sense of the role of technology in society is poorly educated, and poorly prepared to contribute to the next century."

With that in mind, Thayer professors worked to craft courses that would appeal to the broad range of Dartmouth students, making them the most popular technology courses on campus. "We started teaching these courses before they became a requirement," Professor Horst Richter would later say. "Nowadays, we use so much technology — the cell phone, the computer; we cannot even repair our own cars any more, so much technology is in them

… and it behooves students very well to understand something about it."

Duncan created and taught a course, "Engineering and the Future of Society," for Dartmouth freshmen. In 2000, Wilhelm wrote, he was invited to give a welcome lecture for those "pea green" newcomers. His message got their attention, particularly this line: "It is completely conceivable that ours is among the last of generations ever to experience natural biological aging and death." One student's wry reaction: "Oh great — the first thing I hear when I get to Dartmouth is that I'll be coming back to my 50th reunion as a computer!"

Duncan enlisted the support of successful entrepreneurs to inspire, guide and provide seed money for Thayer projects. Some of those projects provided the lessons of success, including GlycoFi, a biological engineering firms. Others provided the lessons of failure — or, perhaps more accurately, could-have-beens — including an early version of a portable MP3 player created by two M.E.M. students that was eclipsed by Apple's new iPod.

Some innovations came with a distinct element of altruism. Students embraced opportunities to design clean water and sustainable housing projects, and in 2003 formed a Dartmouth chapter of Engineers Without Borders. "Many Thayer School students have the desire to use their engineering skills to make a concrete difference," said Tico Blumenthal, who graduated from Thayer in 2005 and was one of the group's founders.

Duncan wrapped up his tenure as dean in 2005, and trustees appointed as his successor Joseph J.

Helble, who had worked as an environmental consultant and headed the chemical engineering department at the University of Connecticut. Duncan said Helble would face his challenges, including some familiar ones: the need to raise money, to define future priorities, and to grapple with a question nearly as old as Dartmouth itself: "I think Dartmouth is in the middle of an identity crisis," Duncan said, "trying to decide whether or not it really is a research university."[241]

Helble was a chemical engineer who earned his undergraduate degree at Lehigh University and his doctorate at MIT. When Thayer came calling in 2005, he was on sabbatical from his UConn post and advising then-U.S. Sen. Joseph Lieberman on environmental policy issues. A decade earlier, he had used his expertise in thermodynamics and air pollution while working as a fellow at the Environmental Protection Agency.

Helble's experience in the capital reflected and shaped his conviction that engineers have an important perspective to add on public policy choices — and taught him how to handle political complexities, according to a narrative of his deanship produced by the school.[242] "He saw people succeed and not succeed, and he saw how politicians communicate and who does it well," said his wife, Becky Dabora, a biochemical engineer.

When he arrived in Hanover, Helble did a lot of listening. "He had a very fresh perspective and a determination to get things done," said Terry McGuire, a 1982 graduate and chair of the school's board of advisors. "But he's also sensitive, so when he walked in, he didn't just command: 'This is what we're going to do.'"

Instead, he took a collaborative approach, said professor Laura Ray. "He would walk around and talk to faculty members individually," she said. "Then he'd take all that information he got from individuals, and he'd assimilate it and he'd formulate a plan." Veteran professor Eric Hansen added, "Joe created an open, collegial climate within the school."

One of Helble's first accomplishments as dean was to resolve an issue that had been hovering without resolution for more than a decade — how to organize the faculty according to thematic areas of focus. Seeing that Thayer engineers were already heavily engaged with Dartmouth Medical School researchers in medical imaging and other health care advances, he proposed engineering medicine as one key focal point. Faculty members embraced the idea and then worked with Helble to come up with two more areas of emphasis: energy and complex systems.

Eric Fossom, an accomplished inventor who joined the Thayer faculty in 2010, praised Helble's leadership. "It's exactly like a small entrepreneurial startup," he said. "We're small, and Joe figured out that you have to be focused."

Faculty members credit Helble with working hard to promote promising junior faculty members. "It's much harder to do it this way, because it takes much longer than if you hire some superstar away from another university," said professor Tillman

Gerngross. But it paid dividends as once-junior faculty members patented inventions, built their teaching skills and returned the investment to students and the school. Professor John Zhang said Helble wants to "get someone here to stay for a long time and to be the best possible version of him or herself, and then carry the vision forward for the school."

Thayer is small compared to other top American engineering schools, and Helble saw that as a plus. Drawing on his political acumen, he also realized that the surging popularity of engineering among incoming students could feel like a threat to some members of Dartmouth's core arts and sciences faculty. "He knew he would have to use every bit of diplomacy he has to show the rest of Dartmouth that engineering wasn't a threat; it was an opportunity," said Thayer board member Chris McConnell '75. Helble's message was that "innovation happens at the intersection of disciplines."

The Thayer dean worked across those disciplines to establish a biomedical sciences major and human-centered design minor, along with modified majors in earth sciences, neuroscience and public policy.

According to the school narrative, Helble worked hard to recruit more women to the Board of Advisors, created a Dean's Council to involve young alumni in charting the school's course and made a point — through Coffee with the Dean events and informal one-on-one chats — to engage students in conversations about their projects, their pursuit of funding and their ideas for education.

At Thayer, students learn not only from their

dean and professors, but also from engineers who built careers beyond Hanover. In 2004, Thayer formed the Corporate Collaboration Council to give students in the Masters in Engineering Management (MEM) program an industry perspective on ways to combine engineering and entrepreneurship. Alumni and other industry leaders serve as mentors, help students secure internships and aid school leaders in constantly refining the program to meet a rapidly shifting technological landscape.

"We find the MEM graduates have the ideal mix of engineering and business capabilities and additional work experience from their internship," John Fletcher, chair of the council and CEO of the strategy consulting firm Fletcher Spaght, told *Dartmouth Engineer*.[243]

Each member of the council agrees to mentor three students and help them find their first job after graduation. "I've really enjoyed the opportunity to be a mentor to current students and then keep in touch with them over the years," said council member and 2008 Thayer graduate Dana Haffner Guernsey, a top official at an energy storage startup company, Ambri.

At Dartmouth, sometimes big discoveries come in small packages. That was certainly the case for a team led by computer science professor Bruce Donald, who worked with Thayer faculty and students to build the world's smallest untethered, controllable robot in 2005.

How small? "About as wide as a strand of human hair and half the length of the period at the end of this sentence," Dartmouth writer Susan

Knapp reported in September 2005. "About 200 of these could march in a line across the top of a plain M&M."[244]

The research was funded in part by the federal Department of Homeland Security, with future applications for the microrobots that include ensuring information security, exploring hazardous environments such as the site of a chemical explosion, and manipulating cells or tissues in biotechnology.

Donald explained that the new devices were "thousands of times smaller in mass" than previous controllable microrobots. Rather than moving on wheels, it "crawls like a silken inchworm, making tens of thousands of 10-nanometer steps every second. It turns by putting a silicon 'foot' out and pivoting like a motorcyclist skidding around a tight turn."

As the 2006-07 academic year began, Thayer faculty and students got a spacious new building in which to teach, learn and innovate. The 64,000-square feet MacLean Engineering Sciences Center was designed not only to dramatically increase the size of the school's facilities but also to pay architectural tribute to Thayer's approach.

"MacLean's distinctive design — mixing traditional with contemporary features — mirrors our approach to engineering education, in which we blend time-tested principles of engineering with innovation and emerging technologies," Helble said at the building's dedication.[245]

The structure — named for lead donors Barry MacLean '60 Th'61 and his wife Mary Ann — features a blend of traditional brick and modern glass on the outside. Inside, the most striking feature is the atrium, in which clear panels reveal laboratories where students and their professors are hard at the work of creating.

"To a Dartmouth engineer, technology is the outcome of an intensive process of research, need assessment, brainstorming, conception, feasibility evaluation, modeling, resource procurement, design, experimentation, analysis, prototype development, iteration, iteration, iteration and then voila — technology," said professor William Lotko, who chaired the building committee. He said architects Fred Koetter and Susie Kim had succeeded in capturing that "messy" process. That was true "especially in the atrium, where it appears that MacLean indeed has been sheared open to reveal the inner workings of engineering."

As the new century began, former Dean Hutchinson had teamed up with Gerngross to form a company, GlycoFi, to capitalize on a breakthrough method of making genetically engineered yeast cells produce human-like proteins. The invention held great promise for the pharmaceutical industry, in which half of all drugs in development depend on such proteins.

That promise paid off in a big way in 2006, when drug giant Merck paid $400 million cash to purchase GlycoFi. "Our acquisition of GlycoFi's scientific expertise, patent estate, and robust technology platform is a significant step toward enabling Merck to discover, optimize, and develop novel biologic drugs to serve the needs of patients worldwide," said Peter S. Kim, president of Merck

Research Laboratories.

Before GlycoFi's innovation, most of the proteins used to make medicine were produced by mammalian cells, *Dartmouth Engineer* reported. But those cells are prone to contamination and expensive to culture, making the yeast cell alternative that much more appealing. The deal was one of the biggest in biotech history, and a milestone in Thayer's history of innovation.[246]

Rock musicians may aspire to be on the cover of *Rolling Stone* magazine, but for an engineering student, it doesn't get much better than making *Popular Mechanics*. In 2006, four students did just that when their invention — which they dubbed the GyroBike — landed one of the magazine's Breakthrough Awards.

"One of my favorite inventions this year is the Gyrobike, created by a group of Dartmouth students," wrote contributing editor Jim Meigs. "It's an elegant, simple solution to the eternal problem of learning to ride a bike."

Students Hannah Murnen, Augusta Niles, Nathan Sigworth and Deborah Sperling invented the bike during their ES 21 class in 2004 and then combined forces to bring it to the marketplace.

"People have been perfecting bikes for over 100 years, and there's been a knowledge of gyroscopes for much longer, but these students were the first to combine them in a device like this," Mcigs wrote. "And they did the work in an introductory engineering class, which shows you don't have to be an expert with an advanced degree to do something important — you just need creativity and resourcefulness."[247]

Since 1995, Thayer students have been designing and racing cars in the Formula SAE program sponsored by the Society of Automotive Engineers. The Dartmouth teams regularly placed in the top 20, generally competing against teams from larger institutions.

But in 2007, Thayer students turned frustration into creativity by creating a competition of their own — the Formula Hybrid competition held at New Hampshire International Speedway in Loudon. The idea was hatched in 2003, when Thayer teams had hoped to enter a hybrid in the Formula SAE competition but a rule change forbade it. So they decided to create their own competition.

Douglas Fraser, Thayer research engineer and Formula Hybrid director, said the competition could lead to innovations in the field. "Students don't go in with preconceived notions," Fraser said. "They sometimes launch off in directions that you wouldn't think would work, but they do."[248]

The hybrid entries differed from the standard Formula SAE vehicles in some key ways, including the use of recycled race car materials and gas consumption at least 15 percent lower than the standard entry. The Dartmouth vehicle used a "series hybrid" system, in which energy from the gas engine is stored in 88 bright blue ultracapacitors, which in turn send energy to the drivetrain.

The project blended mechanical and electrical engineering, allowing students to literally get their hands on unfamiliar technology. "I never would have learned as much about electrical engineering had I not been involved in this project," said Dana Haffner '06, who was pursuing a master's in engineering management. "I've taken classes in electrical engineering, but this is hands-on. There's no comparison."

While Thayer had always emphasized putting engineering discoveries to work in the world, faculty members credit Helble for placing an even greater accent on entrepreneurship. Gerngross, who started five biotech companies, said he might have left Thayer after his commercial success had Helble not been so encouraging. Board member and 1984 graduate Christine Bucklin said that, in turn, helps to attract students. "I believe that if you were to scrape down to some of the things that attract students to the field of engineering, they include being able to create and commercialize technologies."[249]

That encouragement takes many forms. In 2008, Helble led Thayer to create the nation's first PhD program in innovation. The program offers a select group of engineering PhD candidates entrepreneurial training they can use to turn complex research discoveries into applied technologies that hold both commercial and social promise.

The program featured two new innovation courses taught by former Dean Hutchinson, co-founder of GlycoFi, and John Collier, Myron Tribus Professor in Innovation. In addition to their coursework, the students complete an internship at an entrepreneurial enterprise.

The first class of four candidates illustrated the program's accent on using technology to create social good. Ashifi Gogo, for instance, co-founded a

Ghana-based company, mPedigree, that authenticates medicines in developing world countries plagued by counterfeit pharmaceuticals.

In addition to equipping future engineer/ entrepreneurs to put their inventions to work in the world, Helble said, "We expect to train a new generation of professors."[250]

In 2009, one group of Thayer students won a national award for devising a simple but effective arsenic removal method for use in rural Nepal as part of their capstone project. The students created a system that allowed vil-lagers to use locally available materials — three buckets, two steel plates, sand, and a 6-volt battery — to remove dangerous amounts of arsenic from drinking water.

Lindsay Holiday, Dana Leland and Philip Wagner invented the system to address a major public health prob-lem. Their system uses electrocoagulation — the process used in large water treatment facilities — with materials readily available in rural areas. Contaminated water goes into one bucket and an electrical current travels through submerged steel plates to release iron precipitates, which bind to the arsenic. The water is then poured into a second bucket, which filters the water through sand that removes the iron-arsenic particles. Clean water then pours into a third bucket.

The invention — which took water registering arsenic levels at 20 times the safe level to almost nothing — won the students an award in the 2009 Collegiate In-ventors Competition sponsored by the National Inventors Hall of Fame, along with Thayer's Special Faculty Award for Engineering and Service to Humanity. Said Leland, "I hope that our work can help bring clean drinking water to people in need."[251]

Chapter Fourteen
Dartmouth Gets its First Physician President

While all of Dartmouth's presidents had grappled to varying degrees with the question of whether the school should remain a "small college" or a university, that issue did not vex Wright's replacement, Jim Yong Kim, a global health pioneer and Dartmouth's first physician president.

As Dr. Kim prepared to take office in July 2009, he told an audience of faculty, staff and students that Dartmouth has "the perfect constellation of professional schools … in addition to a fantastic undergraduate college," Jennifer Durgin wrote in *Dartmouth Medicine*.[252]

Kim arrived in Hanover with an international reputation as a health care reformer. While at Harvard Medical School, he and classmate Paul Farmer hatched a plan to address global health problems.

The organization they founded, Partners in Health, began by fighting tuberculosis in a remote region of Haiti and went on to become a major player in the public health world.

Kim was also known for his "3 by 5" campaign at the World Health Organization, which aimed to provide life-prolonging retroviral drugs to three million HIV/AIDS patients in low- and middle-income countries by 2005. He received a MacArthur genius grant in 2003 and was named one of Time's 100 Most Influential People in the World in 2006.

Kim came to Dartmouth from Harvard, where he had served as chair of the Department of Global Health and Medicine. Seeing potential in weaving together the work of the undergraduate college and the graduate programs in medicine, engineering, business and the sciences, he combined those resources to create the Dartmouth Center for Health Care Delivery Science.[253]

Health care systems are among "the most complex, scientific delivery systems that exist on the face of the Earth," Kim was quoted as saying in a 2010 *Dartmouth Medicine* article about the center. With help from an anonymous $35 million gift, the center was designed to bring experts from Dartmouth's professional and graduate schools together with health industry leaders to identify ways to improve health outcomes while dialing back the costs.

At Dartmouth, the disciplines would be integrated through new courses at the undergraduate and graduate level, including a new master's degree in health care delivery science. Kim envisioned the medical school and DHMC playing key roles in giving those lessons a real-life trial.

"We're not saying that we're the only ones [studying] health care delivery. There are lots and lots of wonderful researchers" trying to do that, Kim said. However, Dartmouth was uniquely positioned to carry the effort forward, particularly given the pioneering work done by Dr. John Wennberg at what came to be known as the Dartmouth Institute for Health Policy and Clinical Practice, or TDI. The institute already offered three graduate degrees (master's in public health, master of science and PhD) and was home to the Dartmouth Atlas of Health Care.

Wennberg and his colleagues had found that hospitals and regions spending more on health care had no better results than lower-spending ones, and that in some cases the outcome was worse. Such findings had gotten the attention of political leaders including President Barack Obama, and drew sometimes harsh scrutiny to the Dartmouth-based researchers.

Such controversy helped Kim make his case for the new center. "These debates should happen in the contest of a rigorous academic field," he said, rather than a partisan political arena. Influencing public policy would be one of the center's goals. "Some people say that academic institutions cannot influence health policy," he said. "I disagree."[254]

Kim saw another opportunity for Dartmouth to contribute after an earthquake devastated Haiti on Jan. 12, 2010. With his support, Dartmouth physician and medical school professor Jim Geiling and a team of DHMC nurses joined an international relief effort at the University Hospital compound in Port-au-Prince.

The group stayed with a Haitian family associated with Partners in Health, the primary health care provider in the impoverished island nation. A reporter and photographer from the *Valley News* tagged along with the group one day as they rose at first light, packed supplies and headed into their eighth day.

"Brian Birner, a nurse anesthetist from Enfield, loaded a backpack full of supplies he would need for the day: Valium, morphine, ketamine and other hard-to find medical supplies, as well as some personal sundries," wrote reporter Gregory Trotter. " 'Morphine and fruit cocktail, that's all you need,' he joked, holding up a small travel cup of fruit."

The Dartmouth team set up a tent at a hospital compound badly damaged by the quake and its aftershocks, hanging a Big Green pennant outside. The heat was oppressive, the flies ever-present, but the Dartmouth team worked hard to care for their patients.

Sometimes that care consisted of small acts, changing dressings, teaching family members how to attend to their loved ones, engaging patients in a daily "bed dance" to get them moving and smiling at least a bit. Other times, they had to perform heroic acts with almost none of the familiar resources, such as when a 29-year-old woman arrived, bleeding profusely after taking herbal medicine for an abortion.

Blood was in short supply, but they managed to requisition enough to save the woman, whose name was Marielle Oreste. "Her hemoglobin level was incompatible with life," said Deb Stephens, a DHMC recovery room nurse. "It was a big process. We really had to fight to get blood from the blood bank."

"Simply put," Trotter wrote, "the Dartmouth team saved countless lives in the past eight days."[255]

That effort would continue in the months that followed, as the Dartmouth Haiti Response — a collaboration between the college and DHMC — sent medical staff and supplies, along with cash donations, to a nation and health care system struggling to recover.

Kim saw the potential for Dartmouth's graduate and professional schools, along with its medical center, to combine efforts. The Haiti relief project was a vivid example of that, medical school professor Joseph O'Donnell would recall years later. "That was Jim Kim at his best."[256]

At 11 a.m. on a Monday in August 2010 — three hours after beginning their medical school educations at Dartmouth — members of the Class of 2014 got their first patient.

The fictitious "Mr. Barns" was suffering from a long list of symptoms, including a worsening cough, unwanted weight loss and coughing up blood. Before they had taken their first anatomy class or clinical rotation, before they had even gotten their ID cards or learned their way around campus, 90 students were asked to start thinking like the doctors they hoped to become.

The exercise represented a revision of the medical school's orientation program led by Dr.

David Nierenberg, senior associate dean for medical education, Amos Esty wrote in *Dartmouth Medicine*.[257] The goal: to engage students in the big picture before they dove into the nitty gritty details of medical science.

"I wanted to throw them into medicine. I wanted to show them the forest before they began focusing on a few trees," said Nierenberg. The agenda: to do a better job equipping students with the too-often-overlooked tools needed to communicate well with patients and take a critical look at a fast-changing health care system — a system in need of reform.

"I really wanted them to start learning that the health-care system needs to change," he said. "There are too many mistakes. It's disorganized. It's not patient-centered."

The next day, students went to the Dartmouth-affiliated VA Medical Center in White River Junction, Vt. There, they were able to talk to observe O'Donnell, an oncologist and veteran professor, talk with a long-time cancer patient.

"I definitely feel like I won't forget that interaction," first-year student Elizabeth Barton told the magazine. "Taking the case from one we had been reading on paper and making it come alive with a real patient was really moving."

The school's attempts to engage students more broadly in rethinking health care didn't stop at first-year orientation. Spurred by Kim's call for improving the delivery of health care services, the school began to reshape its curriculum, including a reimagined fourth-year course, Health, Society and the Physician.

The course had begun in 1983 and was the first at Dartmouth to take on subjects such as domestic violence, HIV infection, managed care and health care policy reform. It was dramatically retooled in 2010 to make Dartmouth's pioneering work in health-care delivery science a central part of the medical school curriculum.

"We do a very good job of preparing people like you for the practice of medicine. And we do a very good job of preparing you and your colleagues for the practice of research [and] the practice of education," Dr. Wiley "Chip" Souba, whom Kim had appointed as medical school dean, told students in the HSP class. What the school could do better, he continued was to prepare students for "the practice of leadership."

In an article for the spring 2011 issue of *Dartmouth Medicine*, Souba was quoted as saying, "We are beginning the process of curricular reform" at the medical school.[258]

Chapter Fifteen
A New President and a New School

In 2010, faculty teams from Tuck and the Dartmouth Institute for Health Policy and Clinical Practice (TDI) spent six months shaping their new collaborative program — the Master of Health Care Delivery Science program — set to launch the next year.

At a time of rapid change, the 18-month program was designed to equip health care industry professionals (who arrive with substantial work experience and, often, other advanced degrees) with the tools needed to reduce health care costs and improve patient outcomes.

"Teaching people to lead change in complex organizations is a core competency of Tuck," TDI faculty member Eric Wadsworth said. "When you marry that to TDI's expertise in delivery innovation, you get a graduate who will know what to do and how to get it done — a skill set desperately needed in the health care industry."[259]

As the economy recovered from a recession triggered in large part by shoddy ethics and poor decisions by business leaders, American business schools came under increased scrutiny. In educating some of those leaders, had the schools come up short?

While most schools responded by ratcheting up their ethics offerings for students, Danos created a stir at the Association of MBAs International Conference for Deans and Directors in Montreal when he said the crisis stemmed not only from ethical misconduct, but also from a poor grasp of complex facts.

"Some regulators and business leaders did misinterpret their duties, did not keep up with the latest knowledge, misused models, were not brave enough to demand full explanations," Danos told his colleagues at the 2010 meeting.

"The lesson you learn is that it takes more than what I would call conventional ethics to be a responsible leader," Danos explained in a later article posted by Tuck. "The important thing is that you have to keep up, and if you can't keep up, you have to make a choice: 'Either I slow the process down or I get more educated about this.'"

At Tuck, professors tried to improve the prospects for sound judgment by future leaders with "research-to-practice" seminars that gave students a chance to make decisions by drilling deep into the available data. The seminars didn't use case studies or other distilled information, but instead asked students to do their own homework and make the best possible choices.

"When put to such intellectual testing, wrong and even unethical claims will normally get weeded out," said Senior Associate Dean Bob Hansen, who played a key role in shaping the research-to-practice curriculum. "I tell my students that if they think of themselves as leaders of the business world in the future, when they see an issue they've got to take a stand on it and have the courage to ask the hard questions."

Beginning in 2011, Tuck took advantage of its growing network of alumni living and working overseas by creating advisory councils — first in Europe, then in Latin America and Asia — to create stronger connections between those regions and the business school.

Tuck's robust alumni network was one of the factors cited by *The Economist* magazine in giving Tuck the top spot on its annual ranking of MBA programs in 2011. That, the magazine said, is "an important consideration given the often-repeated claim that who you meet in an MBA programme is just as important as what you learn." The rankings dropped the University of Chicago's previously top-ranked business school to second place, saw Harvard slide from fourth to fifth, and gave the third place slot to IMD, a Swiss school.[260]

Carey Albertine, a 2005 graduate, tapped into the alumni network when she and a friend were thinking about starting a publishing house for middle-grade and young adult fiction. Her contacts confirmed her instincts that the publishing industry — which was being disrupted by a flood of self-published titles — had room for outsiders with a brilliant idea.

In 2012, Albertine said goodbye to her job as an executive recruiter and founded In This Together Media, a house specializing in inspiring stories for young girls. Within a year, Tuck news writer Kirk Kardashian reported, the firm had published two titles that were selling well on Amazon and had another six in the pipeline.

Albertine said her firm had identified the sweet spot between traditional publishing and self-publishing, offering authors a supportive publisher and a promising market. "It's the young adult who reads the classics but also wants modern books that don't insult her intelligence."

"Tuck gave me the discipline to work through and solve problems," she told Kardashian. "Even though I'm not an expert on any one thing, Tuck gave me exposure to different specialties so that I know how to get a question answered."[261]

While they are in Hanover, Tuckies have an opportunity to broaden their horizons in a different way. An article by Tuck news writer Jeff Moag captured the scene as, late one weeknight in September, some 60 first-years spilled onto the ice at Hanover's Campion Rink.

All wore the familiar gear of hockey players: skates, helmets, sticks and enough padding to make most any fall painless. While some skated with authority, many wobbled and lurched, leaning so heavily on their sticks for balance that any visitor could quickly discern why this was called the "Tri-pod League."[262]

The tradition of Tuckies playing hockey dates at least to the1950s, when students would use a fire hose to flood the lawn between Stell and Chase halls during the winter. The best of them competed in Dartmouth's intramural league under the banner "Tuck Tycoons." But most were happy with pickup games, a way to blow off steam after the rigors of classwork.

Six decades later, the games were still going strong, if in a somewhat more organized fashion. As music played and the puck whizzed around the ice, newly minted Tuckies not only got some exercise; they got to know each other a little — and to laugh a lot.

"We're all bad hockey players, let's just stipulate that," said Derrick Dease, T'12. "But some people have never seen ice before."

As Kim departs, a 1977 Dartmouth grad takes charge

However bold his vision, Kim's time and in-fluence at Dartmouth would be limited. In March 2012, President Barack Obama picked Kim to lead the World Bank, which was created at the end of World War II to finance post-war reconstruction and in the decades since had become a major player in providing financial and technical help to developing nations.

With his background in global health, Kim seemed a strong choice. The *Boston Globe* quot-ed Mark Weisbrot, co-director of the Center for Economic and Policy Research in Washington, as saying Kim was "the first qualified [World Bank] president in 68 years."

Members of the Dartmouth community reacted with a blend of disappointment and dismay at the news that Kim was leaving barely three years into his tenure. Faculty members faulted him for not spending much time on campus, sidestepping the need for curbing student abuses at fraternity houses and treating the college as a temporary stop on his career climb.

"It's not clear whether he and Dartmouth were a great match," said economics professor David Blanchflower. "The scuttlebutt has been that he was using the school as a stepping stone to something bigger and greater. Maybe this is better for both places."[263]

Kim was succeeded in June 2013 by another of Dartmouth's own, Philip J. Hanlon, a 1977 graduate of the college and a mathematician who rose to become provost for academic affairs at the University of Michigan. In his inaugural speech, Hanlon made clear that he, like his immediate predecessors, would not apologize for the accomplishments of Dartmouth's graduate programs. Instead, he would help them grow.

"The most vexing problems facing mankind — sustaining the environment, battling poverty and disease, building an efficient health care system … require deep thinking and the broad range of perspectives Dartmouth has to offer," Hanlon said. "And our colleagues offer us proof that our scholars are making a difference."

The first of the scholars Hanlon cited were Jack

Wennberg and his associates, "who had the foresight to build the foundation upon which our nation will transform health care delivery." In addition to continuing the effort to provide a top-shelf undergraduate education, Hanlon said he would promote the creation of new knowledge by "creating a Society of Fellows program that will bring dozens of highly qualified postdoctoral fellows to our campus." The fellows would come from a range of disciplines, Hanlon said, and work with faculty members to develop their research and hone their skills at passing along their knowledge through teaching.

A little more than a year later, after Hanlon had spent months reviewing strategic plans and talking with professors and students, Dartmouth's 18th president outlined his vision for about 200 faculty members.

Building on the themes he had sounded at his inauguration, Hanlon said he wanted Dartmouth to stress "experiential learning" and deepen graduate offerings — including an expansion of the Thayer School of Engineering and creation of an umbrella school to coordinate the resources and growth of graduate programs.

Hanlon said Dartmouth had traditionally boasted strong faculty and an exceptional undergraduate program. The time had come, he said, to "fill the middle" by increasing the number of "young scholars" doing graduate and post-doctoral work in Hanover. "Young scholars bring energy and new ideas to the campus," Hanlon told the faculty. "They come to us with a sense of urgency. They are just beginning their academic careers and they are hungry."[264]

One of his chief priorities was to expand the Thayer School, which was doing important work in preparing students to live and work in an increasingly technological world but where he said the number of faculty was "below critical mass." He also called for increasing the role that the Tuck School of Business plays in helping undergraduates acquire business skills.

Environmental studies professor Richard Howarth told the *Valley News* reporter Sarah Brubeck that he liked Hanlon's idea of "filling in the middle." Helping graduate students does not detract from undergraduate teaching, he said; they can actually help younger students enter the world of scholarship.

Hanlon echoed that in an interview before his speech, stressing that Dartmouth would never become a place where — as at many research universities — graduate students were teaching a large number of undergraduate classes. All students would continue to learn directly from professors.

"It's something that's been part of our culture forever," he said. "The direct access to faculty is, I think, above all else what makes the undergraduate experience here so special."

At Tuck, new paths and a new leader

Students come to Tuck not only from business but also the military. Often, they bring with them leadership skills that are, literally, battle-tested. At a 2013 panel sponsored by Tuck's MBA program office — From Combat to Corporate: How Military Experiences Can Translate to Corporate Success

— Tuckies who were also military vets shared their stories.

Before coming to Tuck, Christina Fanitzi was a 23-year-old Army lieutenant trying to establish herself as leader of a platoon of soldiers assigned to a maintenance depot in South Korea, Tuck news writer Jason McClure reported.[265]

"I was the only white person in my platoon," she said of the group, which included veterans of combat in Iraq and Afghanistan. "I was excited and they were not. They did not like me and did not appreciate my 'save the world' attitude."

She got to work, learning how to operate every kind of heavy equipment her platoon operated, wrote down the names of spouses and children back home, and listened to their harrowing stories of war. "It took a lot of time but it was worth it," she recalled. "I was firm and fair … I set the bar high, but I didn't act as if I was above them."

Four years later, Tuck invited veterans and elite athletes to participate in a new program designed to introduce them to the business world and beginning building the skills needed to make their mark in it.

The Next Step: Transition to Business program launched in March 2017, attracting people like Julien Bahain, a three-time Olympic rower who had recently decided to retire from the all-consuming sport. "I was faced with the question, 'What do I do now?' " he said. "I don't have any connection to anything outside of rowing. I didn't have time to create any link to the real world."[266]

Bahain joined 66 other athletes and veterans at the two and a half week program, which featured career coaching, mini-courses in such topics as finance, marketing and negotiation, and talks by leaders including Jet Blue President and CEO Robin Hayes and Jim Craig, goalie for the U.S. "Miracle on Ice" hockey team that beat the Soviet Union at the 1980 Olympics.

Transferring skills wouldn't be hard. Companies like veterans and elite athletes because of their proven determination, competitiveness and ability to perform as part of a team, said Punam Anand Keller, the program's faculty director. "When they're given a task, they can repeat it over and over again until they can beat anybody else doing it."

Jan Ingram, a surface warfare officer in the U.S. Navy, arrived in Hanover eager to make the move from military service to health care administration. At first, "all the military people clustered together and we used all this jargon and acronyms," she said. "But when we started mingling with the athletes, it all clicked. We have a lot in common."

In 2014, Danos announced that he would retire the following year, capping a 20-year tenure that the MBA-tracking Poets & Quaints news organization called "extraordinary" for both its length and accomplishment — so extraordinary that the group named Danos its B-school dean of the year.

When Danos took the job in 1995, Google did not yet exist, Steve Jobs hadn't returned to revolutionize Apple and Tuck had fallen far from its earlier top-five ranking in *Businessweek*, John A. Byrne wrote in a tribute to Danos. The school was, in the words of a professor, "in a vulnerable place, like a major league baseball team with a losing record."[267]

Under his leadership, the school had increased its enrollment by a third, expanded the full-time faculty from 35 to 55, grown the endowment from $59 million to $310 million, and boasted an alumni giving rate of more than 70 percent — far greater than the 20 percent average at other business schools. "Paul Danos transformed Tuck's faculty into a world-class academic powerhouse, built a gorgeous campus, raised a ridiculous amount of money, moved the school into the top of the rankings, and became the most trusted administrator at Dartmouth," veteran professor Paul Argenti told Poets & Quaints. "We shall never see the likes of him again."

While rankings aren't the only measure of a school, they provide a window into progress. Before his arrival. Tuck's highest ranking in the various surveys of business school excellence was third; over the next two decades, it hit the No. 1 spot eight times, Kardashian wrote in a 2015 retrospective about Danos's tenure.

Danos endeared himself to students and faculty not just with grand plans and high standards, but by such small personal touches as hosting a charity crawfish dinner for students to treat them to the food of his childhood, and taking the time to coach faculty members in one-on-one meetings that could last for hours. Accounting professor Leslie Robinson said the sessions are "long because he loves to talk about not just what you're doing but what you should be doing."[268]

In 2015, Tuck got a new dean with a familiar face. Matthew Slaughter, an expert in international

economics, had begun teaching Dartmouth undergraduates in 1994 after receiving his PhD from MIT,
then shifted to the Tuck faculty in 2002. His classes
were among the school's most popular, he founded
Tuck's Center for Global Business and Government, and he had served for two years on President
George W. Bush's Council of Economic Advisors.

With a thin frame and a quick grin, Slaughter stepped readily into the leadership role with a
healthy respect for the past and fresh eyes to the
future. As he began his tenure, Great Britain's
Financial Times profiled the new dean. "The 115-
year history of Dartmouth College's Tuck School
of Business might not impress those in countries
where the door handles are older than the American Constitution," wrote correspondent Jonathan
Moules, "but in the U.S. this counts as a heritage
and a challenge for the new dean."[269]

Slaughter said the school would draw on its
traditions while also trying to position itself in an
increasingly digital and international world. "He de-
scribes Tuck as a 'base camp,' from which students
can return from study trips abroad or from studying
online to reflect on what they have learnt amid
the calm of the New England campus."

On campus, the 560 students — the smallest enrollment of America's elite business schools — the
students can learn from people like finance professor Kenneth French, who invites students to join
him on Saturday morning bike rides, Slaughter said.
"This man is a god of accounting. But you don't just
learn from Ken French in the classroom, you can go
cycling with him on a Saturday and ask questions

about finance."

While acknowledging that "it all sounds very romantic," the author noted that by 2015, Tuck had "tumbled" from 16th to 23rd place in the *Financial Times* ranking of MBA programs. Slaughter replied, "I don't like that we have been slipping a bit in recent years."

But he said Tuck remained a "very solid" school, from which nearly 100 percent graduate with a job or offer in hand. He pledged to do his best to bring a "new energy" to his role.

Slaughter spent his first year working with colleagues to refine the school's mission, vision and strategy statement. While that mission had many components, Slaughter boiled it down to ten words: "Tuck educates wise leaders to better the world of business."

"It is my hope that these words will not only shape our actions and our impact on the world, but will also remind us of the broadest aspirations that led to Tuck's founding more than a century ago — and the responsibility that comes with it."[270]

Central to the vision was nurturing the entrepreneurial spirit of students. In 2018, those creatives got a boost with the formation of a startup incubator at Tuck's Center for Entrepreneurship.

On Wednesday nights, second-year Tuckies and other members of their startups (who could come from inside or outside the Dartmouth community) met in a room outfitted with whiteboards and leather chairs to compare notes and get advice.

The first cohort contained four teams wanting to bring their ideas to market. The ideas included a mobile app to diagnose disease in the aquaculture industry, a personal care line for men, an app called "Gut Check" to help people with digestive problems manage stressors, and "Nudg," a system busy people could use to manage personal and professional relationships.

"One of the main points of the incubator is to create a cohort, so students work together, provide feedback, and [can] be supportive of each other," associate professor Steve Kahl D'91, who led the effort along with adjunct professor Daniella Reichstetter T'07, told Tuck writer Kardashian. "Each week, we go through highs and lows of the week, which is important, because this is an emotional journey. You're figuring out how to wrestle through successes and failures, so they don't paralyze you."[271]

It's not just full-time MBA students who gain start-up skills. Tuck professors joined with their colleagues at Thayer and Dartmouth to teach a group of young African entrepreneurs who come to Hanover as part of the Mandela Washington Fellowship and hope to return with skills to create positive change in their home nations.

Joshua Kiplangat Kirui was part of the group in the summer of 2018. The son of Kenyan farmers, he developed a way to use text messaging to cut out exploitive middlemen and connect farmers directly with grocery stores. Another participant, Lillian Moremi, was a career coach from Botswana determined to reduce rampant youth unemployment.

"We are so full of resources, and we need to tap into those," she said. "And that's the whole point …

to go back home and disrupt the status quo."[272]

The Class of 2020 demonstrated that Tuck had come a long way from serving largely as an extension of a Dartmouth education for young American men. Better than one-third of the class of was international, representing 42 nations, a 10 percent increase from the previous year's class.

The incoming class broke another record, with women constituting 45 percent of the students, a Tuck record. They arrived with an average of five years work experience, coming from 225 different employers.[273]

Even as those students were preparing to begin their careers at Tuck, the school released evaluation criteria for applicants to the highly competitive school. "The pathways students take to Tuck are numerous," said Luke Anthony Pena, executive director of admissions and financial aid. "Yet we've found that no matter their path to Tuck, there are four attributes that our students consistently demonstrate. We're now intentionally highlighting those four qualities for prospective students."

The qualities: "smart, nice, accomplished and aware."

While "nice" might sound fluffy for a school preparing leaders for the sharp-elbowed world of commerce, the word encompasses a broad range of attributes that contribute to success at Tuck and in careers beyond. "What we're looking for is emotional intelligence, empathy, and respect for others," he said. "Tuck is a distinctly collaborative community, so being able to challenge others tactfully and thoughtfully in important."[274]

To help fund the continuing growth of Tuck's reach, Slaughter in 2018 launched a $250 million fundraising campaign called The Tuck Difference: The Campaign for Tomorrow's Wise Leaders.

The campaign's aim was nearly twice that of the school's previous capital campaign, with the new money planned for increasing student scholarships, attracting and supporting scholar-teachers and making improvements in programs and campus facilities.

"The order of these priorities — people, programs, places — is important," Slaughter said in announcing the drive, which began with $132 million in donations already committed. "Our most cherished asset is talent. The dynamism and diversity of our students and our faculty are why Tuck thrives."

Medical school gets a new name
The month after Kim's departure made headlines, Dartmouth's medical school made more by changing its name to reflect the generosity of one of Dartmouth's best-known doctors — although one who had never earned an M.D.

Theodor "Ted" Geisel — aka the legendary children's book author Dr. Seuss — and his wife Audrey had become "the most significant philanthropists to Dartmouth in its history," the college said in April 2012 announcement that the school would henceforth be known as the Geisel School of Medicine. The statement cited the couples' "generosity to Dartmouth during their lifetimes and through their estate plan."

"Ted would be proud to have his name forever

connected to one of America's finest schools of medicine," said Audrey Geisel, widow of a man who graduated from Dartmouth in 1925 and died in 1991. English professor and MALS Chair Donald Pease wrote in a biography of Geisel, "Ted cherished the profound sense of community he found at Dartmouth."[275]

The college did not disclose the amount of the couple's gifts over the years, but *Valley News* staff writer Rick Jurgens would later speculate that it was "somewhere around $50 million, or higher," based on Dartmouth's decisions to name a visual arts center after investor Leon Black, who had given $48 million.[276]

Wiley "Chip" Souba, medical school dean at the time of the name change, said the Geisel gift would enable the school to increase scholarships, recruit and retain talented professors and pay for state of the art technology, among other needs.

The announcement surprised many outside of Dartmouth's inner leadership circle, including medical students, *Dartmouth Medicine* reported. "It was somewhat shocking that on April 4 the school not only completely changed its name but also its identity within what seemed to be a matter of minutes," said fourth-year student Jonathan Zipursky. Renaming the medical school is "great," Zipursky commented, "but I think that it is even more meaningful that the name on the school reflects Theodor Geisel's commitment to education and changing the world for the better."

And what about the "Dr." in front of the writer's name? After running afoul of the rules by throwing a party while an undergrad, Geisel was ordered to give up his extracurricular activities, including writing for the student humor magazine, the *Jack-O-Lantern*. He didn't quite comply, instead taking his middle name, Seuss, adding a "Dr." on the front and emerging with a pen name that would last throughout a storied career.[277]

In December 2014, word came that former President Kim's chief initiative — the Dartmouth Center for Health Care Delivery Science — would no longer exist as a separate entity. Instead, college officials said it would merge with the older Dartmouth Institute for Health Policy and Clinical Practice, more commonly known as TDI. College spokeswoman Diana Lawrence told the *Valley News* that Kim's center had been "created with finite funding" and "consolidation with the Dartmouth Institute was always part of the college's long-term plan."[278]

That same fall, the medical school had some happy news to report: Applications to the entering class had risen 20 percent in just one year — an increase of more than three times the national average.

"Prospective students seem to appreciate the very collaborative working environment that exists here," said Aileen Panitz, assistant admissions director at the Geisel School. "With all of the changes occurring in health care today, prospective students realize that Geisel is at the forefront in terms of preparing the types of physicians that will be needed to address this country's needs."

In 2012, a planning committee had announced an effort to make Dartmouth's medical school a national force by boosting research funding, recruiting up to 100 new faculty researchers and adding a like number of graduate students. Over the next four years, however, leaders at the college and medical school realized that they were going to have to shrink rather than grow in order to eliminate a stubborn $30 million deficit that was putting the school, yet again, at risk.

In 2014, Hanlon replaced Geisel School Dean Souba with longtime professor Duane Compton. Compton's mandate: rescue the budget and, by extension, the school.

Compton, who initially served as interim dean, said he was left with no choice but to eliminate jobs. "That's not something I wake up thinking about — 'Oh, let's figure out how many people we can get off the budget this year,'" he recalled in a 2018 interview. "So yes, that was painful, still is."[279]

Compton said the financial crisis had multiple causes, including a decline in federal research funding and, closer to home, "unregulated growth" that had the school straying too far from its central missions of training doctors and conducting important research. It had also suffered from a decline in federal research funding.

Compton devised a plan that included restructuring the school and eliminating jobs. As he presenting it to college trustees in November 2015, a group of faculty members submitted a petition warning of dire consequences. While expressing support for Compton's efforts to stabilize finances, the petition said the restructuring "has the potential to decimate the Geisel School of Medicine, the Norris Cotton Cancer Center, DHMC's clinical research and patient care, Geisel's contribution to under- graduate and graduate education, and Dartmouth's reputation in the world."[280]

In the end, Compton won approval for a plan that would eliminate 30 jobs but save 285 others by transferring them from the college payroll to that of DHMC. The transferred employees — 182 physicians, researchers and staff in the psychiatry department and 103 faculty and staff doing clinical research — made the switch in July 2016.

John Birkmeyer, the medical center's executive vice president and chief financial officer, said the employee transfer would help DHMC "in strength- ening its academic brand and the research portfolio of its physician faculty."[281]

Joseph Asch, a 1979 Dartmouth graduate, used his online "Dartblog" to scoff at Dartmouth officials blaming federal funding for the school's woes. As- serting that the deficit amounted to nearly $43,000 per medical student, he suggested that "misman- agement, unfounded ambition and pie-in-the-sky budgeting" were to blame.[282]

A *Dartmouth Medicine* article on the reorganiza- tion struck a more upbeat note, saying it would lead to more efficient use of the medical school's re- sources. "The decisive steps we've taken to funda- mentally restructure the school and to align resourc- es within a stable, long-term model will support and augment our mission — to address the world's health problems through research that discovers new knowledge about human health, evaluate and improve systems of care delivery, and train the best of the future generations of physicians and scientists," Compton said.[283]

Even as Compton and other medical school leaders had to deliver some hard news, they also got to celebrate a new building designed to allow medical researchers and clinicians to work together more closely on life-saving discoveries.

The 161,000-square-feet Williamson Translational Research Building opened on the DHMC campus and invited collaborative work between scientists including biomedical researchers, engineers, health policy analysts and the clinicians hoping for better ways to treat their patients.

"Much of what drives innovation in research are the interactions and dialogues that you have across different disciplines," Compton said in 2016. "When these connections can take place under one roof … it provides a much better conduit for facilitating the translation of scientific discoveries into better, safer care for patients."[284]

Construction of the $104 million structure was sparked by a $20 million gift made in 2007 by Dr. Peter Williamson and his wife, Susan. Peter was a 1958 Dartmouth graduate who went on to win renown for his pioneering treatment of epilepsy at DHMC. Sadly, neither Williamson lived to see the building's opening; Peter died in 2008 and Susan in 2015.

After nearly three years as Geisel's interim leader, Duane Compton was named dean of the school in 2017. School overseers and college leaders credited him with having restored financial stability to the school and sharpening its focus on education and research.

"Duane was asked to step into the interim role at a difficult time for Geisel, and he has done a remarkable job of guiding the school into a new and more sustainable path," said Ross Jaffe, chair of the school's board of overseers.[285]

Compton is not a medical doctor, but instead a respected cell and cancer biologist who had been recruited to the faculty in 1993. At the time of his promotion, he had published more than 70 articles, taught numerous undergraduate medical courses and taken under his wing a range of PhD, MD-PhD and postdoctoral students.

"I have been fortunate to work with so many talented young researchers, and I am proud of the discoveries we've made together," he said. "I look forward to continuing my research and teaching."

As patients and physicians alike grappled with the rapidly changing economics of medicine, Dartmouth's medical and business schools combined forces to send a select group of doctor-business-people into the health care marketplace through a combined MD-MBA program.

Originally proposed in the 1990s, the program got a significant boost when 1973 medical school graduate Dr. Norm Payson established a $1.5 million endowment in 2004. Payson had learned to combine medical and business skills on his own, first as a practicing physician, then as a managed-care executive and finally as an investor, consultant and philanthropist.

His donation combined with others to provide scholarships for students to pursue the dual degree through coursework and hands-on experience at both Geisel and Tuck. "I ended up loving it and discovering I had a passion for the business side, as well as the clinical side, of medicine," said 2018 program graduate Dr. Colin Tasi, recalling the class he took early in his Dartmouth career, "Medical Care and the Corporation."

Students spend their first three years focused on medical science and clinical experience at Geisel and DHMC, then shift in year four to business coursework at Tuck. The total program takes five or six years, depending on their choice of pacing, and Dartmouth graduates six to eight MD-MBAs each year.

"I'm extremely grateful for the program," said Dr. Si France, a 2007 MD-MBA graduate who went on to found a national urgent care chain, lead an addiction-treatment company serving rural areas and a program caring for frail senior citizens. "It opened up opportunities I never knew existed and prepared me for a career as a mission-focused physician-entrepreneur."[286]

Heading toward Dartmouth's 250th anniversary year, Geisel in 2018 launched a $250 million fundraising campaign aimed at three goals: "educating complete physicians, pursuing bold ideas and transforming health care."

In announcing the campaign, Compton said the money would be used to refine the medical school's offerings, offer student scholarships, build Geisel's multidisciplinary research centers, and provide "transformative gifts" to the Norris Cotton Cancer Center and TDI, among other purposes.

"At Geisel, we encourage students to become citizens of curiosity — physicians and scientists who will listen deeply to patients, examine accepted wisdom, and tackle tough questions. That's how we create leaders, and that's how we can have the greatest impact."[287]

In an era when the #MeToo movement was drawing greater attention to instances of sexual misconduct by powerful men, Dartmouth was roiled by allegations that three professors in the Department of Psychological and Brain Sciences had subjected female graduate students and post-doctoral scholars to a sexually abusive environment.

Professors Todd Heatherton, Paul Whalen and Bill Kelley were placed on paid leave and barred from campus in October 2017 while the allegations were investigated. Following the inquiries, Dean of the Faculty of Arts and Sciences Elizabeth Smith recommended that all three be fired. Before the college could act on that recommendation, however, Whalen and Kelley resigned and Heatherton retired.

In November 2018, a group of female science students filed a $70 million class action lawsuit against Dartmouth, accusing college administrators of ignoring the abuse for more than 16 years, as the professors "leered at, groped, sexted, intoxicated and even raped female students."[288]

In 2019, the college and the women who had sued over a "21st century Animal House" atmosphere reached a $14.4 million settlement, the New York Times reported. President Hanlon said Dartmouth had moved quickly to put in place safeguards against future abuse. "Through this process, we

293

have learned lessons that we believe will enable us to root out this behavior immediately if it ever threatens our campus community again." 289

Over the years, Dartmouth's health care network had grown to include regional hospitals and a growing responsibility to care for the region's sickest patients. In December 2018, DHMC announced plans for a $130 million expansion that would add 60 new inpatient beds, expanded emergency services and — by extension — new training opportunities for medical students and residents, the *Valley News* reported.

"For some time now, we've seen demand for our care dramatically grow, and we've had success with our member hospitals in both states in making sure patients receive the right care, at the right time, close to home," said Dartmouth-Hitchcock CEO Joanne Conroy. "But the increasing demands for Dartmouth-Hitchcock's specialty and high-acuity care, in all disciplines, requires us to expand our capacity."

The expansion announcement came just weeks after the Dartmouth-Hitchcock system reported an operating surplus of $47.5 million on a $2-billion operating budget, the newspaper reported. That was a big improvement from the 2017 and 2016 fiscal years, which saw Dartmouth-Hitchcock post operating losses of $7 million and $12.2 million, respectively.[290]

Thayer grows quickly, broadens reach

In 2003, Thayer students had established a Dartmouth chapter of Engineers Without Borders. Two years after that, they founded their own organization, which eventually came to be known as Dartmouth Humanitarian Engineering. The group has students working in developing countries on such projects as clean water, pico-hydropower and sanitation.

In 2012, students belonging to the group installed a zero-emissions hydroelectric generating station on the Rugaragara River in Rwanda — and then came up with a way for impoverished residents to afford bringing electricity to their homes for the first time.

After engineering the hydro system to provide power to the villages of Rugote and Nyamirambo, the students found most villagers didn't have enough money to buy a battery to store the power for use in lighting dwellings and charging cell phones. So they worked with local business owners to create a rental system in which customers could rent batteries from the businesses on a monthly basis.

"There are over 300 families living in close proximity to the site — about two kilometers or less — many of which are experiencing the benefits of having electricity in their village for the first time," student Kevin Francfort told *Dartmouth Engineer*.[291]

The signature introductory engineering course, ES 21, has left its mark on many a Thayer student. One, George Boateng, decided to team up with six Ghanian friends to bring the lessons to youths in their native country.

Beginning in 2013, Project iSWEST (Innovating Solutions with Engineering, Science & Technology) has offered high school students an abbreviated version of ENGS 21. "The thing that blew my mind about [ES 21] was that students without advanced engineering classes could go through a design and innovation process and actually build solutions to real-life problems and start companies out of it," said Boateng, who graduated from Thayer in 2017.

The project was based at the University of Ghana in Legon, offering free admission to girls in an attempt to inspire the widest possible range of young innovators. "Our vision," said Boateng, who went on to work as a research scientist at Dartmouth and a tutor in the Dartmouth Emerging Engineers program, "is to inspire a revolution for youth across Africa to create solutions to their communities' problems."[292]

In 2014, Dean Joseph Helble and three Thayer colleagues won a national award for their work in creating the Dartmouth Engineering Entrepreneurship Program. The program, which aims to prepare students to be leaders in creation and use of technology, was awarded the Bernard M. Gordon Prize for Innovation in Engineering and Technology Education by the National Academy of Engineering.

Joining Helble in the award were professor and 1977 graduate John Collier, former Dean Hutchinson and professor Robert Graves. Collier transformed Thayer's introductory engineering class into an opportunity for budding engineers to develop a project idea, research and build the technology and try to win funding to bring it to market.

Hutchinson had launched the school's Master of Engineering Management (MEM) program in 1989, tapping the faculty expertise of Tuck School profes-

sors to equip future engineers with needed management and entrepreneurship skills. Graves took
over leadership of the M.E.M. program in 2003 and
established the Corporate Collaboration Council to
invite industry leaders to mentor students and give
them internship opportunities. Helble was lauded
for launching the PhD in Innovation Program in
2008.

The Gordon Prize came with $500,000, half
of which was given to recipients and the rest to
the school to fuel further innovation efforts. Elsa
Garmire, Thayer professor and former dean, nomi-
nated her colleagues for the prize. "I hope," she said,
"that engineering programs across the country will
be inspired to replicate our approach to engineering
entrepreneurship."[293]

Dartmouth's football team headed into the fall
2015 season with its best preseason ranking in 18
years — and a training program bolstered by the
first robotic mobile tackling dummy, courtesy of an
inventive former Big Green player and his Thayer
classmates.

Thayer student and former defensive tackle El-
liot Kastner had approached Dartmouth coach Bud-
dy Teavens with the project, designed to cut injuries
and increase opportunities for players to practice
blocking and tackling. Teavens, nationally known
for his efforts to reduce injuries, embraced it.

"Health is a huge thing in our game, and certainly in this league," said the coach, who as a quarter-
back had led the Big Green to the 1978 Ivy League
championship.[294]

The Mobile Virtual Player (MVP) runs on

wheels, is self-righting and operated by remote control. It was designed to simulate football players' size, weight and agility, allowing them to minimize head and neck injuries while still making full contact during practice.

Replacing live players with machines held the added benefit of giving more practice reps to second- and third-team athletes. The researchers applied for a patent, developed a business plan through the Dartmouth Entrepreneurial Network and geared up to market the MVP to football teams ranging from peewee to professional.

Helble created a veritable inventor's hall of fame in the hallway outside the dean's office in Cummings Hall, where the walls are lined with more than 200 patents held by Thayer faculty members, staff and students — all resulting, Helble notes, from research done on the Dartmouth campus.

The growing inventiveness of the Thayer faculty drew attention far beyond Hanover. In 2015, professor Robert Dean was named a fellow of the National Academy of Inventors, joining professors Eris Fossum, Tillman Gerngross, Elsa Garmire and Axel Scherer in that distinction.

Being named an NAI fellow represents the highest honor for academic inventors "who have demonstrated a prolific spirit of innovation in creating or facilitating outstanding inventions that have made a tangible impact on quality of life, economic development and the welfare of society."

A faculty member since 1961, Dean held 28 U.S. patents at the time of the honor, numerous foreign patents and other patents pending. He headed a company, Synergy Innovations, which developed products and processes including ones intended to help elderly people avoid falling and, if they did, to rise safely from the floor.

Three years later, Professor Rahul Sarpeshkar was named an NAI fellow. A professor of both engineering and computational science, Sarpeshkar has made significant advances in such areas as medical devices and electronics, ultra-low power, analog and bio-inspired design.

"I loved the sizzle in the brain created by an invention that solves a problem you have been working on intensely," said Sarpeshkar.[295]

In 2016, Dartmouth became the first national research institution to award more undergraduate engineering degrees to women than to men. Women made up 52 percent of the group, a dramatically higher share than the 19 percent average nationwide.

"We've been able to attract more students, and especially women, by letting them use engineering to solve real-world challenges," said Helble. "They quickly learn how their creativity and engineering skills can make a real difference."

Gabriella Grangard was one of the graduates. She and a team of classmates invented a new kind of cerebral shunt for treating hydrocephalus, a condition in which excessive fluid and pressure inside the cranium can lead to pain, disability and even death. Another, Shinri Kamei, led a team that built an ergonomic serving tray to reduce injuries and accidents for restaurant waitstaff.

As recently as the period between 1997 and 2001, women made up only 20 percent of engineering majors. But the percentage of women grew rapidly as word got out that Dartmouth offered a curriculum — and culture — that was decidedly female-friendly.

Women cited a number of factors for choosing the engineering path in a 2015 *Dartmouth Engineer* magazine article written by Anna Fiorentino. One would have made generations of Dartmouth leaders proud: a focus on blending specialized technical education with a broad base in the liberal arts.

"I chose Thayer because I loved that I would be able to have a diverse course of study that includes both the engineering and the liberal arts side of the school," said Kelsey Kittelsen '17, who added to her engineering major a focus on studio art and a new minor in human-centered design. "All my close girlfriends are in the engineering program."[296]

Students and faculty members said female students often enjoy Thayer's project-based approach to learning. "Learning at Thayer goes beyond the technical aspects of engineering and considers how people relate to engineering problems, which is of particular interest to me," said Rachel Margolese '16.

Female or male, students didn't need to arrive at Dartmouth with lots of experience handling tools and machinery. Professor Vicki May noted, "All students are introduced to tools in the machine shop, which I think is empowering for everyone."

Women arrived in classes and labs to find a growing number of role models, include female teaching assistants and a cadre of female professors. "Success in coursework is not and has never been dependent on gender," said professor Jane Hill. "We have reached a critical mass, and with that status people are more informed about what engineering can be and the cool things that evolve from the experience at Thayer."

Still, female students said they would like to see more female professors at Thayer. When the article appeared, women accounted for only about one in five of the core faculty members.

As Thayer grows, said Allison Brouckman '15, "I would love to see more female and other minority group professors join the ranks of the impressive engineering faculty."

The success Thayer has achieved in promoting women engineers pleased not just the school, its faculty and students but also Helble's spouse. Dabora said she was happy that their two daughters would encounter a very different climate than she did a generation before. "They're growing up in a different time."

One of their daughters, Michaela, a dual-degree student from Bowdoin College, earned her BE from Thayer in 2017. "Joe handed her the diploma, gave her a big hug, and didn't make a big deal out of it, but that must've been wonderful for him," said Thayer graduate and board member Samantha Scollard Truex. "How nice to be able to provide education for all students across the globe, and one from his own home."[297]

Thayer's small size had always been considered one of its chief virtues, allowing undergraduate and graduate students and professors to work together in a tight, collaborative community. But as demand for engineering courses increased, including among Dartmouth undergraduates majoring in other subjects, and as the world of technology become increasingly computer-based, Helble had a bold vision — doubling the size of the school and integrating it with the Computer Sciences department in a new building at the west end of campus.

Some Thayer board members were initially skeptical. "I was one of the more vocal opponents, initially, because I thought part of the magic of Thayer is how small it is," board member and 1986 graduate Scott Sandell told Senz for the school's narrative. But Helble took his usual patient and methodical approach, listening to concerns, presenting persuasive facts and working toward consensus. "He responded to my concerns with logic and data and brought me around to his point of view, effectively and legitimately," Sandell said.[298]

Central to Helble's pitch was the way the physical and digital worlds had converged and produced an array of new technologies, including robotics, cybersecurity and computational biology. The notion of bringing computer sciences and engineering closer had long been discussed at Dartmouth, but Helble managed at last to move it forward.

He found an ally in Harry Farid, chair of the computer science department. Farid recalled raising the question when he joined the faculty two decades earlier. "Nobody was willing to touch it," he said, "because everyone felt like it was too big of a hurdle to even talk about this kind of unification of a school and a department."

But Helble and Farid joined forces and, meeting by meeting, conversation by conversation, won people over. Some Thayer board members who attended the duo's presentations to alumni in 2017 and 2018 came away impressed with the way they blended strong reasoning, passionate argument and a touch of humor. "It was almost like they were a two-man comedy team selling the virtues of combining computer science and engineering, which is a little hard to make exciting, frankly," said Samantha Truex. "I thought to myself, I can't think of better leaders."

Helble also "turned out to be an outstanding fundraiser," said board member Peter Fahey, who said Helble took the lead in the $200 million fund-raising campaign for the new building. "I don't think you would have perceived that from Joe 15 years ago, but he's grown into that."

By any measure, it's a big deal. "You have to appreciate the scale of the project," says Farid. "It is massive. It will be the single largest building project on campus in its history. It is bringing together two big departments to grow them substantially."[299]

A key donor came from the ranks of Thayer alumni. Some college graduates go out into the world, ind success and only look back at the 5-year reunion mark. Not Barry MacLean, a 1960 Dart-mouth and 1961 Thayer School graduate and head of MacLean-Fogg, an Illinois-based manufacturing company with more than 4,500 employees scattered across the globe.

MacLean had served better than four decades on Thayer's Board of Overseers and made generous inancial contributions along the way — particularly in 2016, when he pledged $25 million. MacLean's gift was the largest in Thayer's century and a half, with $15 million to help design and build the new engineering building and the other $10 million to match donations for creating endowed professorships.

"Engineering is recognized as a solution to many of the world's challenges, such as hunger, space exploration, or extending life," MacLean said. "All those issues have engineering aspects, and students today are focused on trying to make a better world. Seeing young people going farther than you ever expected is really rewarding, and helping them on their way is a great joy to me."[300]

MacLean intended his gift to lead the way in the $200 million building campaign. It would also pave the way for meeting a surging demand among students for a Thayer education — the school whose early decades featured just a handful of students had grown to include 110 engineering majors in the 2016 senior class alone — while increasing faculty size to preserve a low student-faculty ratio and community spirit.

Finally, it would help advance the goal set by Thayer leaders and Dartmouth President Phil Hanlon for providing engineering educational opportunities not just to Thayer students but to all Dartmouth undergraduates, to help them succeed in an increasingly high-tech world.

Hanlon applauded MacLean's generosity and leadership. "Though his example," Hanlon said, "I take great confidence that the exceptional experiential learning opportunities offered by Thayer today may soon be available to all Dartmouth students, instilling in them the skills and wisdom to lead with impact."[301]

In 2017, Thayer professor Eric Fossum won engineering's version of the Oscar, the Queen Elizabeth Prize for Engineering, for his work in inventing the complementary metal-oxide-semiconductor, or CMOS image sensor.

Don't know what CMOS means? Pick up your smart phone, take a selfie and think about the technology that allowed you to do that. Then, thank Fossom.

"The Queen Elizabeth Prize honors individuals whose innovations have quite literally changed the world, and this is exactly what Eric Fossom has done," said Dartmouth President Hanlon. "His CMOS image sensor has brought us everything from medical advances to pictures from Mars to cameras in our pockets. And he continues to innovate here at Dartmouth, where he is committed to teaching the next generation of engineers."[302]

Fossom's pionering work began when he was working at NASA's Jet Propulsion Laboratory in the 1990s, trying to find a way to put a reliable camera in space. The existing charge-coupled device (CCD) technology was clunky, power-hungry and vulnerable to radiation damage. Fossom's breaththrough was inventing a sensor that could measure light where it lands — allowing engineers to put electronics on a tiny chip.

Early versions of the chip didn't perform as well as CCDs, limiting their use in the consumer marketplace. But refinements in the technology combined with the arrival of cell phones in the early 2000s led to a boom for Fossom's invention, the creation of two successful companies and what Fossom thought was going to be his retirement.

"I have to say retirement was great — I got to do all the things I always wanted to do," Fossom told *Dartmouth Engineer* writer Hannah Silverstein. "And then when I got to the bottom of my bucket list, I started to wonder, what is the best thing to do with the rest of my life?"

Teaching. He approached Helble, offering to teach a course, maybe two, at Thayer. That evolved into a full-time job, in which he not only taught but also became director of the school's Innovation Program and associate provost of entrepreneurship and technology transfer. Oh, and an inventor/educator whose restless mind led him and his students into the lab in search of more breakthroughs.

As Dartmouth entered 2019 and prepared to celebrate the 250th anniversary of its founding, a $200 million construction project marked a new era in the growth of technological education — a building designed to integrate engineering, computer science and entrepreneurship.

The West End project provides room to grow for Thayer, Dartmouth's computer science department and the Dartmouth Entrepreneurial Network, Dartmouth News writer Susan Boutwell reported. "Engineering and computer science have a natural synergy that will spark collaboration and innovation through their overlapping work in robotics, imaging, protein engineering, and other areas of technological advancement," said Hanlon. "In addition, locating Dartmouth's entrepreneurial enterprise in the west end will speed translation of ideas into real-world applications."[303]

The building rises up next to the MacLean Engineering Sciences Center and Cummings Hall. With a growing demand for graduate study slots and more than two out of three Dartmouth undergraduates enrolling in engineering or computer science courses, Helble said the time was right. "We are bursting at the seams," Helble said. "Our time to grow is now."

The center will give students a chance to participate in "the fourth industrial revolution," said Helble. "This is the time for engineering and computer science to dissolve the artificial boundary between the computational and the physical worlds."

In May 2018, President Hanlon announced that Helble would become Dartmouth's next provost. "As an educational trailblazer, Joe Helble is eminently suited to help shape Dartmouth's future at this time of dynamic change and opportunity."

For several years, Thayer board members had wondered whether they might lose their talented dean to another university. While Thayer would miss having Helble's talents to itself, they said, he had proven himself worthy of a job focusing on uniting the efforts of all of Dartmouth's schools and departments, both graduate and undergraduate.

"Whether it's Tuck or computer science or the medical school, Joe has worked really hard to be sure that the relationships between Thayer and those entities are a two-way street and that there's benefit for everyone," observed board member Charlie Nearburg. "That's why I think he's an excellent choice for provost, because he's demonstrated that he sees the big picture and we're all in this together in trying to make this a better Dartmouth."[304]

The first new graduate school in a century

In January 2016, Dartmouth trustees made one of President Hanlon's hopes a reality, creating Dartmouth's first new graduate school since the Tuck School was founded in 1900. The School of Graduate and Advanced Studies, Hanlon said, would "enhance the impact of our current research enterprise, help attract the most talented students and faculty, and promote collaborative interdisciplinary efforts while maintaining Dartmouth's high expectations for quality and excellence."[305]

The new school would not erect a building or hire its own faculty. Instead, it would tie together the master's, PhD and post-doctoral work being done by students in all of Dartmouth's departments and schools. Its first dean was F. Jon Kull, a 1988 Dartmouth graduate and internationally known structural biologist and biochemist who had been serving as dean of graduate studies.

"Dartmouth will be a destination for graduate students and postdoctoral fellows who want to be expertly trained in their field … and become thoughtful leaders, ready to tackle the world's most pressing challenges and important questions," Kull said after the new school was formed.

On one level, creating the school was simply an organizational move, consolidating administration for some 800 students in 16 PhD programs and 12 masters programs, along with 250 postdoctoral students. But on another, it was intended to signal the growing importance of graduate studies at Dartmouth and to make it easier for professors and students in those programs to win funding for their research and create new interdisciplinary offerings.

A little more than two years later, in April 2018, the school was renamed the Frank J. Guarini School of Graduate and Advanced Studies in honor of a "historic gift" — the amount was unspecified — to support graduate study. Guarini had graduated from Dartmouth in 1946 after coming to the school as part of the Navy V-12 program, then gone on to build a career as a U.S. congressman, delegate to NATO and representative to the United Nations.

It was the latest in a series of gifts Guarini had given to his alma mater. "This latest gift from Frank is a remarkable act of generosity and a historic investment in the education of future generations," Hanlon said. "We are committed to providing outstanding graduate programs, among the very best in the world, and Frank shares that commitment."[306]

Two and a half centuries after Eleazar Wheelock had first heard that cry for knowledge in the New Hampshire wilderness, Dartmouth College entered its next century with a brand new graduate school — and an identity shaped in powerful ways by the educators and students who had made it "a university in all but name."

Epilogue: At 250 years, Dartmouth's Leaders Look Ahead

As Dartmouth prepared to mark its 250th year in 2019, the author sat down with two college presidents and the deans of the graduate programs to ask: Is Dartmouth a "small college," a university or a unique combination of the two?

James Wright, President, Dartmouth College 1998-2009

After taking the presidency, Wright wasted no time in cutting straight to the question. In an April 6, 1998 speech, he declared that "Dartmouth is a research university in all but name, and we are not going to be deflected from our purposes."

Two decades later, Wright sits in his office behind a bakery south of campus and explains that he wanted to signal that "university is not a dirty word." During the tenure of his predecessor, James O. Freedman (1987-1998), alumni, faculty, students and administrators had debated the question of whether Freedman had gone too far in turning Dartmouth into a research university.

"I wanted to be clear," Wright says. "Dartmouth has been a university in all but name for many years."[307]

The college has one of the nation's oldest medical schools, a first-of-its kind engineering school and America's original graduate school of business, Wright points out. At the same time, Dartmouth had always made clear that providing an excellent education to undergraduates had long been its defining mission.

The two are not mutually exclusive, he says. Nor are the goals of excellence in teaching and original research.

During his tenure (in which he served as dean of the faculty as well as a longtime history professor), Wright says he recruited faculty members "who are on the cutting edge of whatever their field of research was ... and couldn't wait to share it" with students — both undergraduate and graduate.

Graduate study and research at Dartmouth has long enriched undergraduates, Wright says, as professors and graduate students give younger students a chance to participate in original research projects and envision their futures as scholars, researchers, professors and practitioners.

When Wright took over as president, he tried to bring the professional schools more to the center of the Dartmouth culture. Known for decades as "associated schools," he says, "they were more on the periphery."

The medical school was not only providing first-rate educations to future physicians but also engaged in cutting edge research into the causes and treatment of disease and the science of measuring health care outcomes. "When I became president, I was increasingly impressed by the strength of the students and faculty over there, so I looked for ways to engage them more with the college."

With its 5-year program blending an undergraduate liberal arts education and top-shelf graduate training, the Thayer School has always served a broad group of students. Its emphasis on collaboration and innovation means the school graduates students "who can in their careers move into positions of leadership more and more because they know how to work as a team. They know how to bring people from different disciplines together."

At Tuck, meanwhile, teamwork also plays a central role in a way unmatched by most schools. "Tuck in many ways is a remarkable mirror of what the undergraduate college is in terms of teaching, focus on students and collaborative work."

Did he or other college leaders ever consider expanding Dartmouth's portfolio of graduate programs to include a law school, divinity school or PhD program in a strong liberal arts field such as history? Wright says that during the presidency of David McLaughlin in the 1980s, there was some talk of Dartmouth forging a relationship with Vermont Law School, which had a strong program in environmental law.

But he said that idea, and others, were soon dispatched so the college could maintain its focus on a carefully curated group of graduate offerings.

"I don't think we've ever seen our niche based on size or quantity. We've been focused more on quality," he says. "I don't think Dartmouth is afraid to grow but I think we also understand that our scale is important."

F. Jon Kull, Dean, Frank J. Guarini School

Placing formerly separate graduate programs under one organizational umbrella serves many purposes, says Kull. On a practical level, it provides focused attention to the programs that have become an increasingly large part of Dartmouth's academic life, makes fundraising simpler and — importantly — makes it easier to emphasize and create programs that cut across traditional disciplinary lines.

Take, for instance, the Ecology, Evolution, Ecosystems and Society (EEES) program, Kull says. Students pursuing graduate degrees in the program learn from professors with expertise not only in environmental studies, but also biology, ecology, evolution, environmental economics, geography, anthropology, and engineering.

"It's putting environmental studies into a context," he explains. "How does environmental change affect society, and how do societies affect environmental change? Just looking at the science is one thing, but these days you can't just look at science by itself."[308]

Dartmouth's professional schools in medicine, engineering and business date back to, respectively, 1797, 1867 and 1900. By contrast, most of the growth in its master's and PhD programs in the arts and sciences divisions has come in the last half century — and the pace of innovation is increasing.

313

"Many things at Dartmouth are really high quality, but small," Kull observes. The Guarini School has the ability to stitch together seemingly disparate disciplines into a coherent whole that — as with the EEES program — can equip graduate and post-doctoral students with a unique and practical set of skills.

It also makes it easier to win recognition and funding for the high-level research being done in Hanover. "When the world looks at Dartmouth versus Harvard, they're going to think of Harvard as a place that does cutting edge research," he says. "We want people to recognize Dartmouth as a place where the faculty does really great research."

And what of those who say graduate study has little or no place at a college known for the excellence of its undergraduate programs? Kull dismisses that criticism as outdated, noting that the presence of strong graduate students and research programs is a draw for strong faculty members.

"If we didn't have graduate programs, we wouldn't have the same faculty," he says. "No faculty member who's going to look at a job at Harvard chemistry or Harvard biology is going to look at Dartmouth if we don't have a graduate program."

And that, in turn, draws on the college's traditional strength in a well-rounded liberal arts education. "We have a strong reputation in the liberal arts," he says. "We want to train our PhD students to be out-of-the-box thinkers and look at things from multiple perspectives."

Duane Compton, Dean, Geisel School of Medicine

Compton, a prominent cell and cancer biologist, leads a school with nearly 900 students in MD, PhD, MPH and MS programs, 900 clinical and research faculty, 650 staff members and more than 1,000 affiliated faculty. He says that presiding over budget cuts was a stressful but necessary job.

With the budget stabilized, Compton says the challenge is crafting a medical education and research approach that keeps up with — and gets ahead of — the quickening pace of discovery in medical knowledge. Sixty years after the school's 1797 founding, medical techniques were still primitive. "We were still in the Civil War and the solution was to cut the limb off and good luck if you survive the infection."

Today, he says, knowledge and teaching constantly need to be updated — especially in fields such as genetics, biochemistry, cell biology, reproductive health, psychiatry and cardiovascular treatment. "Antibiotics are only about 40 years old. The human genome [project] was finished about 10, 12 years ago," he says. Taking a pen and a piece of paper, he shows the trajectory of medical knowledge growing "exponentially instead of linearly."[309]

What distinguishes Dartmouth's medical schools from peer institutions? "There's a certain community spirit here that's hard to replicate in other places," he says. Noting that students are taught largely by full professors rather than the adjunct faculty members common at other schools, he adds that "those barriers don't exist here."

Nor do barriers exist between the medical school and other parts of Dartmouth, graduate and undergraduate. "I can't even imagine what Dartmouth would look like without the medical school," he says. "We're so integrated into the fabric of what's going on here."

He ticks off the collaborative programs: With Tuck, a master's degree program in health care delivery science. At Thayer, about half the engineering faculty members work with medical school faculty on biomedical research. With Dartmouth's arts and sciences divisions, the medical school shares PhD programs in molecular and cell biology, experimental and molecular medicine, and quantitative biomedical sciences. In the undergraduate realm, about a quarter of incoming Dartmouth freshmen choose pre-health majors and get the opportunity to participate in laboratory research and shadow physicians.

Students at the medical school have an "intellectual fierceness about them" that mirrors the fierce spirit of dis-covery Eleazar Wheelock and Nathan Smith brought to Hanover in the late 18th century. "There's an innovative spirit that fills everyone here," he says. "I mean, some-thing drove someone to paddle up the Connecticut River and stop here."

"We're not pushing the geography boundary anymore; we're pushing the science boundaries," he says. "People ask me what's going to happen in the next ten years ... I have no idea. I can't wait."

Joseph Helble, Dean, Thayer School of Engineering from 2005 to 2018, Dartmouth Provost October 2018

While Thayer's enrollment lagged behind Dartmouth's other profession-al schools for many years, that's changed. Helble says that of all the schools, Thayer has experienced the most growth — since he took over as dean, the student population has doubled and the tenured or tenure-track faculty has grown from 25 to the mid-40s.

While engineering might at one point have seemed a field for people who wanted to build roads, bridges and dams, the explosion of computer technology has made it a booming field with plenty of sex appeal. Apple, Google, Facebook, YouTube and Amazon are just some of the firms that have made tech a cutting-edge place to build a career.

In addition, the design movement has made clear to students that there is plenty of room for creativity and making a difference in ways that are measured not only in commercial value, but also in social good. That ability is enhanced by a feature that remains unique at Dartmouth: the requirement that future engineers have a solid grounding in the liberal arts.

Thayer graduates often end up at small or me-dium-sized companies where the ability to see the big picture, be flexible and work as part of a team are valued. Increasingly, Thayer students and their

317

professors start those companies themselves. When Helble began as dean, he says, one in four professors had started a company based on their work — that number has soared toward 50 percent.

"This is what we're showing our students by example," says Helble. "You've got an idea — go out and make it happen."[310]

Thayer professors and students work closely with colleagues at the Tuck School of Business and Geisel School of Medicine. Thayer has also continued its historic connection with the undergraduate college, not just through the engineering science majors who will complete their education at Thayer but also in an innovative minor in human-centered design led by Thayer professor Peter Robbie and computer science professor Lorie Loeb, which has become one of Dartmouth's most popular.

Moving forward, Helble would like to see the school add capacity so that every Dartmouth student can take courses in engineering design and computer science, to prepare them to function effectively in a technological world.

"A liberal arts education helps you understand and interpret the world," he says. "And when you add engineering on that fundamental foundation, you now have the tools and the capability not just to understand the world but to design technologies to go out and change it."

Matthew Slaughter, Dean, Tuck School of Business

In discussing Tuck's present and future, Slaughter looks to its founding in 1900 as the nation's first graduate school of business. The school, he says, is "a hallmark not just for Dartmouth but for all of education as one of innovation."

The school's founding benefactor, Edward Tuck, saw the need for an American school to groom a generation of business leaders for an emerging — but not fully formed — international economy. In the 21st century, Tuck graduates are entering a world that's in a similar state of rapid growth and flux.

Tuck tries to prepare business leaders for that challenge with an education rooted in teamwork and interdisciplinary knowledge. That effort reaches across boundaries at the school as well.

"All of the different pieces of Dartmouth thrive best when we are seeking points of connectivity across the school," Slaughter says. He points as an example to the master's degree in health care delivery science coordinated with the medical school, in which health care industry leaders can chart a better way for a system coping with financial challenges and whirlwind scientific advances. "We want to educate future health care leaders to reform the system for the better."[311]

Even as Tuck students graduate to six-figure

starting salaries, the school tries to infuse them with a sense of social responsibility, to remain true to Edward Tuck's adage that "altruism is the highest and best form of egoism." For most Tuck MBAs, the two years at Dartmouth will be their final formal education, but the school encourages them to be lifelong learners committed to acting wisely in the world.

"There's a big parallel with how we do education at Tuck and how Dartmouth does it," says Slaughter.

The curriculum changes with the times, he says, with an increasing emphasis on smart analysis of data, close attention to emerging markets and the global revolution in technology and trade. "We're constantly experimenting."

The 2008 financial crisis undercut not only the nation's economic health but also people's faith in the ethical compasses of business leaders. Tuck has responded by weaving into leadership courses ethical questions ranging from "How far into your supply chain do you have to think about child labor?" and "Is it moral for individuals to default on their mortgages?" In class, professors and students contemplate contemporary situations with guidance from such classical thinkers as Aristotle and Kant.

The average student arrives with five years of experience in the business world, and they increasingly hail from nations across the globe. "As great as the Tuck faculty are," says Slaughter, "the students learn as much from each other."

Philip J. Hanlon, President, Dartmouth College 2013-present

In his office overlooking the Green, Baker Library and the not-so-small college founded two and a half centuries earlier by Eleazar Wheelock, Dartmouth's 18th president reflects on a question nearly as old as the institution itself.

"I have worked at four great universities during my career," Philip J. Hanlon says, listing MIT, Cal Tech, Michigan and Dartmouth. "Only one of them called itself a university."

"The names are not really about what we are," he continues. "They are really about what we value."[312]

Dartmouth has effectively been a university since Nathan Smith founded its medical school in 1797, Hanlon says. "There's no question we're a university" — but one with "an unusually strong" commitment to the undergraduate experience.

That experience is enhanced, not diminished, by the presence and growth of Dartmouth's robust and growing graduate programs. Most universities build silos of knowledge and operation that make it hard to weave connections across the "academic generations" — undergraduate students, graduate and post-doctoral learners, and members of the faculty.

321

"Dartmouth can be a campus without the kind of barriers that limit other institutions," he says. "Because of our scale, because of our intimacy, we could really be the campus without barriers."

Creating the Guarini School helped advance that goal, and signaled Dartmouth's commitment to ensuring that all students have the opportunity to collaborate rather than to compete for the attention of faculty members and the institution. Such collaboration helps today's scholars build on the tradition encouraged by former President John Sloan Dickey, bringing the lessons learned in Hanover into the wider world.

"He did not want the ivory tower, where we just sit here and think about ourselves," Hanlon says. Instead, Dickey told the Dartmouth community, "The world's problems are your problems."

Hanlon says he appreciates the concerns expressed by alumni who fear losing the college's historic commitment to undergraduate education. But he says it's "a mistaken belief that it's a zero-sum game, that if we give more resources to graduate students that we'll be giving fewer resources to undergraduates."

Instead, he said undergraduates will benefit from the opportunity to work alongside more advanced students in their disciplines, and to tap into the ferment of new interdisciplinary programs pioneered at the graduate level. Will Dartmouth follow the lead of universities that have many undergraduate courses taught by graduate students? "We have no intention of ever doing that. We expect that the preponderance of our classes will be taught by regular faculty."

Breaking new ground in graduate study is nothing new at Dartmouth, home to the nation's first graduate school of business, the first engineering school of its kind and one of the nation's first medical schools.

"Dartmouth, despite its deserved reputation as a fantastic undergraduate institution, has led the way in innovating in graduate studies," Hanlon says. "It's an unknown story, a really important one."

All Epilogue images courtesy of Dartmouth College.

Acknowledgements

It is daunting, to say the least, to attempt a history of a school with Dartmouth's rich tradition of graduate study, scholarship and spirited debate about whether Daniel Webster's beloved "small college" is really a university in all but name. I am happy to report, however, that I had plenty of help from the gifted historians who came before, beginning with Leon Burr Richardson and his lyrical two-volume *History of Dartmouth College* published in 1932. This book draws on more than a hundred other sources, small and large, all listed in the bibliography and notes that follow. Any mistakes in distilling their work and words are mine alone.

I also owe a debt to the people who provided me with encouragement and advice. They include Donald M. Pease, Jr., a busy scholar and professor of literature who also finds time to chair the Master of Arts in Liberal Studies department and co-chair the college's 250th anniversary celebration, and who gave me the opportunity to undertake this project; Barbara S. Kreiger, who leads the MALS creative writing unit and became my inspiring mentor as I tried to hone my craft as a student in that program, with this as my final project; Christopher S. Wren, a veteran *New York Times* foreign correspondent, author and MALS professor who has cheered my efforts at every turn; the Guarini School's Amanda A. Skinner and Ellie Nan Storck, who worked hard to bring this project from typewritten page to bound book; and Diana Maria Solis, who provided gourmet meals, the sharp eye of a first reader, and loving encouragement at every step. Finally, I send love and gratitude to my adult children, Amelia and Alex, who make me proud as they author their own histories in the world.

About the Author

Jeffrey Good is a veteran journalist who served as the editor of the *Valley News*, won the Pulitzer Prize in Editorial Writing, and authored (with contributor Susan Goreck) *Poison Mind*, the nonfiction account of a Florida murder investigation. He is currently Director of Communnications for Acceleration Academies, a network of public high school drop out reenagement programs.

Note: This book covers Dartmouth's history up to its 250th anniversary in 2019. The Covid-19 pandemic that began in 2020 brought great challenges to the college and its graduate programs, but that period arrived after this volume was completed. It will provide the opening pages of the history of Dartmouth's next 250 years.

References

Alden, Ebenezer. 1820. *An address, delivered in Hanover, N.H. before the Dartmouth Medical Society, on their first anniversary, Dec. 28th, 1819*. Boston: Printed by James Loring.

Alsop, Ron. And the winner is ... Dartmouth's Tuck School. *Wall Street Journal*, May 9, 2001.

Alumni Letter Writers. College or university? *Dartmouth Alumni Magazine.* March 1989.

Andrews, Richard. The new curriculum. *Tuck Today.* Summer 2000.

Asch, Joseph. Geisel chaos: Phil blames the feds. in Dartblog [database online]. September 30, 2015. Available from http://www.dartblog.com/data/2015/09/012240.php (accessed October 18, 2018).

Bagamery, Anne, Rob Albright, and Lee Michaelides. The rise of research. *Dartmouth Alumni Magazine.* February 1989.

Baldwin, John C. Mapping the future. *Dartmouth Medicine.* Summer 2000.

Berry, Patricia E. Dartmouth's most influential women (and one man). *Dartmouth Alumni Magazine.* March 1997.

Bildner, Allen, Mary Stelle Donin, Dartmouth College Oral History Project, and Dartmouth College. Class of 1947. 2008. *Oral history interview with Allen Bildner*, http://www.dartmouth.edu/~library/rauner/archives/oral_history/worldwar2/Bildner_Allen.html.

Bird, Harry H., Daniel L. Daily, and Dartmouth College Oral History Project. 2002. *Oral history interview with Dr. Harry Bird*, http://ead.dartmouth.edu/html/doh20.html.

Boutwell, Susan. Integrating engineering, computer science, entrepreneurship. in Dartmouth News [database online]. March 28, 2018. Available from https://news.dartmouth.edu/news/2018/03/integrating-engineering-computer-science-entrepreneurship (accessed December 27, 2018).

Britton, Katharine F. Vital Signs: Measuring the time that clinicians spend on teaching activities. In Dartmouth Medicine [database online]. Summer 2004. Available from https://dartmed.dartmouth.edu/summer04/html/vs_measuring.shtml (accessed October 20, 2018).

Broehl, Wayne G. 1999. *Tuck and Tucker: The origin of the graduate business school*. Hanover, N.H.: University Press of New England.

Broehl, Wayne G., Jane Louise Carroll, and Dartmouth College Oral History Project. 1998. *Oral history interview with Wayne Broehl*, http://ead.dartmouth.edu/html/doh21.html.

Brown, Nancy M. DMS researcher documents incidence of needless Paps. In Dartmouth Medicine [database online]. Fall 2004. Available from https://dartmed.dartmouth.edu/fall04/html/vs_paps.shtml (accessed October 20, 2018).

Brown, Francis. 1969. *A Dartmouth Reader*. Hanover, N.H.: Dartmouth Publications.

Brubeck, Sarah. New Dartmouth President Phil Hanlon dis-

327

cusses his agenda. *Valley News*, November 5, 2013.

Byrne, John A. B-school dean of the year: Dartmouth's Paul
Sanos. In Fortune [database online]. December 23,
2014. Available from http://fortune.com/2014/12/23/
dartmouth-paul-danos-business-school-dean-of-the-year/
(accessed January 5, 2019).

Carey, Patricia Slater, Mary Stelle Donin, Dartmouth College
Oral History Project, and Dartmouth College. Class of
1944. 2008. *Oral history interview with Patricia Slater
Carey*, http://www.dartmouth.edu/~library/rauner/ar-
chives/oral_history/worldwar2/Carey_Harry.html.

Carmichael, Mary. World Bank pick draws praise, unsettles
Dartmouth. In Boston Globe [database online]. March
23, 2012. Available from https://www.bostonglobe.com/
metro/2012/03/23/choice-jim-kim-lead-world-bank-
draws-praise-but-unsettles-dartmouth/kdiF55P4koi-
AwVtH3XzpwJ/story.html (accessed September 27,
2018).

Carter, Laura S. DMS's new dean is a pediatrician and a pharmacologist. In Dartmouth Medicine [database online].
Summer 2003. Available from https://dartmed.dartmouth.
edu/summer03/html/vs_dean.shtml (accessed October
12, 2018).

Critical concept. In Dartmouth Medicine [database online].
Spring 2005 (accessed October 20, 2018).

Beyond Nightingale. In Dartmouth Medicine [database
online]. Fall 2005. Available from https://dartmed.
dartmouth.edu/fall05/html/beyond_nightingale.php
(accessed October 20, 2018).

In our midst. In Dartmouth Medicine [database online]. Fall 2002. Available from https://dartmed.dartmouth.edu/fall02/html/in_our_midst.shtml (accessed October 20, 2018).

Carter, Laura S., and Mathews, Cara A. Opening doors. In Dartmouth Medicine [database online]. Fall 2006. Available from https://dartmed.dartmouth.edu/fall06/html/opening_doors.php (accessed October 25, 2018).

Collins, Jim. An enviable tension (James Wright). *Dartmouth Alumni Magazine.* November 1998.

Compton, Duane. Geisel launches $250M fundraising campaign. In Dartmouth Medicine [database online]. Spring 2018. Available from https://geiselmed.dartmouth.edu/news/2018/geisel-fundraising-campaign/ (accessed November 27, 2018).

Cooper, Megan M. Kosovar exchange is a "profound educational experience" for DMS. In Dartmouth Medicine [database online]. Fall 2000. Available from https://dartmed.dartmouth.edu/fall00/html/vs_kosovar.shtml (accessed November 20, 2018).

Dandrea, Alyssa. Dartmouth faces class-action lawsuit following professor misconduct allegations. *Concord Monitor*, November 15, 2018.

Dankert, Clyde E. 1979. *Dartmouth College and Dartmouth University*. Hanover, N.H. C. Dankert.

Danos, Paul. Tuck at 100. In Tuck School [database online]. 2000. Available from www.tuck.dartmouth.edu/about/history/tuck100.html (accessed November 2, 2018).

329

Tuck nonprofit fellows program. May 8, 2002. Tuck
School.

Dartmouth College. Dartmouth announces the Frank J.
Guarini school of Graduate and Advanced Studies. In
Dartmouth News [database online]. April 27, 2018.
Available from https://news.dartmouth.edu/
news/2018/04/dartmouth-announces-frank-j-guarini-
school-gradu-ate-and-advanced-studies (accessed
February 12, 2019).

1870. *Centennial celebration at Dartmouth
College, July 21, 1869*. Hanover, N.H.: J.B. Parker.

Dartmouth Medicine. Celebrating two centuries of medicine at Dartmouth. *Dartmouth Medicine.* Summer-Fall
1997.

Dartmouth Medicine. Timeline of Dartmouth Medical
School's first 200 years. Summer-Fall 1997.
Dean, Tim. Dartmouth's MD-MBA program: Training change
agents in health care. In Dartmouth Medicine [database
online]. Spring 2017Available from https://dartmed.dart-
mouth.edu/spring17/html/features_md-mba_program/
(accessed October 27, 2018).

Charting a course for success. In Dartmouth Medicine
[database online]. Fall 2016. Available from https://
dartmed.dartmouth.edu/fall16/html/course_for_success/
(accessed December 2, 2018).

Closing the gap. In Dartmouth Medicine [database
online]. Available from https://dartmed.dartmouth.edu/
spring16/html/closing_the_gap/ (accessed November 27,
2018).

Doyle-Burr, Nora. Dartmouth runs off professors, gives few details on misconduct. *Valley News*, July 22, 2018.

Dartmouth-Hitchcock Medical Center announces $130 million expansion. *Valley News*, December 7, 2018.

Durgin, Jennifer. Part of the process. in Dartmouth Medicine [database online]. Summer 2011. Available from https://dartmed.dartmouth.edu/summer11/html/part_of_the_process.php (accessed February 5, 2019).

Public health pioneer Jim Yong Kim is named president of Dartmouth. In Dartmouth Medicine [database online]. Summer 2009. Available from https://dartmed.dartmouth.edu/summer09/html/vs_president.php (accessed January 5, 2019).

Delivering the goods. In Dartmouth Medicine [database online]. Fall 2010. Available from https://dartmed.dartmouth.edu/fall10/html/delivering_the_goods.php (accessed January 5, 2019).

Endicott, Karen. Engineering revealed. In Dartmouth Engineer [database online]. September 2006. Available from https://engineering.dartmouth.edu/magazine/engineering-revealed (accessed January 7, 2019).

The trembling edge of science. *Dartmouth Alumni Magazine.* April 1998.

Esty, Amos. A view of the forest. In Dartmouth Medicine [database online]. Winter 2010. Available from https://dartmed.dartmouth.edu/winter10/html/a_view_of_the_forest.php (accessed January 26, 2019).

Fieldsteel, Robert, Joyce Fieldsteel, Mary Stelle Donin,

Dartmouth College Oral History Project, and Dartmouth College. Class of 1943. 2007. *Oral history interview with Bob Fieldsteel and Joyce Fieldsteel*, http://www.dartmouth.edu/~library/rauner/archives/oral_history/worldwar2/Fieldsteel_Robert.html.

Fiorentino, Anna. Our Place. Dartmouth Engineer Spring 2015. Available from https://engineering.dartmouth.edu/magazine/our-place (accessed September 17, 2018).

Fiorentino, Anna. Mastering engineering management. in Dartmouth Engineer [database online]. Fall 2014 (accessed January 4, 2019).

Fish, Tim. Andy Beckstoffer: Napa valley's most powerful grapegrower. *Wine Spectator.* June 15, 2017.

Freedman, James O. 1996. *Idealism and liberal education.* Ann Arbor, MI: University of Michigan Press.

Is "the College" a college? *Dartmouth Alumni Magazine.* Winter 1988.

Frye, Ellen. 2007. *Knowledge with know-how: Thayer school of engineering at Dartmouth.* Hanover: University Press of New England.

Geisel School. Duane Compton named dean of Geisel School of Medicine. In Dartmouth News Release [database online]. Spring 2017.Available from https://news.dartmouth.edu/news/2017/04/duane-compton-named-dean-geisel-school-medicine (accessed December 27, 2018).

Off to great places. in Dartmouth Medicine [database online]. Spring 2012. Available from https://dartmed.

dartmouth.edu/spring12/html/great_places/ (accessed December 27, 2018).

Good, Jeffrey, Interview with MALS Director Wole Ojurong-be Hanover, NH, September 21, 2018.

"Interview with Thayer School Dean Joseph Helble" Hanover, NH, September 20, 2018.

"Interview with Dartmouth President Phil Hanlon" Hanover, NH, September 19, 2018.

"Interview with Guarini School Dean F. Jon Kull" Hanover, NH, September 19, 2018.

"Interview with MALS Chair Donald Pease" Hanover, NH, September 19, 2018.

"Interview with former Dartmouth President James Wright" Hanover, NH, September 18, 2018.

"Interview with Geisel School Dean Duane Compton" Hanover, NH, September 18, 2018.

"Interview with Former Dartmouth Medical School Dean James Strickler" Hanover, NH, October 31, 2018.

"Interview with Tuck School Dean Matthew Slaughter" Hanover, NH, October 25, 2018.

"Interview with Geisel School Professor Joseph O'Donnell" Hanover, NH, October 24, 2018.

Graham, Robert B. Liberating the Ph.D. *Dartmouth Alumni Magazine.* October 1970.

Guest, Robert H. 1981. *A brief history of the Amos Tuck*

School. Hanover, N.H.: Alumni Office, Amos Tuck School, Dartmouth College.

Hall, Alexandra. A giant passes. In Dartmouth News [database online]. January 18, 2013. Available from https://www.tuck.dartmouth.edu/news/articles/a-giant-passes (accessed February 8, 2019).

Heinrichs, Jay. Now for the hard part. *Dartmouth Alumni Magazine.* February 1991.

Hennessey, John William, Jane Louise Carroll, and Dartmouth College Oral History Project. 1996. *Oral history interview with John W. Hennessey*, http://ead.dartmouth.edu/html/doh28.html.

Hill, Ralph Nading, John Sloan Dickey, Stearns Morse, F. William Andres, and Ernest Roberts. 1964. *The college on the hill: A Dartmouth chronicle*, ed. Ralph Nading Hill. Hanover, N.H.: Trustees of Dartmouth College.

Hopkins, Ernest Martin. 1919. *Dartmouth College: An interpretation of purpose*. Dartmouth college reprints, series 1, no.3. Hanover, N.H.

Hutchinson, Charles E., Mary Stelle Donin, and Dartmouth College Oral History Project. 2003. *Oral history interview with Charles E. Hutchinson*, http://ead.dartmouth.edu/html/doh30.html.

Jamison, Peter. Alumni vie for influence over college mission. *Valley News via Concord Monitor*, August 27, 2007.

Jurgens, Rick. Dartmouth center to fold into institute for health policy. *Valley News*, December 17, 2014.

Despite endowment, challenges abound. *Valley News*, March 22, 2016.

Geisel cuts 30 jobs, moves 285. *Valley News*, April 20, 2016.

Geisel dean to discuss plan for cuts. *Valley News*, November 6, 2015.

Kardashian, Kirk. Tuck center for Entrepreneurship launches startup incubator. In Tuck Communications [database online]. October 23, 2018. Available from https://www.tuck.dartmouth.edu/news/articles/tuck-center-for-entrepreneurship-launches-startup-incubator (accessed December 8, 2018).

The right stuff. in Dartmouth News [database online]. June 18, 2015. Available from https://www.tuck.dartmouth.edu/news/articles/the-right-stuff (accessed October 20, 2018).

Tuck executive group welcomes a new group of business leaders. In Tuck Communications [database online]. July 25, 2011. Available from https://www.tuck.dartmouth.edu/news/articles/tuck-executive-program-welcomes-a-new-group-of-business-leaders (accessed December 14, 2018).

Tuck bridge turns 20. In Tuck News [database online]. January 18, 2017. Available from https://www.tuck.dartmouth.edu/news/articles/tuck-bridge-turns-20 (accessed December 3, 2018).

Tuck and Dartmouth team up to teach Christmas spirit. In Tuck Communications [database on-

line]. December 18, 2012. Available from https://
www.google.com/search?q=Tuck+and+Dart-
mouth+team+up+to+teach+christmas&rlz=1C-
5CHFA_enUS627US636&oq=Tuck+and+Dart-
mouth+team+up+to+teach+christmas&aqs=-
chrome..69i57.14590j0j4&sourceid=chrome&ie=UTF-8
(accessed October 22, 2018).

Leadership lessons for young African entrepreneurs.
Tuck News. August 1, 2018. Available from https://
www.tuck.dartmouth.edu/news/articles/leadership-les-
sons-for-young-african-entrepreneurs (accessed December 11, 2018).

Keating, Kim "World Record: Two of Every Three Tuck
Alumni Give Back" (News release, Tuck School, July 5,
2007) (accessed December 2, 2018).

Kemeny, John G., and A. Alexander Fanelli. 1999. *John
Kemeny speaking: Selected addresses, talks & interviews
by John G. Kemeny from the years of his presidency of
Dartmouth College, 1970-1981* [Speeches.]. Hanover,
N.H.: Dartmouth College.

Kimball, William Phelps. 1971. *The first hundred years of the
Thayer School of Engineering at Dartmouth College.*
Hanover, N.H.: University Press of New England.

Knapp, Susan. Dartmouth researchers build world's smallest
robot. in Dartmouth Engineer [database online]. September 26, 2005. Available from http://www.dartmouth.
edu/~vox/0506/0926/microrobot.html (accessed October
27, 2018).

Kohr, Justine M. Business for good. In Tuck News [database

online]. October 2, 2015. Available from https://www.tuck.dartmouth.edu/news/articles/business-for-good-tuck-works-with-upper-valley-nonprofits-on-allwin-day (accessed September 30, 2018).

Lapierre, Kathryn LoConte. Humanitarian engineering: Zero-emissions hydroelectric power. In Dartmouth Engineer [database online]. Winter 2013.Available from https://engineering.dartmouth.edu/magazine/humanitarian-engineering-zero-emissions-hydroelectric-power (accessed October 27, 2018).

Leavens, Robert French, and Arthur Hardy Lord. 1965. *Dr. Tucker's Dartmouth*. Hanover, N. H.: Dartmouth Publications.

Levinson, Robert A., Mary Stelle Donin, Dartmouth College Oral History Project, and Dartmouth College. Class of 1946. 2010. *Oral history interview with Robert A. Levinson*, http://www.dartmouth.edu/~library/rauner/archives/oral_history/worldwar2/Levinson_Robert.html.

LoConte, Kathryn. Students' arsenic removal system wins national prize. In Dartmouth Engineer [database online]. Winter 2010. Available from https://engineering.dartmouth.edu/magazine/awards-students-arsenic-removal-system-wins-national-prize (accessed October 21, 2018).

LoConte, Kathryn. Leading edge: Nation's first Ph.D. innovation program. In Dartmouth Engineer [database online]. Winter 2009. Available from https://engineering.dartmouth.edu/magazine/leading-edge-nations-first-phd-innovation-program (accessed October 27, 2018).

Long, Carl F., Christopher M. Burns, and Dartmouth College Oral History Project. 2001. *Oral history interview with Carl F. Long*, http://ead.dartmouth.edu/html/doh35.html.

Lunardini, Rosemary. Cause for celebration: A 50th and a 50/50 ratio. In Dartmouth Medicine [database online]. May 2010. Available from https://dartmed.dartmouth.edu/fall10/html/vs_celebration.php (accessed November 27, 2018).

Lunardini, Rosemary, and Dana Cook Grossman. Thoughts on change. *Dartmouth Medicine.* Summer-Fall 1997.

Mahar, Maggie. Braveheart: Jack Wennberg. In Dartmouth Medicine [database online]. Winter 2007. Available from https://dartmed.dartmouth.edu/winter07/html/braveheart.php (accessed October 20, 2018).

Marquard, Bryan. John W. Hennessey Jr., 92; brought gender and racial diversity to Dartmouth's Tuck School. *Boston Globe*, January 17, 2018.

Martin, Douglas. David McLaughlin, 72, ex-president of Dartmouth, dies. *New York Times*, August 27, 2004.

McCollum, Robert W., Daniel L. Daily, and Dartmouth College Oral History Project. 2002. *Oral history interview with Robert W. McCollum*, http://ead.dartmouth.edu/html/doh38.html.

McLaughlin, David T., Howard Coffin, Dean Bornstein, Frederick B. Whittemore, Edward Connery Lathem, and Perpetua Press. 2007. *Choices made: A memoir*. Hanover, N.H.: Privately printed.

McClure, Jason. Tuck veterans see benefits, challenges in soldiering before business school. In Tuck Communications [database online]. April 2, 2013 Available from http://mytuck.dartmouth.edu/s/1353/05-myTUCK/15/index.aspx?sid=1353&gid=5&calcid=5150&calpgid=2285&pgid=2190&crid=0&cid=5150 (accessed January 12, 2019).

Melocik, Cathy. Bettering the world of business — and nature. *Tuck Today.* Summer 2017.

Michaelides, Lee. Investigating a shiny killer. *Dartmouth Alumni Magazine.* February 1989.

Mitchell, Katrina. Creating connections. *Dartmouth Medicine.* Fall 2003.

Moag, Jeff. In Tuck Communications [database online]. December 2, 2011. Available from https://www.tuck.dartmouth.edu/news/articles/a-league-of-our-own (accessed December 12, 2018).

Moules, Jonathan. Dean of Dartmouth Tuck focuses on 115-year heritage. *Financial Times*, October 30, 2015.

Munter, Mary. 1990. *Tuck School history*. Hanover, N.H.: The Amos Tuck School of Business Administration, Dartmouth College.

Nordhoff, Andrew. First national study on kids and smoking in movies has major impact. In Vox of Dartmouth [database online]. December 5, 2005 Available from http://www.dartmouth.edu/~vox/0506/1205/movies.html (accessed November 20, 2018).

Platt, Bill. Trustees establish school of graduate and advanced studies. In Dartmouth News [database online]. January 27, 2016. Available from https://news.dartmouth.edu/

news/2016/01/trustees-establish-school-graduate-and-advanced-studies (accessed October 9, 2018).

Dartmouth football kicks off high-tech season. in Dartmouth News [database online]. August 25, 2015. Available from https://news.dartmouth.edu/news/2015/08/ dartmouth-football-kicks-high-tech-season (accessed February 27, 2019).

Putnam, Constance E. 2004. *The science we have loved and taught: Dartmouth medical school's first two centuries*. Lebanon, NH: University Press of New England.

Richardson, Leon B. 1932. *History of Dartmouth College*. Hanover, N.H.: Dartmouth College Publications.

Rieser, Leonard M. Graduate study - past and present. *Dartmouth Alumni Magazine.* November 1965.

Senz, Kristen, Marcia Craig Jacobs, Karen Endicott, and Molly Howard. 2018. *Helble: A tribute to Joseph J. Helble, dean.* Thayer School of Engineering.

Shribman, David M., and Edward Connery Lathem. 1999. *Miraculously builded in our hearts: A Dartmouth reader*. Hanover, N.H.: Dartmouth College: University Press of New England distributor.

Silverstein, Hannah. Eric Fossum wins engineering's biggest prize. In Dartmouth News [database online]. February 1, 2017. Available from https://news.dartmouth.edu/ news/2017/02/eric-fossum-wins-engineerings-biggest-prize (accessed November 18, 2018).

Thayer School. Educational innovation: Faculty awarded national prize. in Dartmouth Engineer [database on-

line]. Spring 2014. Available from https://engineering.
dartmouth.edu/magazine/educational-innovation-facul-
ty-awarded-national-prize (accessed November 7, 2019).

Ghana's adaptation of Dartmouth's intro to engineering
course is flourishing in its 4th year. In Thayer School
News Release [database online]. September 19, 2017
(accessed January 7, 2019).

$25 million gift propels expansion of Dartmouth en-
gineering. May 16, 2016. Available from https://news.
dartmouth.edu/news/2016/05/25-million-gift-propels-ex-
pansion-dartmouth-engineering (accessed October 22,
2018).

Dartmouth makes history by graduating a majority
female engineering class. in Thayer News Release
[database online]. June 16, 2016Available from https://
engineering.dartmouth.edu/news/dartmouth-makes-his-
tory-by-graduating-a-majority-female-engineering-class
(accessed December 27, 2018).

Engineers without borders: Students earn social justice awards. in Dartmouth Engineer [database online].
January 2006. Available from https://engineering.
dartmouth.edu/magazine/engineers-without-borders-stu-
dents-earn-social-justice-awards (accessed January 7,
2019).

Innovations: GlycoFi bought by Merck. in Dartmouth
Engineer [database online]. Fall 2006. Available from
https://engineering.dartmouth.edu/magazine/innova-
tions-glycofi-bought-by-merck (accessed October 23,
2018).

341

Sarpreshkar elected to the national academy of inventors. in Dartmouth Engineer [database online]. December 17, 2018Available from https://engineering.dartmouth.edu/news/sarpeshkar-elected-to-the-national-academy-of-inventors (accessed January 8, 2019).

Thayer students inspire hybrid race car competition. In Vox of Dartmouth [database online]. April 16, 2007. Available from http://www.dartmouth.edu/~vox/0607/0416/hybrid.html (accessed November 17, 2018).

Thayer School. Historical timeline. Undated.

The Economist. The top thirty. *The Economist.* October 15, 2011.

Thomas, Danielle. Students win grants and honors for free clinic. In Dartmouth Medicine [database online]. Spring 2007. Available from https://dartmed.dartmouth.edu/spring07/html/vs_students.php (accessed January 5, 2019).

Trotter, Gregory. Day in the life, with death. *Valley News*, January 31, 2010.

Tuck School. For Tuck, a refined vision. in Tuck News [database online]. September 26, 2016. Available from https://www.tuck.dartmouth.edu/news/articles/tuck-announces-refined-mission-vision-and-strategy (accessed January 2, 2019).

The next 10. In Tuck Communications [database online]. September 24, 2010. Available from https://www.tuck.dartmouth.edu/news/articles/the-next-10 (accessed October 13, 2018).

Tuck welcomes the record-setting class of 2020. in Tuck Communications [database online]. September 11, 2018. Available from https://www.tuck.dartmouth.edu/news/articles/tuck-welcomes-the-record-setting-class-of-2020 (accessed December 17, 2018).

The road ahead. in Tuck Communications [database online]. Sept. 22, 2010. Available from https://www.tuck.dartmouth.edu/news/articles/the-road-ahead (accessed October 19, 2018).

Healthy debate. In Tuck Communications [database online]. November 25, 2010. Available from https://www.tuck.dartmouth.edu/news/articles/healthy-debate (accessed November 12, 2018).

Next step: Business skills for veterans and athletes. In Tuck Communications [database online]. November 14, 2016. Available from https://www.tuck.dartmouth.edu/news/articles/next-step-business-skills-for-veterans-and-athletes (accessed February 28, 2019).

Tuck announces new criteria for MBA admissions. In Tuck Communications [database online]. June 11, 2018. Available from https://www.tuck.dartmouth.edu/news/articles/tuck-announces-new-criteria-for-mba-admissions (accessed October 22, 2018).

Tuck announces $250-million capital campaign for tomorrow's wise leaders. In Tuck Communications [database online]. April 27, 2018. Available from https://www.tuck.dartmouth.edu/news/articles/tuck-announces-250-million-capital-campaign-for-tomorrows-wise-leaders (accessed January 8, 2019).

Tucker, William Jewett. My generation: an autobiographical interpretation. 1919, Houghton Mifflin Company, Boston.

Ward, Logan. GyroBike: Preventing scraped knees. in Popular Mechanics [database online]. December 18, 2009Available from https://www.popularmechanics.com/technology/a1399/4212854/ (accessed November 12, 2018).

Widmayer, Charles E. Uncle Sam at Dartmouth. *Dartmouth Alumni Magazine.* April 1967.

Widmayer, Charles E. 1977. *Hopkins of Dartmouth: The story of Ernest Martin Hopkins and his presidency of Dartmouth College*. Hanover, N.H.: Published by Dartmouth College through the University Press of New England.

Widmayer, Charles E., and David T. McLaughlin. 1991. *John Sloan Dickey: A chronicle of his presidency of Dartmouth College*. Hanover, N.H.: Dartmouth College : Distributed by University Press of New England.

Wood, John B. John Kemeny of Dartmouth. *Boston Globe*, December 17, 1972.

Notes

Chapter One: A Voice in the Wilderness

1   Richardson, Leon B. 1932. *History of Dartmouth College*. Hanover, N.H.: Dartmouth College Publications. This section draws heavily on Richardson's elegant (though citation-free) history of the college's first century and a half. The direct quotations come from pages 14, 17, 18, 23, 28, 33, 38, 49, 50, 56, 82, 110, 115, 121, 132, 188.

2   Hill, Ralph Nading, John Sloan Dickey, Stearns Morse, F. William Andres, and Ernest Roberts. 1964. *The college on the hill: A Dartmouth chronicle*, ed. Ralph Nading Hill. Hanover, N.H.: Trustees of Dartmouth College, pg. 29. This volume, edited by Hill with historical essays written by him and others, adds lively perspectives to Richardson's history.

3   Shribman, David M., and Edward Connery Lathem. 1999. *Miraculously builded in our hearts: A Dartmouth reader*. Hanover, N.H.: Dartmouth College: University Press of New England distributor, 399. Like its predecessor volume by Brown (cited below), this is a wide-ranging and delightful collection of writings on Dartmouth's history by people who experienced and, in many cases, shaped it.

4   Brown, Francis. 1969. *A Dartmouth Reader*. Hanover, N.H.: Dartmouth Publications, 16.

5   Hill, 22.

6   Wheelock, in Brown, 16-17.

7   Hill, 68.

8   Putnam, Constance E. 2004. *The science we have loved and taught: Dartmouth medical school's first two centuries*. Lebanon, NH: University Press of New England. All uncited material in this section is from Putnam's thorough and useful history. The direct quotations are from pages 4-9, 15 and 26.

9   Richardson, 229-30.

10   Dartmouth Medicine. Timeline of Dartmouth Medical

School's first 200 years. Summer-Fall 1997.
11   The colorful quotes in this section are from Richard
      son, pp. 248, 252, 259, 274.
12   Wright, in Putnam, xiv.
13   Except where noted, this account of The Dartmouth
      Case comes from Richardson, 294-345.
14   Hill, 66.
15   Mecklin, in Brown, 192.

Chapter Two: The Medical School Thrives
16   Richardson, 379.
17   Ibid, 381.
18   Putnam, 41-2.
19   The Hale story comes from Richardson, 447-449.
20   Dartmouth Medicine timeline.
21   Putnam, 56-7.
22   Shribman and Lathem, 154.
23   Dartmouth Medicine timeline and Hill, 229.
24   This section is drawn from Richardson, 389-92.
25   Except where noted, this section is drawn from Rich
      ardson, 420-22.
26   Putnam, 46.
27   Hill, 105-6.
28   This section on women and student life comes from
      Putnam, 78-85.
29   Putnam, 85.

Chapter Three: The College Moves Toward Becoming a University
30   The first part of this section is drawn from Richardson,
      422-427.
31   Brown, 54-7.
32   Most of the material on the first century and a half of
      Thayer School comes from two sources: the 1971 *The
      First Hundred Years of the Thayer School of Engineering
      at Dartmouth College* written by William Phelps Kim-
      ball with contributions from other authors, and the 2007
      Knowledge with Know-How, a collection of historical ac-
      counts distilled from Kimball's book and, for subsequent
      years, the research and views of a variety of authors, all
      edited by Ellen Frye.

33   Kimball, William Phelps. 1971. *The first hundred years of the Thayer School of Engineering at Dartmouth College*. Hanover, N.H.: University Press of New England, 1.

34   Kimball, 5-6.

35   Frye, Ellen. 2007. *Knowledge with know-how: Thayer school of engineering at Dartmouth*. Hanover: University Press of New England, 16.

36   Kimball, 53.

37   Ibid, 27.

38   Thayer School. Historical timeline. Undated.

39   Hill, Ralph Nading, John Sloan Dickey, Stearns Morse, F. William Andres, and Ernest Roberts. 1964. *The college on the hill: A Dartmouth chronicle*, ed. Ralph Nading Hill. Hanover, N.H.: Trustees of Dartmouth College, 99.

40   Putnam, 69-70.

41   Richardson, 523.

42   Hill, 107.

43   Hill, 108.

44   Putnam, 94-8.

45   Putnam, 104-5.

46   Dartmouth College. 1870. *Centennial celebration at Dartmouth College, July 21, 1869*. Hanover, N.H.: J.B. Parker. The full texts of all speeches quoted in this section can be found in this slim but fascinating volume stored in the Rauner Library overlooking the Dartmouth Green.

Chapter Four: Presidents Debate "College v. University" Question

47   Except where noted, this section is drawn from Richardson, 543 and 587-629.

48   Hill, 165.

49   Richardson, 669.

50   Leavens, Robert French, and Arthur Hardy Lord. 1965. *Dr. Tucker's Dartmouth*. Hanover, N. H.: Dartmouth Publications.

51   Hill, 294.

52   Hill, 296; Leavens and Lord, 28.

347

53   Tucker, William Jewett. My generation: an autobi-
      ographical interpretation. 1919, Houghton Mifflin Com-
      pany, Boston, New York, 269-70, 349-353.
54   Richardson, 702.
55   Richardson, 703
56   Hill, 186.

Chapter Five: A New Century Brings an American Original
57   Broehl, Wayne G. 1999. *Tuck and Tucker: The origin of
      the graduate business school*. Hanover, N.H.: University
      Press of New England, 1-31.
58   Leavens and Lord, 161.
59   Munter, Mary. 1990. *Tuck School history*. Hanover,
      N.H.: The Amos Tuck School of Business Administra-
      tion, Dartmouth College.
60   Ibid.
61   Hill, 296.
62   Leavens and Lord, 164.
63   Broehl, 33.
64   Richardson, 737.
65   Broehl, 37.
66   Leavens and Lord, 162.
67   Except where noted, the rest of this section is drawn
      from Guest, 3-4, and Broehl, 42-44, 54, 72-5.
68   Richardson, 737.
69   This section on Tucker's views draws on Leavens and
      Lord, 165-8.
70   Except where noted, material in this section on the
      Thayer School is drawn from Kimball, pp. 19-22, 39-41,
      55 and 58.
71   This excerpt of Eastman's autobiography comes from
      Shribman, 57.
72   The first part of this section is drawn from Putnam, 112-
      115.
73   Richardson, 736.
74   Richardson, 727-8.
75   The account of the Flexner report comes from Putnam,
      118-135.

Chapter Six: World Wars Bring Dramatic Change

76   Shribman, 67-9.
77   Widmayer, Charles E. 1977. *Hopkins of Dartmouth: The story of Ernest Martin Hopkins and his presidency of Dartmouth College*. Hanover, N.H.: Published by Dartmouth College through the University Press of New England, 4.
78   Ibid, 158.
79   Hopkins, Ernest Martin. 1919. *Dartmouth College: An interpretation of purpose*. Dartmouth college reprints, series 1, no.3. Hanover, N.H.
80   Widmayer, 161.
81   Ibid, 78-9.
82   Ibid, 101.
83   Ibid, 42.
84   Ibid, 51.
85   Ibid, 269-73.
86   From Shribman, 142-4.
87   This section on Thayer is drawn from Kimball's *First Hundred Years* and its distillation in *Knowledge with Know-How*.
88   Kimball, 45.
89   This paragraph and the ones that follow are based largely on material from Kimball, 63-85.
90   Guest, 5.
91   Munter, 10-11.
92   Guest, 6.
93   This entertaining account of Tuck and Hopkins in Paris comes largely from Hill, 309-311.
94   Widmayer, 74.
95   Hill, 311.
96   Wellman, Harry R. Amos tuck school: Original graduate school of business administration. *Dartmouth Alumni Magazine.* May 1945, 15-18.
97   Fieldsteel, Robert, Joyce Fieldsteel, Mary Stelle Donin, Dartmouth College Oral History Project, and Dartmouth College. Class of 1943. 2007. *Oral history interview with Bob Fieldsteel and Joyce Fieldsteel*, http://www.dartmouth.edu/~library/rauner/archives/oral_history/

worldwar2/Fieldsteel_Robert.html

98   Levinson, Robert A., Mary Stelle Donin, Dartmouth
      College Oral History Project, and Dartmouth College.
      Class of 1946. 2010. *Oral history interview with Robert
      A. Levinson*, http://www.dartmouth.edu/~library/rauner/
      archives/oral_history/worldwar2/Levinson_Robert.html

99   Bildner, Allen, Mary Stelle Donin, Dartmouth College
      Oral History Project, and Dartmouth College. Class of
      1947. 2008. *Oral history interview with Allen Bildner*,
      http://www.dartmouth.edu/~library/rauner/archives/
      oral_history/worldwar2/Bildner_Allen.html

100   Carey, Patricia Slater, Mary Stelle Donin, Dartmouth
      College Oral History Project, and Dartmouth College.
      Class of 1944. 2008. *Oral history interview with Patricia
      Slater Carey*, http://www.dartmouth.edu/~library/rauner/
      archives/oral_history/worldwar2/Carey_Harry.html

101   Except where noted, this section draws on Putnam's
      history, pp. 137-78.

102   Widmayer, 121.

103   Putnam, 146.

104   This section on faculty legends is based on Putnam,
      154-70.

105   Dartmouth Medicine timeline.

106   Ibid.

107   This section on troubles at the school comes from Put-
      nam, 161-78.

108   Shribman, 158-71.

109   Widmayer, Charles E., and David T. McLaughlin. 1991.
      *John Sloan Dickey: A chronicle of his presidency of
      Dartmouth College*. Hanover, N.H.: Dartmouth College :

      Distributed by University Press of New England, 139.

Chapter Seven: An Era of Reinvigoration and "Refounding"

110   Putnam, 183-4.

111   Widmayer, Dickey, 124.

112   Putnam, 186.

113   Widmayer, Dickey, 126-7.

114   Putnam chronicles the visit and its aftermath on pp. 191-
      99.

115 Information on the medical school "refounding" project comes from Widmayer, Dickey, 126-156.

116 Putnam, 199-202.

117 Widmayer, Dickey, 172.

118 Lunardini, Rosemary. Cause for celebration: A 50th and a 50/50 ratio. In Dartmouth Medicine [database online]. May 2010. Available from https://dartmed.dartmouth.edu/fall10/html/vs_celebration.php (accessed November 27, 2018).

119 Widmayer, Dickey, 132-3.

120 Unless noted, information on the conflict comes from Putnam, 218-243.

121 Widmayer, Dickey, 134.

122 Kimball, 87-9.

123 Ermenc in Kimball, 90.

124 Widmayer, Dickey, 138.

125 Ibid, 137.

126 Ermenc in Kimball, 93.

127 Ibid, 94.

128 Long, Carl F., Christopher M. Burns, and Dartmouth College Oral History Project. 2001. *Oral history interview with Carl F. Long*, http://ead.dartmouth.edu/html/doh35.html.

129 Widmayer, Dickey, 159.

130 Hansen in Frye, 24.

131 Widmayer, 100, 151.

132 Converse in Kimball, 98-100.

133 Widmayer, Tucker, 73.

134 Guest, 8.

135 Broehl, Wayne G., Jane Louise Carroll, and Dartmouth College Oral History Project. 1998. *Oral history interview with Wayne Broehl*, http://ead.dartmouth.edu/html/doh21.html.

136 Hall, Alexandra. A giant passes. In Dartmouth News [database online]. January 18, 2013. Available from https://www.tuck.dartmouth.edu/news/articles/a-giant-passes (accessed February 8, 2019).

137   Hennessey, John William, Jane Louise Carroll, and Dartmouth College Oral History Project. 1996. *Oral history interview with John W. Hennessey*, http://ead. dartmouth.edu/html/doh28.html.
138   Munter, 14-15.
139   Fish, Tim. Andy Beckstoffer: Napa valley's most power-ful grapegrower. *Wine Spectator.* June 15, 2017, p. 42.
140   Guest, 10.
141   Kemeny, John G., and A. Alexander Fanelli. 1999. *John Kemeny speaking: Selected addresses, talks & interviews by John G. Kemeny from the years of his presidency of Dartmouth College, 1970-1981* [Speeches.]. Hanover, N.H.: Dartmouth College. The story of the 1974 speech is found on pp. 84-87.
142   Hennessey oral history transcript, 15.
143   Ibid, 45.
144   Marquard, Bryan. John W. Hennessey Jr., 92; brought gender and racial diversity to Dartmouth's Tuck School. *Boston Globe*, January 17, 2018.
145   Hennessey, oral history, 132.
146   Broehl, oral history transcript, 18.
147   Hennessey, oral history, 26-34.

Chapter Eight: Moving into 1960s, Research Booms
148   Hill, 193.
149   Brown's address, titled "What Makes a College New," is found in Shribman, 233-40.
150   Widmayer, Dickey, 169-70.
151   Rieser, Leonard M. Graduate study - past and present. *Dartmouth Alumni Magazine.* November 1965, 32-35.
152   Widmayer, Charles E. Uncle Sam at Dartmouth. *Dart-mouth Alumni Magazine.* April 1967.
153   "A Candid Conversation with Dartmouth's John Sloan Dickey," June 1969 Yankee magazine, in Shribman, 269-275.
154   Kemeny, John G., and A. Alexander Fanelli. 1999. *John Kemeny speaking: Selected addresses, talks & interviews by John G. Kemeny from the years of his presidency of Dartmouth College, 1970-1981* [Speeches.]. Hanover,

N.H.: Dartmouth College, 64-65.

155   Wood, John B. John Kemeny of Dartmouth. *Boston Globe*, December 17, 1972, 10-12.

Chapter Nine: Stability, Growth and Women on the Rise

156   Graham, Robert B. Liberating the Ph.D. *Dartmouth Alumni Magazine.* October 1970.

157   Good, Jeffrey. "Interview with MALS Chair Donald Pease" Hanover, NH, September 19, 2018).

158   Good, Jeffrey, "Interview with MALS Director Wole Ojurongbe" Hanover, NH, September 21, 2018).

159   Putnam, 245.

160   Good, Jeffrey. "Interview with Geisel School Professor Joseph O'Donnell" Hanover, NH, October 24, 2018).

161   Putnam, 246.

162   Good, Jeffrey. "Interview with Former Dartmouth Medical School Dean James Strickler" Hanover, NH, October 31, 2018).

163   Putnam, 247.

164   Bird, Harry H., Daniel L. Daily, and Dartmouth College Oral History Project. 2002. *Oral history interview with Dr. Harry Bird*, http://ead.dartmouth.edu/html/doh20.html.

165   Putnam, 277.

166   Putnam, 279.

167   Good, O'Donnell interview.

168   Dartmouth Medicine. Celebrating two centuries of medicine at Dartmouth. *Dartmouth Medicine.* Summer-Fall 1997, 39.

169   Ibid, 47.

170   Ibid, 49.

171   Mahar, Maggie. Braveheart: Jack Wennberg. In Dartmouth Medicine [database online]. Winter 2007. Available from https://dartmed.dartmouth.edu/winter07/html/braveheart.php (accessed October 20, 2018). This article is the source of most of the information about Wennberg in this section.

172   Wilhelm, Doug, in Frye, Ellen. 2007. *Knowledge with know-how: Thayer school of engineering at Dartmouth.*

Hanover: University Press of New England. Unless otherwise noted,Wilhelm's chapter on Long, pp. 31-46, is the source for this account of his tenure.

173   Long, Carl F., Christopher M. Burns, and Dartmouth College Oral History Project. 2001. *Oral history interview with Carl F. Long*, http://ead.dartmouth.edu/html/doh35.html.

174   Wilhelm, in Frye, 37.

175   Ibid, 42.

176   Hennessey oral history, 104.

177   Munter, 16.

178   Guest, 13.

179   Hennessey, oral history interview transcript, 61.

180   Kardashian, Kirk. Tuck executive group welcomes a new group of business leaders. In Tuck Communications [database online]. July 25, 2011. Available from https://www.tuck.dartmouth.edu/news/articles/tuck-executive-program-welcomes-a-new-group-of-business-leaders (accessed December 14, 2018).

181   Kemeny, John G., and A. Alexander Fanelli. 1999. *John Kemeny speaking: Selected addresses, talks & interviews by John G. Kemeny from the years of his presidency of Dartmouth College, 1970-1981* [Speeches.]. Hanover, N.H.: Dartmouth College, 90-95.

182   Guest, 15.

183   Melocik, Cathy. Bettering the world of business — and nature. *Tuck Today.* Summer 2017, 18-19.

184   Carter, Laura S., and Mathews, Cara A. Opening doors. In Dartmouth Medicine [database online]. Fall 2006. Available from https://dartmed.dartmouth.edu/fall06/html/opening_doors.php (accessed October 25, 2018). My account of the nursing school is drawn from this article.

Chapter Ten: The 1980s Bring a New President and New Challenges

185   Martin, Douglas. David McLaughlin, 72, ex-president of Dartmouth, dies. *New York Times*, August 27, 2004.

186   McLaughlin, David T., Howard Coffin, Dean Bornstein, Frederick B. Whittemore, Edward Connery Lathem, and

Perpetua Press. 2007. *Choices made: A memoir*. Hanover, N.H.: Privately printed, 176-7.
187 McLaughlin, 187-9.
188 Ibid, 190.
189 Ibid, 196.
190 Putnam, 275.
191 McCollum, Robert W., Daniel L. Daily, and Dartmouth College Oral History Project. 2002. *Oral history interview with Robert W. McCollum*, http://ead.dartmouth.edu/html/doh38.html. This section on McCollum is based on the oral history transcript.
192 McLaughlin, 173.
193 Wilhelm, in Frye, 61.
194 Hutchinson, oral history.
195 Wilhelm, in Frye, 64. The rest of this section is drawn from the Wilhelm chapter on Hutchinson's tenure, 61-89.

Chapter Eleven: A 'Liberal Arts University'
196 Freedman, in Shribman, 350-4.
197 Freedman, James. Is "the College" a college? *Dartmouth Alumni Magazine.* Winter 1988, 28-34.
198 Alumni Letter Writers. College or university? *Dartmouth Alumni Magazine.* March 1989, beginning on pg. 8.
199 Bagamery, Anne, Rob Albright, and Lee Michaelides. The rise of research. *Dartmouth Alumni Magazine.* February 1989, 24-32.
200 Bagamery, 32.
201 Heinrichs, Jay. Now for the hard part. *Dartmouth Alumni Magazine.* February 1991, 16-18.
202 Berry, Patricia E. Dartmouth's most influential women (and one man). *Dartmouth Alumni Magazine.* March 1997, 18.
203 Michaelides, Lee. Investigating a shiny killer. *Dartmouth Alumni Magazine.* February 1989, 29.
204 Endicott, Karen. The trembling edge of science. *Dartmouth Alumni Magazine.* April 1998, 22-31.
205 Ibid, 30.

Chapter Twelve: The Professional Schools Mature

206   Warren, Anita, in Frye, "Learning to Fly: Thayer School as Business Incubator," 47-52.

207   Wilhelm, in Frye, 79.

208   Ibid, 80.

209   Ibid, 82-88.

210   Ibid, 91-100.

211   This section is based on material from Putnam, 250-86.

212   Putnam, 259.

213   Ibid, 260-2.

214   Putnam and *Dartmouth Medicine* timeline.

215   Lunardini, Rosemary, and Dana Cook Grossman. Thoughts on change. *Dartmouth Medicine.* Summer-Fall 1997, 92-97.

216   Information in this section comes from Munter's compact history of the school.

217   Kardashian, Kirk. The right stuff. in Dartmouth News [database online]. June 18, 2015. Available from https://www.tuck.dartmouth.edu/news/articles/the-right-stuff (accessed October 20, 2018).

218   Ibid.

219   Kardashian, Kirk. Tuck bridge turns 20. In Tuck News [database online]. January 18, 2017. Available from https://www.tuck.dartmouth.edu/news/articles/tuck-bridge-turns-20 (accessed December 3, 2018).

220   Wright, in Shribman, 404-408.

221   Collins, Jim. An enviable tension (James Wright). *Dartmouth Alumni Magazine.* November 1998, 28-9.

222   Ibid.

223   Good, Jeffrey. "Interview with former Dartmouth President James Wright" Hanover, NH, September 18, 2018).

224   Jamison, Peter. Alumni vie for influence over college mission. *Valley News via Concord Monitor*, August 27, 2007.

Chapter Thirteen: Entering a New Century

225   Kohr, Justine M. Business for good. In Tuck News [database online]. October 2, 2015. Available from https://www.tuck.dartmouth.edu/news/articles/business-for-

good-tuck-works-with-upper-valley-nonprofits-on-all-win-day (accessed September 30, 2018).

226   Danos, Paul. Tuck at 100. In Tuck School [database online]. 2000. Available from www.tuck.dartmouth.edu/about/history/tuck100.html (accessed November 2, 2018).

227   Andrews, Richard. The new curriculum. *Tuck Today.* Summer 2000, 15-22.

228   Alsop, Ron. And the winner is ... Dartmouth's Tuck School. *Wall Street Journal*, May 9, 2001.

229   Tuck School. The next 10. In Tuck Communications [database online]. September 24, 2010. Available from https://www.tuck.dartmouth.edu/news/articles/the-next-10 (accessed October 13, 2018).

230   Baldwin, John C. Mapping the future. *Dartmouth Medicine.* Summer 2000, 53.

231   Cooper, Megan M. Kosovar exchange is a "profound educational experience" for DMS. In Dartmouth Medicine [database online]. Fall 2000. Available from https://dartmed.dartmouth.edu/fall00/html/vs_kosovar.shtml (accessed November 20, 2018).

232   Mitchell, Katrina. Creating connections. *Dartmouth Medicine.* Fall 2003, 32-5.

233   Carter, Laura S. In our midst. In Dartmouth Medicine [database online]. Fall 2002. Available from https://dartmed.dartmouth.edu/fall02/html/in_our_midst.shtml (accessed October 20, 2018).

234   Carter, Laura S. DMS's new dean is a pediatrician and a pharmacologist. In Dartmouth Medicine [database online]. Summer 2003. Available from https://dartmed.dartmouth.edu/summer03/html/vs_dean.shtml (accessed October 12, 2018).

235   Britton, Katharine F. Vital Signs: Measuring the time that clinicians spend on teaching activities. In Dartmouth Medicine [database online]. Summer 2004. Available from https://dartmed.dartmouth.edu/summer04/html/vs_measuring.shtml (accessed October 20, 2018).

236   Brown, Nancy M. DMS researcher documents incidence of needless Paps. In Dartmouth Medicine [database

online]. Fall 2004. Available from https://dartmed.dart-mouth.edu/fall04/html/vs_paps.shtml (accessed Octobert 20, 2018).

237   Nordhoff, Andrew. First national study on kids and smoking in movies has major impact. In Vox of Dartmouth [database online]. December 5, 2005Available from http://www.dartmouth.edu/~vox/0506/1205/mov-ies.html (accessed November 20, 2018).

238   Carter, Laura S., and Mathews, Cara A. Opening doors. In Dartmouth Medicine [database online]. Fall 2006. Available from https://dartmed.dartmouth.edu/fall06/html/opening_doors.php (accessed October 25, 2018).

239   Thomas, Danielle. Students win grants and honors for free clinic. In Dartmouth Medicine [database online]. Spring 2007. Available from https://dartmed.dartmouth.edu/spring07/html/vs_students.php (accessed January 5, 2019).

240   Unless otherwise noted, the information about Duncan's tenure comes from a chapter about the dean written by Doug Wilhelm in *Knowledge with Know-How*, 107-134.

241   Wilhelm, 134.

242   Senz, Kristen, Marcia Craig Jacobs, Karen Endicott, and Molly Howard. 2018. *Helble: A Tribute to Joseph J. Helble, Dean.* Thayer School of Engineering. Unlike many institutional tributes, this one — based on inter-views conducted by Senz — is not only laudatory but also thorough and journalistically sound. It serves as the source for this introductory section on Helble.

243   Fiorentino, Anna. Mastering engineering management. in Dartmouth Engineer [database online]. Fall 2014 (accessed January 4, 2019).

244   Knapp, Susan. Dartmouth researchers build world's smallest robot. in Dartmouth Engineer [database online]. September 26, 2005. Available from http://www.dart-mouth.edu/~vox/0506/0926/microrobot.html (accessed October 27, 2018).

245   Endicott, Karen. Engineering revealed. In Dartmouth Engineer [database online]. September 2006. Available from https://engineering.dartmouth.edu/magazine/engi-

neering-revealed (accessed January 7, 2019).

246   Thayer School. Innovations: GlycoFi bought by Merck. in Dartmouth Engineer [database online]. Fall 2006. Available from https://engineering.dartmouth.edu/magazine/innovations-glycofi-bought-by-merck (accessed October 23, 2018).

247   Ward, Logan. GyroBike: Preventing scraped knees. in Popular Mechanics [database online]. December 18, 2009Available from https://www.popularmechanics.com/technology/a1399/4212854/ (accessed November 12, 2018).

248   Thayer School. Thayer students inspire hybrid race car competition. In Vox of Dartmouth [database online]. April 16, 2007. Available from http://www.dartmouth.edu/~vox/0607/0416/hybrid.html (accessed November 17, 2018).

249   Senz et al, 29.

250   LoConte, Kathryn. Leading edge: Nation's first Ph.D. innovation program. In Dartmouth Engineer [database online]. Winter 2009. Available from https://engineering.dartmouth.edu/magazine/leading-edge-nations-first-phd-innovation-program (accessed October 27, 2018).

251   LoConte, Kathryn. Students' arsenic removal system wins national prize. In Dartmouth Engineer [database online]. Winter 2010. Available from https://engineering.dartmouth.edu/magazine/awards-students-arsenic-removal-system-wins-national-prize (accessed October 21, 2018).

Chapter Fourteen: Dartmouth Gets its First Physician President

252   Durgin, Jennifer. Public health pioneer Jim Yong Kim is named president of Dartmouth. In Dartmouth Medicine [database online]. Summer 2009. Available from https://dartmed.dartmouth.edu/summer09/html/vs_president.php (accessed January 5, 2019).

253   Ibid.

254   Durgin, Jennifer. Delivering the goods. In Dartmouth Medicine [database online]. Fall 2010. Available from

https://dartmed.dartmouth.edu/fall10/html/delivering_
the_goods.php (accessed January 5, 2019).

255   Trotter, Gregory. Day in the life, with death. *Valley News*, January 31, 2010, 1a.

256   Good, O'Donnell interview.

257   Esty, Amos. A view of the forest. In Dartmouth Medicine [database online]. Winter 2010. Available from https://dartmed.dartmouth.edu/winter10/html/a_view_
of_the_forest.php (accessed January 26, 2019).

258   Durgin, Jennifer. Part of the process. in Dartmouth Medicine [database online]. Summer 2011. Available from https://dartmed.dartmouth.edu/summer11/html/
part_of_the_process.php (accessed February 5, 2019).

Chapter Fifteen: A New President and a New School

260   The Economist. The top thirty. *The Economist.* October 15, 2011.

261   Kardashian, Kirk. Tuck and Dartmouth team up to teach Christmas spirit. In Tuck Communications [database online]. December 18, 2012. Available from https://www.google.com/search?q=Tuck+and+Dart-
mouth+team+up+to+teach+christmas&rlz=1C-
5CHFA_enUS627US636&oq=Tuck+and+Dart-
mouth+team+up+to+teach+christmas&aqs=-
chrome..69i57.14590j0j4&sourceid=chrome&ie=UTF-8
(accessed October 22, 2018).

262   Moag, Jeff. In Tuck Communications [database online]. December 2, 2011. Available from https://www.tuck.
dartmouth.edu/news/articles/a-league-of-our-own (accessed December 12, 2018).

263   Carmichael, Mary. World Bank pick draws praise, unsettles Dartmouth. In Boston Globe [database online]. March 23, 2012. Available from https://www.boston-
globe.com/metro/2012/03/23/choice-jim-kim-lead-
world-bank-draws-praise-but-unsettles-dartmouth/kdiF-
55P4koiAwVtH3XzpwJ/story.html (accessed September 27, 2018).

264   Brubeck, Sarah. New Dartmouth President Phil Hanlon discusses his agenda. *Valley News*, November 5, 2013.

265   McClure, Jason. Tuck veterans see benefits, challenges in soldiering before business school. In Tuck Communications [database online]. April 2, 2013Available from http://mytuck.dartmouth.edu/s/1353/05-myTUCK/15/index.aspx?sid=1353&gid=5&calcid=5150&calpgid=2285&pgid=2190&crid=0&cid=5150 (accessed January 12, 2019).

266   Kardashian, Kirk. Where business is next. in Tuck Today [database online]. May 17, 2017Available from https://www.tuck.dartmouth.edu/news/articles/tuck-next-step-transition-to-business-for-military-and-athletes (accessed October 22, 2018).

267   Byrn, John A. *Fortune*, December 23, 2014. http://fortune.com/2014/12/23/dartmouth-paul-danos-business-school-dean-of-the-year/ (accessed January 5, 2019).

268   Kardashian, Kirk. The right stuff. in Dartmouth News [database online]. June 18, 2015. Available from https://www.tuck.dartmouth.edu/news/articles/the-right-stuff (accessed October 20, 2018).

269   Moules, Jonathan. Dean of Dartmouth Tuck focuses on 115-year heritage. *Financial Times*, October 30, 2015.

270   Tuck School. For Tuck, a refined vision. in Tuck News [database online]. September 26, 2016. Available from https://www.tuck.dartmouth.edu/news/articles/tuck-announces-refined-mission-vision-and-strategy (accessed January 2, 2019).

271   Kardashian, Kirk. Tuck center for Entrepreneurship launches startup incubator. In Tuck Communications [database online]. October 23, 2018. Available from https://www.tuck.dartmouth.edu/news/articles/tuck-center-for-entrepreneurship-launches-startup-incubator (accessed December 8, 2018).

272   Kardashian, Kirk. Leadership lessons for young African entrepreneurs. Tuck Communications, August 1, 2018. Available from https://www.tuck.dartmouth.edu/news/articles/leadership-lessons-for-young-african-entrepreneurs (accessed December 11, 2018).

273   Tuck School. Tuck welcomes the record-setting class of 2020. in Tuck Communications [database online].

September 11, 2018. Available from https://www.tuck.dartmouth.edu/news/articles/tuck-welcomes-the-record-setting-class-of-2020 (accessed December 17, 2018).

274   Tuck School. Tuck announces new criteria for MBA admissions. In Tuck Communications [database online]. June 11, 2018. Available from https://www.tuck.dartmouth.edu/news/articles/tuck-announces-new-criteria-for-mba-admissions (accessed October 22, 2018).

275   Geisel School. Off to great places. in Dartmouth Medicine [database online]. Spring 2012. Available from https://dartmed.dartmouth.edu/spring12/html/great_places/ (accessed December 27, 2018).

276   Jurgens, Rick. Despite endowment, challenges abound. *Valley News*, March 22, 2016.

277   "Off to great places," in Dartmouth Medicine.

278   Jurgens, Rick. Dartmouth center to fold into institute for health policy. *Valley News*, December 17, 2014

279   Good, Jeffrey. "Interview with Geisel School Dean Duane Compton" Hanover, NH, September 18, 2018).

280   Jurgens, Rick. Geisel dean to discuss plan for cuts. *Valley News*, November 6, 2015.

281   Jurgens, Rick. Geisel cuts 30 jobs, moves 285. *Valley News*, April 20, 2016.

282   Asch, Joseph. Geisel chaos: Phil blames the feds. in Dartblog [database online]. September 30, 2015. Available from http://www.dartblog.com/data/2015/09/012240.php (accessed October 18, 2018).

283   Dean, Tim. Charting a course for success. In Dartmouth Medicine [database online]. Fall 2016. Available from https://dartmed.dartmouth.edu/fall16/html/course_for_success/ (accessed December 2, 2018).

284   Dean, Tim. Closing the gap. In Dartmouth Medicine [database online]. Available from https://dartmed.dartmouth.edu/spring16/html/closing_the_gap/ (accessed November 27, 2018).

285   Geisel School. Duane Compton named dean of Geisel School of Medicine. In Dartmouth News Release [database online]. Spring 2017.Available from https://news.dartmouth.edu/news/2017/04/duane-compton-named-

dean-geisel-school-medicine (accessed December 27, 2018).

286   Dean, Tim. Dartmouth's MD-MBA program: Training change agents in health care. In Dartmouth Medicine [database online]. Spring 2017Available from https://dartmed.dartmouth.edu/spring17/html/features_md-mba_program/ (accessed October 27, 2018).

287   Compton, Duane. Geisel launches $250M fundraising campaign. In Dartmouth Medicine [database online]. Spring 2018. Available from https://geiselmed.dartmouth.edu/news/2018/geisel-fundraising-campaign/ (accessed November 27, 2018).

288   Dandrea, Alyssa. Dartmouth faces class-action lawsuit following professor misconduct allegations. *Concord Monitor*, November 15, 2018.

289   290 Hartocollis, Anemona. Dartmouth reaches $14 million settlement in sexual abuse lawsuit. New York Times, August 6, 2019.

290   Doyle-Burr, Nora. Dartmouth-Hitchcock Medical Center announces $130 million expansion. *Valley News*, December 7, 2018.

291   Lapierre, Kathryn LoConte. Humanitarian engineering: Zero-emissions hydroelectric power. In Dartmouth Engineer [database online]. Winter 2013.Available from https://engineering.dartmouth.edu/magazine/humanitarian-engineering-zero-emissions-hydroelectric-power (accessed October 27, 2018).

292   Thayer School. Ghana's adaptation of Dartmouth's intro to engineering course is flourishing in its 4th year. In Thayer School News Release [database online]. September 19, 2017 (accessed January 7, 2019).

293   Thayer School. Educational innovation: Faculty awarded national prize. in Dartmouth Engineer [database online]. Spring 2014. Available from https://engineering.dartmouth.edu/magazine/educational-innovation-faculty-awarded-national-prize (accessed November 7, 2019).

294   Platt, Bill. Dartmouth football kicks off high-tech season. in Dartmouth News [database online]. August 25, 2015. Available from https://news.dartmouth.edu/

news/2015/08/dartmouth-football-kicks-high-tech-season (accessed February 27, 2019).

295   Thayer School. Sarpreshkar elected to the national academy of inventors. in Dartmouth Engineer [database online]. December 17, 2018Available from https:// engineering.dartmouth.edu/news/sarpeshkar-elected-to-the-national-academy-of-inventors (accessed January 8, 2019).

296   Fiorentino, Anna. Our place. *Dartmouth Engineer*, Spring 2015. Available from https://engineering.dartmouth.edu/magazine/our-place (accessed September 17, 2018).

297   Senz et al, 18.

298   Ibid, 36.

299   Ibid, 42.

300   Thayer School. $25 million gift propels expansion of Dartmouth engineering. May 16, 2016. Available from https://news.dartmouth.edu/news/2016/05/25-million-gift-propels-expansion-dartmouth-engineering (accessed October 22, 2018).

301   Ibid.

302   Silverstein, Hannah. Eric Fossum wins engineering's biggest prize. In Dartmouth News [database online]. February 1, 2017. Available from https://news.dartmouth.edu/news/2017/02/eric-fossum-wins-engineerings-biggest-prize (accessed November 18, 2018).

303   Boutwell, Susan. Integrating engineering, computer science, entrepreneurship. in Dartmouth News [database online]. March 28, 2018Available from https://news.dartmouth.edu/news/2018/03/integrating-engineering-computer-science-entrepreneurship (accessed December 27, 2018).

304   Senz et al, 49.

305   Platt, Bill. Trustees establish school of graduate and advanced studies. In Dartmouth News [database online]. January 27, 2016. Available from https://news.dartmouth.edu/news/2016/01/trustees-establish-school-graduate-and-advanced-studies (accessed October 9, 2018).

306   Dartmouth College. Dartmouth announces the Frank J.

364

Guarini school of Graduate and Advanced Studies. In Dartmouth News [database online]. April 27, 2018Available from https://news.dartmouth.edu/news/2018/04/ dartmouth-announces-frank-j-guarini-school-graduate-and-advanced-studies (accessed February 12, 2019).

Epilogue: At 250 years, Dartmouth's Leaders Look Ahead

307   Good, Jeffrey. "Interview with former Dartmouth President James Wright" Hanover, NH, September 18, 2018.

308   "Interview with Guarini School Dean F. Jon Kull" Hanover, NH, September 19, 2018.

309   "Interview with Geisel School Dean Duane Compton" Hanover, NH, September 18, 2018.

310   "Interview with Thayer School Dean Joseph Helble" Hanover, NH, September 20, 2018.

311   "Interview with Tuck School Dean Matthew Slaughter" Hanover, NH, October 25, 2018.

312   "Interview with Dartmouth President Phil Hanlon" Hanover, NH, September 19, 2018.

www.ingramcontent.com/pod-product-compliance
Lightning Source LLC
Chambersburg PA
CBHW070632150426
42811CB00050B/276